Lecture Notes in Computer Science 13750

More information about this subseries at https://link.springer.com/bookseries/8851

Ngoc Thanh Nguyen · Ryszard Kowalczyk ·
Jacek Mercik · Anna Motylska-Kuźma (Eds.)

Transactions on Computational Collective Intelligence XXXVII

Springer

Editor-in-Chief
Ngoc Thanh Nguyen 🆔
Institute of Informatics
Wroclaw University of Technology
Wroclaw, Poland

Co-Editor-in-Chief
Ryszard Kowalczyk
Faculty of Information
and Communication Technology
Swinburne University of Technology
Hawthorn, Victoria, VIC, Australia

Guest Editors
Jacek Mercik
WSB University in Wroclaw
Wroclaw, Poland

Anna Motylska-Kuźma
University of Lower Silesia
Wroclaw, Poland

ISSN 0302-9743   ISSN 1611-3349   (electronic)
Lecture Notes in Computer Science
ISSN 2190-9288   ISSN 2511-6053   (electronic)
Transactions on Computational Collective Intelligence
ISBN 978-3-662-66596-1   ISBN 978-3-662-66597-8   (eBook)
https://doi.org/10.1007/978-3-662-66597-8

Preface

It is our pleasure to present to you the thirty-seventh volume of Transactions on Computational Collective Intelligence (LNCS volume 13750), which comprises the post-proceedings of The seventh seminar on "Quantitative Methods of Group Decision Making", held at WSB University in Wroclaw, Poland, on November 26, 2021. The seminar was organized, financed, and supported by WSB University, giving us the excellent opportunity to listen to and discuss 13 presentations given by researchers from a number of different universities. The volume contains nine high-quality, carefully reviewed papers[1].

The first paper, "The decline of the Buchholz tiebreaker system: a preferable alternative" by Josep Freixas, is devoted to a simple method of undoing tiebreaks in sports competitions with a large number of competitors and a relatively small number of rounds of competition. Such methods are common in many games including Chess, Go, Bridge, and Scrabble, among others. Tiebreaking methods decide in strict order the prizes to be received, and one of the most commonly used is the well-known Buchholz method, based on the arithmetic mean of the scores obtained by the opponents. The alternative method that is proposed in this paper, which is quite close to the median of the scores obtained by the opponents, is also a weighted average of the opponents' scores, whose weights are based on the binomial distribution. The main objective of the paper is to compare the proposed method with that of Buchholz, highlighting the many advantages. Even today Buchholz's method and its variants are routinely used as the first and second tiebreaker criteria, such as in the rapid and blitz chess world championships that took place in December 2021; however, the author believes that Buchholz's method should be replaced by the one proposed in the paper.

In the second paper entitled "Constructing Varied and Attractive Shortlists from Databases: A Group Decision Approach" David M. Ramsey and Aleksander Mariański study a game theoretic approach to the number of offers being placed on a short list. Thanks to the Internet, basic information can be found about a very large number of offers at very little cost. Many sites give basic information about real estate offers, including price, size, location, and number of rooms. Information of this kind is sufficient to assess whether an offer is potentially attractive or not, but it does not suffice in making an ultimate decision. The number of real estate offers in a city may be very large. In such a case, it can be beneficial to use an automatic procedure to first eliminate offers that do not satisfy the basic criteria of an individual or family and then construct a shortlist of varied and potentially attractive offers. This article recalls an algorithm that derives such a shortlist for an individual searcher. The novelty of this article lies in adapting this algorithm to scenarios in which a group decision is made. A practical example based on real estate offers in Warsaw is used to illustrate the algorithm.

---

[1] Hereafter description of the papers are taken directly from summaries prepared by their authors.

In the third paper, "Algorithms for measuring indirect control in corporate networks and effects of divestment", Jochen Staudacher, Linus Olsson, and Izabella Stach present algorithms for measuring indirect control in complex corporate shareholding networks and investigates the importance of mutual connections in the network in the sense of shareholdings of one firm in another. Their algorithms rely on the concept of power indices from cooperative game theory. They focus on a variant of the implicit power index by Stach and Mercik based on the absolute Banzhaf index. They extend this algorithm by determining the number of regressions in an adaptive network-dependent manner taking into account the màximal length of a path to each controlled company in the network and by a model for the oat, i.e., the set of unidentified small shareholders. The method is compared with existing algorithms and the authors discuss the importance of linkages by investigating divestment of shares for a theoretical network with 21 players.

The fourth paper, "Lies, Damned Lies, and Crafty Questionnaire Design" by Jarl K. Kampen, Ynte K. van Dam, and Johannes Platje, deals with the (well-established in the literature) fact that particular design features of questionnaires affect the distribution and association of collected data. They present a survey approach called Crafty Questionnaire Design (CQED) that allows predictability and replicability of outcomes, expected of the natural sciences, to be achieved in the social sciences. Two independent proof-of-principle experiments, studying interpersonal and institutional trust of Polish and Mexican students (n=1402), show that using different versions of a questionnaire offers predictably different outcomes. CQED promises a large gain in efficiency of research in terms of sample size required and number of replications needed. This knowledge can safeguard the social scientific researcher against unpleasant surprises and inconvenient results. Knowledge about the principles of CQED could also be a tool for editors as well as reviewers of social scientific journals to scrutinize the methodological soundness and improve the relevance of publications.

In the fifth paper entitled "Solidarity Measures" Izabella Stach and Cezarino Bertini regard some measures for sharing (public) goods or budgets among members with different participation quotas in a binary decision-making process. The main characteristic of such measures is that they should have elements of solidarity with those who have a weak quota of participation in the process. These measures seem appropriate for deals that require solidarity, which contrasts with the classic power indices such as the Shapley and Shubik index or the Banzhaf index. Moreover, they provide a new representation for two power indices — the Public Help Index ξ (proposed by Bertini and Stach in 2015) and the particularization of the solidarity value proposed by Nowak and Radzik in 1994 (the ψ index) — in a simple game using null player free winning coalitions, consider some their properties in simple games.

In the sixth paper, "Transportation problem with fuzzy unit costs. Z-fuzzy numbers approach", Barbara Gładysz considers the classic version of the transportation problem which uses determinstic parameters (the unit transport costs, capacities, and amounts demanded) while in real life problems these parameters are not deterministic. One way of modeling such problems is by using the concept of fuzzy numbers. As proposed in this work on transportation models, she assumes that demand and supply are deterministic numbers and the uncertainty associated with the transport costs is modeled using Z-fuzzy numbers, an ordered pair of fuzzy numbers $Z = (A, B)$. A Z-fuzzy number is associated with a real-valued uncertain variable, X, with the first component, A, playing the role of a fuzzy restriction, $R(X)$, on the values which X can take, written X as A is , where A is a fuzzy set. B is a measure of the reliability (certainty) of A. This allows uncertainty to be included in the model, next to the estimated value of the parameter (in this case, the unit transport cost value), by taking into account an expert's opinion as to their certainty regarding this estimation.

The seventh paper, "The New Ecological Paradigm, Functional Stupidity and the University Sustainability – a Polish Case Study" by Johannes Platje, Anna Motylska-Kuźma, Marjolein Caniels, and Markus Will, addresses the New Ecological Paradigm (NEP) that reflects fragility in nature, limits to growth, and the perceived ability of mankind to deal with all kinds of challenges to sustainable development. Functional stupidity (FS) concerns the willingness to use and apply knowledge, while being able to go beyond short-term, myopic goals. Both concepts bear on the capacity to create a policy for, and redefine goals to achieve, sustainable development. This study aims to provide a picture of the adherence to the New Ecological Paradigm and the level of functional stupidity of a group of business and economics students. By means of a survey and a teaching intervention, data was gathered among Polish business and economics students (N=428) in April and May of 2019. Fuzzy logic was found suitable to analyse the data, as worldviews tend to be general and imprecise. The results show that the worldviews of the students are very similar and do not depend on specific characteristics like gender, employment, etc. The only exception is the direction of the study, which showed a little influence on the specific view. What is very interesting is that the purposeful intervention did not change specific views and the lack of reflection and justification may have convinced students that human intervention, when using a system approach, can prevent different types of adverse side effects, which is related to a belief in unlimited growth. Adherence to the New Ecological Paradigm is neutral or positive.

In the eighth paper, entitled "The Polish market of equity crowdfunding - pre and during pandemic COVID-19 situation", Przemysław Klocek and Anna Motylska-Kuźma identify the changes in the Polish market of equity crowdfunding on the cusp of disturbing external factors, such as the COVID-19 pandemic. The authors analyzed data from the four leading equity crowdfunding platforms (beesfund, crowdway, findfunds, and crowdconnect) through the prism of the basic efficiency factors. Comparing the results obtained before the pandemic to the years 2020 and 2021 shows that the Polish equity crowdfunding market is very resistant to unpredictable conditions such as COVID-19 pandemic and develops in a very stable way, in the meantime experiencing a challenging process of professionalization and matching national legislation to the requirements of the EU.

In the last paper entitled "A Model of a Parallel Design Environment for the Development of Decision-making IoT Systems" Anna Róża Łuczak, Konrad Stróżański, and Cezary Orłowski present a model building a parallel design environment using containerization processes for Internet of Things (IoT) systems supported by local environments and their orchestration. According to the current dominant approach in IT, which is the maximum automation of the software development process, special emphasis is placed on the processes of continuous integration and continuous delivery (CI / CD). They are supported by such solutions as Docker Compose, Swarm, and

Pipeline. CI / CD is a response to common problems related to software development such as slow product growth, lack of transparency in the cooperation of the development team, lack of predictability and the possibility of estimating project duration, late implementation of changes, repeatable errors caused by the human factor, and many others. These challenges translate into the final product and customer satisfaction, and thus the success of the project or even the financial result of the enterprise. Although continuous integration and delivery are not new concepts (the first mention of continuous integration dates back to 1991), thanks to the continuous improvement of these methods, many tools and new approaches are created. Therefore, in this paper, the authors consider the problems of building a decision-making system using continuous integration and continuous delivery processes. For this purpose, a model of the decision-making process was built using both of the above-mentioned processes, and then it was verified in a parallel design environment.

We would like to thank all authors for their valuable contributions to this issue and all reviewers for their opinions which helped to keep the papers of high quality. Our very special thanks go to Ngoc-Thanh Nguyen, who encouraged us to prepare this volume and helped us to publish it in due time and in good order.

November 2022   Anna Motylska-Kuźma
                                                                  Jacek Mercik

Transactions on Computational Collective Intelligence

This Springer journal focuses on research in applications of the computer-based methods of Computational Collective Intelligence (CCI) and their applications in a wide range of fields such as semantic web, social networks and multi-agent systems. It aims to provide a forum for the presentation of scientific research and technological achievements accomplished by the international community.

The topics addressed by this journal include all solutions of real-life problems, for which it is necessary to use CCI technologies to achieve effective results. The emphasis of the papers published is on novel and original research and technological advancements. Special features on specific topics are welcome.

Contents

The Decline of the Buchholz Tiebreaker System: A Preferable Alternative

Josep Freixas[✉]

Escola Politécnica Superior d'Enginyeria, Departament de Matemàtiques,
Universitat Politècnica de Catalunya, Manresa, Spain
josep.freixas@upc.edu

Abstract. We propose a simple method of undoing tiebreaks in sport competitions with a large number of competitors and relatively small number of rounds of competition. Such methods are common in many games including Chess, Go, Bridge or Scrabble, among others. Tiebreaking methods decide in strict order the prizes to be received. One of the most commonly used methods is the well-known Buchholz method, based on the arithmetic mean of the scores obtained by the opponents. The alternative method that we propose in this paper, which is quite close to the median of the scores obtained by the opponents, is also a weighted average of the opponents' scores, whose weights are based on the binomial distribution. The main objective of the article is to compare the proposed method with that of Buchholz, highlighting the many advantages over it.

Unfortunately, even today Buchholz's method and its variants are routinely used as the first and second tiebreaker criteria. It is the used as a first and second criteria in the rapid and blitz chess world championships that took place in December 2021. We believe that Buchholz's method should be replaced by the one proposed here as soon as possible.

Keywords: A system to break ties in sports competitions · Ordered weighted averages · Pascal's numbers · Binomial and Normal distributions · Buchholz's method

1 Introduction

The Swiss-system sport tournament, [12], seeks to provide a clear winner in a format with a large number of competitors and a relatively small number of rounds of competition. These tournaments are often called open tournaments. The system was first employed at a chess tournament in Zurich in 1895, hence the name 'Swiss system', and now used in many games including Chess [11], Go [1,3,13], Bridge and Scrabble, among others. Thus, in a Swiss-system tournament each competitor (team or individual) does not play all the other competitors. Pairings are selected using a set of rules designed to ensure that each competitor plays opponents with a similar running score, but does not play the same opponent

© Springer-Verlag GmbH Germany, part of Springer Nature 2022
N. T. Nguyen et al. (Eds.): Transactions on Computational Collective Intelligence XXXVII,
LNCS 13750, pp. 1–20, 2022.
https://doi.org/10.1007/978-3-662-66597-8_1

more than once. Players in chess competitions are usually granted one point (1) for a win, a half (1/2) point for a draw, and no points (0) for a loss. The system also intends to balance colors (in chess or go), [3].

The winner is the competitor with the highest aggregate points earned in all rounds. All competitors play in each round unless there is an odd number of them. In this case, the unpaired player does not play that round but is awarded the same number of points as for winning a game (e.g., one point for a chess tournament). The player is reintroduced in the next round and is not left over again.

In the final classification there are many ties since the number of competitors is much greater than the number of rounds. Then tie-breaks are used to rank players within point groups.

From now on we will mainly focus on the game of chess, although everything that is described below is also valid for other sports that use the Buchholz method (i.e., the sum of all opponents' scores) as a tiebreaker.

1.1 Tie-Break Systems

Strength of schedule is the idea behind the methods based on the games already played: that the player that played the harder competition to achieve the same number of points should be ranked higher. Harry Golombek points out deficiencies in most of the tie-break systems and recommends the Buchholz system and the cumulative system, see page 322 in [8] for Swiss tournaments. A number of results have made it apparent that the search for a perfect tiebreaker is a chimera, see e.g., [6,7,9,10]. However, we should not settle for an old and outdated method that can be greatly improved.

Tie-breaks are needed when prizes are indivisible, such as titles, trophies, or qualification for another tournament. Otherwise players often share the tied spots, with cash prizes being divided equally among the tied players. After the last round, players are ranked by their score. If players remain tied, a tie-break score is used, such as the Buchholz chess rating, which is described in detail in Sect. 2. If the players are still tied after one tie-break system is used, another system is used, and so on, until the tie is broken. Most of the methods are numerical methods based on the games that have already been played. For instance, the first three tie-breaks according to the regulations for the International Chess Federation (acronym FIDE) open world rapid & blitz championships that took place from 25 to 31 December, 2021 were:

1. Buchholz Cut 1;
2. Buchholz;
3. Average Elo rating of opponents.

For any Swiss chess tournament for individuals (not teams), FIDE's 2019 recommendation, see [5], for the two first tie-breaks are: Buchholz Cut 1 and Buchholz.

A player's Elo rating is represented by a number which may change depending on the outcome of rated games, see [2] for a complete description. It is important to note that the first two criteria are those recommended by FIDE and are applied in most open tournaments. It is necessary to set the tiebreaker methods to be used and the order in which they are applied.

The rest of the paper is organized as follows. Section 2 reviews Buchholz's tiebreaker method and some of its variants, which are all based on means of opponents' scores. In Sect. 3 we discuss an alternative tiebreaker method based on the median opponents' scores. In Sect. 4 we propose a new set of measures which are closer (in statistical terms) to the median than to the mean and point out its many advantages over Buchholz's set of measures. In Sect. 5 we highlight and discuss in detail the large number of advantages of the new method in contrast to Buchholz's method. The conclusion ends the paper in Sect. 6.

2 Final Scores and Buchholz Tie-Breakers

There are many different tie-break systems, some of them popular, some rather obscure. Confusion has been caused by the terminology as one system can be known under different names in different countries. Tie-breaker methods, recommended by FIDE and Chess Federation's Official Rules of Chess (USCF), are grouped according to several principles. Sum of opposition's scores, opposition's weighted scores, player's progressive score, number of wins, opposition's ratings, etc.

The first criterion is simply a particular case of the second one that we call here, weighted averages of the scores obtained by the opponents. Sum of opposition's scores refers only to the Buchholz method and each of its variants.

In this article we analyze the most commonly used tie-breaker method, the Buchholz chess rating, with the main of its variants. The Buchholz method has virtues but numerous weaknesses that, as we will see, are alleviated by the method that we propose to apply from now on as its replacement.

The proposed method, which is an ordered weighted average (OWA, [17,18]) of the scores obtained by the opponents, has the same strengths but considerably improves the weaknesses of the Buchholz method. This is argued in Sects. 4 and 5.

Unfortunately, even today the Buchholz method and its variants are routinely used as the first and second tiebreaker criteria. See, for example, the regulations for the rapid chess and blitz world championships that took place in December 2021, [4]. In the remainder of this section we describe the Buchholz method and some of its variants.

- Buchholz (FIDE) or Solkoff (USCF). (Hereafter abbreviated B).
  This is the sum of opponents' scores. The idea is that the same score is more valuable if achieved against players with better performances in a given tournament. It has been used since the Swiss system was invented. As shown in this paper it has some weaknesses.
- Median-Buchholz (FIDE) or Median/Harkness (USCF). (Hereafter abbreviated B_{-1}^{-1}).

Same as above but discarding the highest and the lowest opposition's scores. Its idea is to eliminate distortions in Buchholz values caused by taking into account games against run-away winners and bottom placed players.

- Buchholz after discarding the lowest score or Buchholz cut 1. (Hereafter abbreviated B_{-1}).
  Same as for B but only discarding the lowest opposition score. It prevents a penalty due to have played against an opponent who withdrew from the tournament before the end or did a very poor performance.
- Buchholz after discarding the two lowest scores and the highest score. (Hereafter abbreviated B_{-2}^{-1}).
  Same as for B but discarding the two lowest opposition's scores and the highest one. Its idea is to eliminate distortions in Buchholz values caused by taking into account games against a run-away winner and two bottom placed players.

We now describe two examples, obtained from past tournaments, which will be used later on.

Example 2.1. Assume three players A, E and I win a 9-round tournament with 7 of the 9 maximum achievable points. The first classified has a prize of 5,000 euros, the second of 3,000 euros and the third of 1,500 euros. The tie-breaker system applied determines the prize for each of them. The scores obtained by their opponents in the tournament are represented from lowest to highest in the following table.

Table 1. Tie-breaking according to four Buchholz methods: B, B_{-1}, B_{-1}^{-1}, B_{-2}^{-1}.

Player	Opponents' scores	B	B_{-1}	B_{-1}^{-1}	B_{-2}^{-1}
A	4 - 5 - 5.5 - 5.5 - 5.5 - 6 - 6 - 7 - 7	51.5	47.5	40.5	35.5
E	4 - 4.5 - 5 - 5.5 - 6 - 6 - 6.5 - 6.5 - 7	51	47	40	35.5
I	4 - 4 - 4 - 6 - 6 - 6.5 - 6.5 - 6.5 - 7	50.5	46.5	39.5	35.5

From Table 1 we observe:

- B, B_{-1}, and B_{-1}^{-1} provide the ordering: $A > E > I$, while
- B_{-2}^{-1} provides the triple tie: $A = E = I$.

None of these four measures gives the ranking $I > E > A$, which it would be more reasonable since player I is the one who has faced the largest number of opponents who have occupied leading positions. The same argument is used to compare E and A. Indeed, the number of opponents who scored 6 or more in the final standings is: 6 for I, 5 for E, and 4 for A, and, the number of opponents who scored 6.5 or more in the final standings is: 4 for I, 3 for E and 2 for A. The difficulty that I has had to overcome in the tournament seems to be greater than that of E and that of A.

Example 2.2. Assume five players A, E, I, O and U tie at 7 points each and occupy positions from third to seventh. The tiebreaker criteria will serve to assign the prizes for these players. The scores obtained by their opponents in the tournament are represented from lowest to highest in the following table.

Table 2. Tie-breaking according to four Buchholz methods: B, B_{-1}, B_{-1}^{-1} and B_{-2}^{-1}.

Player	Opponents' scores	B	B_{-1}	B_{-1}^{-1}	B_{-2}^{-1}
A	4 - 4.5 - 5.5 - 6 - 6 - 6.5 - 6.5 - 7 - 9 - 10	65	61	51	46.5
E	4 - 5.5 - 5.5 - 5.5 - 5.5 - 6 - 7 - 7 - 9 - 10	65	61	51	45.5
I	4.5 - 6 - 6 - 6 - 6.5 - 6.5 - 6.5 - 7 - 7 - 9	65	60.5	51.5	45.5
O	5 - 5.5 - 5.5 - 5.5 - 6 - 6.5 - 7 - 7 - 7 - 10	65	60	50	44.5
U	6 - 6 - 6 - 6.5 - 6.5 - 6.5 - 6.5 - 7 - 7 - 7	65	59	52	46

From Table 2 we observe:

- The ordering for B is: $A = E = I = O = U$.
- The ordering for B_{-1} is: $A = E > I > O > U$.
- The ordering for B_{-1}^{-1} is: $U > I > A = E > O$.
- The ordering for B_{-2}^{-1} is: $A > U > E = O > I$.

Here are some often exhibited weaknesses of Buchholz methods, illustrated in the previous examples.

- *Little discrimination.* Persistence of ties between competitors in the four variants.
- *Strong dependence on extreme opponents' scores.* Extreme opponents' scores often decide in case of similar players' performances.
- *Inconsistency of its variants.* The different variants of the method based on discarding some of the extreme opponents' scores usually provide different rankings.
- *Lack of responsiveness.* When the results of all the competitors are considered, there is not particularly high level of correlation between the number of points gained by a competitor and the corresponding tie-break score(s). When the number of rounds is small, this correlation coefficient is close to zero. The round-to-round correlation coefficient improves, but it does so very slowly.

Some strengths of the Buchholz method are:

- *Representativeness.* All (or almost all for its variants) opponents' scores are considered.
- *Computational simplicity.* Maybe this aspect was an important strength at the beginning of the last century.

3   The Median as a Tiebreaker System

As described in Sect. 2, the Buchholz method is just the arithmetic mean of the sum of the opponents' scores multiplied by the number of rounds. Both the sum and the arithmetic mean provide the same orderings. Thus, multiplying the mean by the number of rounds (i.e., the sum) is *redundant* and harmless for ranking purposes. Therefore we can interpret the arithmetic mean as a normalization of the Buchholz method.

Similarly, the indices that we introduce in this and the next section are measures of centralization multiplied by the number of rounds.

Outliers are frequent in tournaments. They can be due to extreme scores of some opponents, and much worse, due to player withdrawals or byes (authorized absences, which means not adding points, to not play any rounds). A first obvious observation is that Buchholz's method depends in excess on extreme performances of opponents.

It should be noted that in Swiss tournaments it is common for a few withdrawals and the request for a few byes. Having faced one or more players who have subsequently retired or made one or more byes is catastrophic when applying the Buchholz method. Nevertheless, withdrawals and byes are very rare in highly competitive open tournaments, e.g., in the world rapid and blitz chess championships.

It is a well-known fact that in general, when some data contain outliers it is preferable to use the median to the arithmetic mean. In fact, the value of the mean would be dominated by the outliers rather than the representative scores. So, someone who is considering to use the mean needs to check the data for outliers. This general principle questions Buchholz's method as a tiebreaker method based on opponents' scores.

The method most taught academically to identify outliers is the *Tukey test* [14], which takes as a reference the difference between the third quartile Q_3 and the first one Q_1, i.e., $Q_3 - Q_1$ or interquartile range, IQR. An outlier is an observation whose value is either more than 1.5 times the IQR below the lower quartile or more than 1.5 times the IQR above the upper quartile. For instance, in Example 2.2 the score of the best opponents for players A, E, I, O, are outliers according to Tukey's test. The coefficient 1.5 of Tukey's test should be lowered when the number of data (rounds in our case) is relatively small as is in open tournaments.

Undoubtedly, *the most representative opponent(s)* in the tournament among all those who have faced is the one (or those two if the number of rounds is even) whose final score occupies the median among all the opponents' scores. A second level of the most representative opponents in the tournament are those immediately before and after the median. In this way we could mention the first (the median), second, third, etc. levels of the most representative opponent(s). These levels are of great importance in the method that we propose in Sect. 4. Instead, the Buchholz method does not discriminate among these levels and the median method just considers the first level.

Taking the median instead of the mean, we may consider the same variants.

- The non-normalized median (Hereafter abbreviated M).
  This is the median of the opponents' scores multiplied by the number of rounds, n. The median is the central number in the ordered scores of the opponents if n is odd, or the mean of the two central numbers if n is even.
- The non-normalized median minus the worst opponents' score. (Hereafter abbreviated M_{-1}).
  Same as for M but only discarding the lowest opponent's score.

Note that other versions are equivalent to either M or M_{-1}. For instance, $M_{-1}^{-1} = M$ or $M_{-2}^{-1} = M_{-1}$.

From Table 1 we observe:

- M provides the ordering: $E = I > A$, while
- M_{-1} provides the ordering: $I > E > A$.

From Table 2 we observe:

- The ordering for M is: $I = U > A = O > E$.
- The ordering for M_{-1} is: $A = I = O = U > E$.

In both examples, but also in general, the next weakness is even sharper than for the Buchholz method.

- *Little discrimination.* Persistence of (many) ties between competitors in the two variants.

This flaw invalidates the non-normalized median (or the median multiplied by the number of rounds) as a tie-breaking system since discrimination is the most important property that a tiebreaker method must fulfill.

4   A New Tie-Breaker System Statistically Closer to the Median Than to the Mean

The objective of this section is to propose a new tie-breaking system for tournaments, especially those that use the Swiss system (as for example in Chess, Go, Bridge or Scrabble tournaments). The proposed system (described in Subsect. 4.1) admits the same variants (described in Subsect. 4.2) as the Buchholz system with respect to discarding opponents' scores. Therefore, both tie-breaking systems *are perfectly comparable and applicable to the same situations*. We claim that the proposed method in this paper has the following good properties:

- *Discrimination.* It easily breaks ties.
- *Near independence from extreme opponents' scores.* Extreme opponents' scores minimally affect the new proposed tiebreaker method.
- *Consistency of all its variants.* The different variants of the method based on discarding some of the opponents' scores usually give the same order.

- *Responsiveness.* There is a high level of correlation between the number of points gained by a competitor and the corresponding tie-break score(s), even when the number of rounds is small.
- *Regularity.* The results obtained by opponents of a similar level are the most relevant to determine the score of the proposed new tiebreaker method.
- *Representativeness.* All (or almost all for its variants) opponents' scores are considered.
- *Computational simplicity.* It is a weighted average of the opponents' scores, therefore it is very simple to be computed.

It should be noted that the new method satisfies the first five desirable properties to a clearly greater degree than the Buchholz method does. The sixth and the seventh properties are strengths of both methods. Regarding the seventh property, the simplicity of calculation, it can be said that the Buchholz method is somewhat simpler, since it is just a sum or a mean of the opponents' scores multiplied by the number of rounds. The new method is an alternative weighted average of opponents' scores, which is not much more complex!

From a strictly mathematical view point there are two strong arguments in favor of the new method in contrast to the Buchholz one:

- The Buchholz method is the mean multiplied by the number of rounds of the tournament. Similarly, the proposed method can be thought as a 'number' multiplied by the number of rounds of the tournament, where the 'number', which is also a central measure of the opponents' scores, is statistically closer to the median than to the mean of the opponents' scores. As is well-known, the median has many advantages over the mean, such as less variability, greater independence from outliers, less manipulability, etc.
- The weights associated to the opponents' scores are all the same for the mean and define a uniform discrete distribution. Instead, the weights associated to the opponents' scores for the non-normalized version of the new method come from a *binomial distribution*, which is continuously approximated by the *normal distribution*. Thus, in this respect, the proposed method is based on the most important discrete and continuous distributions.

4.1   The New Proposal

Let n be the number of rounds of a chess tournament (or another particular sport) where the number of participants is considerable higher than n. Assume that the opponents' scores of a given player are:

$$x_1 \leq x_2 \leq \cdots \leq x_n, \tag{1}$$

i.e., they are taken in non-decreasing ordering. We consider the *Pascal's numbers*:

$$p_i^n = \binom{n-1}{i-1} \quad \text{for all } i = 1, 2, \ldots, n \tag{2}$$

which are well-defined for all positive integers n. A well-known property of Pascal's numbers, in (2), is $\sum_{i=1}^{n} p_i^n = 2^{n-1}$ for all positive integer n. Then, we compute the following weighted average

$$f^n = \frac{\sum_{i=1}^{n} p_i^n}{2^{n-1}} \cdot x_i \tag{3}$$

If the coefficients in (3) are defined as

$$q_i^n := \frac{p_i^n}{2^{n-1}} \tag{4}$$

for all integers $n > 1$ and $i < n$, then (3) can simply be written as

$$f^n = \sum_{i=1}^{n} q_i^n \cdot x_i \tag{5}$$

where $\sum_{i=1}^{n} q_i^n = 1$. We should interpret the number f^n as a central measure of the opponents' scores, which is closer to the median than to the mean.

Then, the F-tie-breaking score (hereafter abbreviated as F) associated to each player is defined as

$$F = f \cdot n \tag{6}$$

where, as said, n stands for the number of rounds which is known in advance, so we identify f^n with f (and F^n with F) in (6). Obviously, nothing would change if it were used f instead of F. However, we use the latter index in analogy with the Buchholz tie-breaking method, which uses B instead of the mean, b. Compare expressions (5) and (6) above with (7) and (8) below.

Similarly, consider the constant numbers $c_i^n := \frac{1}{n}$ for each integer $n > 1$ and $i < n$, which obviously satisfy $\sum_{i=1}^{n} c_i^n = 1$. Let

$$b^n = \sum_{i=1}^{n} c_i^n \cdot x_i. \tag{7}$$

be the mean of the opponents' scores. The Buchholz tiebreaking method is:

$$B = b \cdot n \tag{8}$$

where we identify b^n with b (and B^n with B) in (8).

Before presenting the three variants of the method, we show some coefficients of the numerators used. We refer to the well-known Pascal triangle.

The numerators, given in (2), of the coefficients q_i^n, given in (4), used to compute the F-index appear in Table 3. As the number of rounds is fixed and known in advance we just need to take the numbers p_i^n in the n-th row in Table 3

Table 3. The numbers of Pascal's triangle, p_i^n for all $n = 1, \ldots, 9$ and $i = 0, \ldots, n-1$.

$$
\begin{array}{ccccccccccc}
 & & & & & 1 & & & & & \\
 & & & & 1 & & 1 & & & & \\
 & & & 1 & & 2 & & 1 & & & \\
 & & 1 & & 3 & & 3 & & 1 & & \\
 & 1 & & 4 & & 6 & & 4 & & 1 & \\
1 & & 5 & & 10 & & 10 & & 5 & & 1 \\
\end{array}
$$

$$
\begin{array}{ccccccccccccc}
1 & & 6 & & 15 & & 20 & & 15 & & 6 & & 1 \\
1 & & 7 & & 21 & & 35 & & 35 & & 21 & & 7 & & 1 \\
1 & & 8 & & 28 & & 56 & & 70 & & 56 & & 28 & & 8 & & 1 \\
\end{array}
$$

and standardize them to get q_i^n. For instance, the numbers in the penultimate row are used to calculate the F-index for a 8-round tournament.

We conclude this subsection by remarking again that for the purpose of breaking ties it is equivalent to consider either B or b as well as F or f. As B is the standard index for chess we will use F for the new index, nevertheless, both b and f have more direct interpretations.

4.2   The Three Analogous Variants

In this subsection we introduce variants of the F-index, analogous to those defined for the B-index.

- The new proposal minus the worst result. (Hereafter abbreviated F_{-1}).
  We just remove x_1 in (1), and redefine the remaining scores x_i for $i > 1$ as $x_i := x_{i+1}$ and then apply the previous method by replacing everywhere n by $n - 1$. That is, we take

$$
f^{n-1} = \frac{\sum_{i=1}^{n-1} p_i^{n-1}}{2^{n-2}} \cdot x_i = \sum_{i=1}^{n-1} q_i^{n-1} \cdot x_i \tag{9}
$$

instead of (3) and then F in (6) is redefined as

$$
F_{-1} = f^{n-1} \cdot (n-1) \tag{10}
$$

- The new proposal minus the best and the worst results. (Hereafter abbreviated F_{-1}^{-1}).
  We just remove x_1 and x_n in (1), and redefine the scores x_i for $i > 1$ and $i < n$ as $x_i := x_{i+1}$ and then apply the first proposed method by replacing everywhere n by $n - 2$. That is, we take

$$
f^{n-2} = \frac{\sum_{i=1}^{n-2} p_i^{n-2}}{2^{n-3}} \cdot x_i = \sum_{i=1}^{n-2} q_i^{n-2} \cdot x_i \tag{11}
$$

instead of (3) and then F in (6) is redefined as

$$F_{-1}^{-1} = f^{n-2} \cdot (n-2) \tag{12}$$

- The new proposal minus the best and the two worst results. (Hereafter abbreviated F_{-2}^{-1}).
  We just remove x_1, x_2 and x_n in (1), and redefine the scores x_i for $i > 2$ and $i < n$ as $x_i := x_{i+2}$ and then apply the first proposed method by replacing everywhere n by $n-3$. That is, we take

$$f^{n-3} = \frac{\sum_{i=1}^{n-3} p_i^{n-3}}{2^{n-4}} \cdot x_i = \sum_{i=1}^{n-3} q_i^{n-3} \cdot x_i \tag{13}$$

instead of (3) and then F in (6) is redefined as

$$F_{-2}^{-1} = f^{n-3} \cdot (n-3) \tag{14}$$

The numerators of the coefficients, q_i^{n-1}, q_i^{n-2} and q_i^{n-3} used to respectively compute the F_{-1}, F_{-1}^{-1} and F_{-2}^{-1} indices appear in Table 3. As the number of rounds is fixed and known in advance we just need to take the respective numbers in the $(n-1)$-th, $(n-2)$-th and $(n-3)$-th row in Table 3. For instance, the numbers in the penultimate row are used to calculate the F-index for a 8-round tournament, or the F_{-1}-index for a 9-round tournament, or the F_{-1}^{-1}-index for a 10-round tournament, or the F_{-2}^{-1}-index for a 11-round tournament.

Example 4.1. (Example 2.1 revisited)

Consider again Example 2.1. Table 4 provides now the results for the F-index and its variants, obtained from expressions (9) to (14). Opposing results are observed for the Buchholz tie-breaking system and the proposed new method. Indeed, while F, F_{-1}, F_{-1}^{-1} and F_{-2}^{-1} give the same ranking: $I > E > A$; the Buchholz methods B, B_{-1} and B_{-1}^{-1} provide the reversed ranking $A > E > I$.

Table 4. Tie-breaking scores according to the four proposed methods: F, F_{-1}, F_{-1}^{-1} and F_{-2}^{-1} respectively analogous to B, B_{-1}, B_{-1}^{-1} and B_{-2}^{-1}.

Player	Opponents' scores	F	F_{-1}	F_{-1}^{-1}	F_{-2}^{-1}
A	4 - 5 - 5.5 - 5.5 - 5.5 - 6 - 6 - 7 - 7	49.92857	46.46875	39.75781	34.6875
E	4 - 4.5 - 5 - 5.5 - 6 - 6 - 6.5 - 6.5 - 7	52.20070	47.75000	40.74218	36
I	4 - 4 - 4 - 6 - 6 - 6.5 - 6.5 - 6.5 - 7	53.05078	49.03125	41.67187	37.125

Example 4.2. (Example 2.2 revisited)

Consider again Example 2.2. Table 5 provides now the results for the F-index and its variants.

From Table 5 we observe the following:

Table 5. Tie-breaking scores according to the four proposed methods: F, F_{-1}, F_{-1}^{-1} and F_{-2}^{-1} respectively analogous to B, B_{-1}, B_{-1}^{-1} and B_{-2}^{-1}.

Player	Opponents' scores	F	F_{-1}	F_{-1}^{-1}	F_{-2}^{-1}
A	4 - 4.5 - 5.5 - 6 - 6 - 6.5 - 6.5 - 7 - 9 - 10	62.7051	57.9902	50.0625	44.8438
E	4 - 5.5 - 5.5 - 5.5 - 5.5 - 6 - 7 - 7 - 9 - 10	60.4199	56.3027	47.9375	43.4219
I	4.5 - 6 - 6 - 6 - 6.5 - 6.5 - 6.5 - 7 - 7 - 9	64.1895	58.5703	51.3438	45.5
O	5 - 5.5 - 5.5 - 5.5 - 6 - 6.5 - 7 - 7 - 7 - 10	62.5488	57.9551	50	45.1172
U	6 - 6 - 6 - 6.5 - 6.5 - 6.5 - 6.5 - 7 - 7 - 7	65	58.9922	52	45.8281

- For F, F_{-1}, and F_{-1}^{-1} the ordering is: $U > I > A > O > E$.
- For F_{-2}^{-1} the ordering is: $U > I > O > A > E$.

From these two examples we observe that, in contrast to Buchholz's method, the new method:

- totally discriminates among tied players. In fact, the four methods give a strict order in the two examples,
- is more homogeneous. No variation in the rankings provided by the different versions for Example 2.1 and almost no variations for Example 2.2. So, few ranking reversal among the different variants of the new index.

5   Strengths of the Proposed Index

In this section we provide some additional arguments on the goodness of the new index, mainly in contrast with Buchholz one. We assume that two players x and y finish the tournament tied and that the results obtained by their respective opponents are taken in order as in (1). We write, for example, $B(x)$ for x's Buchholz score, $M(x)$ for x's median score, and $F(x)$ for x's F-score.

5.1   Focusing on the Scores of the Most Representative Opponents

Opponents' scores in the interquartile range are the most transparent reflection of the tournament the player has made. Scores in the interquartile range are the only ones that are surely free of outliers and therefore should be of greater importance in the tie-breaking method selected. The interquartile range is a good measure of dispersion for skewed distributions. The opponents' scores of an arbitrary player are often skewed, so central opponents' scores explain much better the strength of the opponents that the player had to face.

For example, in a 9-round tournament, the median of the opponent's score, x_5, explains just 11.1% of the Buchholz tiebreaker method, while 27.3% of the F-tiebreaker method and 100% of the median tiebreaker method. The three central opponent's scores (the second centrality level) x_4, x_5, x_6 explain 33.3% of the B-method, while 71.1% of the F-method. The five central opponent's scores (the third centrality level) x_3, x_4, x_5, x_6, x_7 only explain 55.5% of the B-method, while 93.3% of the F-method.

Note that when the number of rounds is greater than 9, the sum of the weights of the opponents' scores included in the interquartile range is not so far from 1 for the F-method, but tends to 0.5 for the B-method, which makes it tremendously dependent on extreme opponents' scores.

5.2 Ordered Weighted Averages

Any way of aggregating the different scores into a unique result is a *scoring system*. An interesting particular class of scoring systems are the *ordered weighted averages* (OWA for short), which are defined as follows:

Let n be the number of tournament rounds, and let $w = (w_1, \ldots, w_n)$ be a vector of non-negative real numbers such that $\sum_{i=1}^{n} w_i = 1$ and the opponents' scores of a player are ordered as in (1). Then, the vector w defines the OWA of these values by:

$$w(x_1, \ldots, x_n) = \sum_{i=1}^{n} w_i x_i \tag{15}$$

The numbers w_i are the weights of the OWA.

OWA operators were introduced by Yager [17] in the context of multicriteria decision making. An overview of these operators can be found in [18].

The coefficients c_i^n for B, q_i^n for F and these for M:

$$w_i^n = \begin{cases} (\overbrace{0, \ldots, 0}^{(n-1)/2}, 1, \overbrace{0, \ldots, 0}^{(n-1)/2}) & \text{if } n \text{ is odd} \\ (\overbrace{0, \ldots, 0}^{n/2-1}, \frac{1}{2}, \frac{1}{2}, \overbrace{0, \ldots, 0}^{n/2-1}) & \text{if } n \text{ is even} \end{cases}$$

define OWAs, as well as the coefficients for its variants: B_{-1}, B_{-1}^{-1}, B_{-2}^{-1}, M_{-1}, F_{-1}, F_{-1}^{-1} and F_{-2}^{-1}. Let $\mathcal{C}$ be the set of ten OWAs formed by B, M, F and all of its variants.

Next, we describe some properties for the OWAs:

1. *Idempotency:* $w(a, \ldots, a) = a$.
2. *Boundedness:* If $x_1 \leq \cdots \leq x_n$ then $x_1 \leq w(x_1, \ldots, x_n) \leq x_n$.
3. *Monotonicity:* If $x_1 \leq y_1, \ldots, x_n \leq y_n$ then $w(x_1, \ldots, x_n) \leq w(y_1, \ldots, y_n)$.
4. *Concavity:* $w_i \leq w_j$ if $i < j$ and $j \leq \lceil \frac{n}{2} \rceil$, and $w_i \geq w_j$ if $i < j$ and $\lfloor \frac{n}{2} \rfloor + 1 \geq i$.
5. *Symmetry:* $w_i = w_{n+1-i}$ for all $i = 1, 2, \ldots, n$.
6. *Strict monotonicity:*
   If $x_1 \leq y_1, \ldots, x_n \leq y_n$ and $(x_1, \ldots, x_n) \neq (y_1, \ldots, y_n)$ then $w(x_1, \ldots, x_n) < w(y_1, \ldots, y_n)$.
7. *Strict concavity:* $w_i < w_j$ if $i < j$, and $j \leq \lceil \frac{n}{2} \rceil$ and $w_i > w_j$ if $i < j$ and $\lfloor \frac{n}{2} \rfloor + 1 \geq i$.

Proposition 5.1. *The F-method is the only one in $\mathcal{C}$ that satisfies the seven properties above.*

PROOF. The ten OWAs in $\mathcal{C}$ satisfy: idempotency, boundedness, monotonicity and concavity.

Symmetry is satisfied by: B, B_{-1}^{-1}, M, F, F_{-1}^{-1}.

Strict monotonicity, which is equivalent to strict positivity, i.e., $w_i > 0$ for all i, is only satisfied by B and F, since they are the only measures within the set $\mathcal{C}$ with all positive coefficients.

Strict concavity is only satisfied by F and F_{-1}^{-1} because they are symmetric, a necessary but not sufficient condition for strict concavity, and satisfy: $w_i < w_j$ if $i < j$, and $j \leq \lceil \frac{n}{2} \rceil$ and $w_i > w_j$ if $i < j$ and $\lfloor \frac{n}{2} \rfloor + 1 \geq i$. The other three symmetric measures in the set $\mathcal{C}$ are: B, B_{-1}^{-1} and M. As these measures have many coefficients being the same, it happens that strict concavity fails for B if $n \geq 3$, and it fails for B_{-1}^{-1} and M if $n \geq 5$.   □

5.3   Binomial and Normal Distributions Support the Proposed Method

The coefficients c_i^n of the B-index follow a discrete uniform distribution, whereas the coefficients q_i^n of the F-index follow a binomial distribution $B(n-1, p)$ with probability $p = 1/2$ and the number of trials $n - 1$ stands for the number of rounds minus 1. Then the central opponents' scores are prioritized over the extreme ones. As is well-known, for large n this binomial distribution can be understood as a discretized approximation of the normal distribution with mean equal to $(n-1)/2$ and standard deviation equal to $\sqrt{n-1}/2$. Indeed, let h be the density function of such a normal distribution and X be the associated random variable. Then, when n increases the coefficients q_i^n become close to

$$q_i^n \approx \frac{h(a_i)}{\sum\limits_{j=1}^{n} h(a_j)}$$

where the numbers a_i for $i = 1, \ldots, n$ are obtained from the inverse of the distribution function $F(a_i) = P(X \leq a_i) = (i - 1) \cdot \frac{1}{n} + \frac{1}{2n}$.

5.4   Discrimination

Due to the method of selecting pairs using the Swiss system, it is common for tied players in the final standings to have a fairly similar Buchholz index. Rarely does this index differ by more than the number of rounds n in the tournament and in most cases their B-indices differ by very small amounts. Moreover, observe that the index B is either an integer number or an integer number plus a half. Therefore, it is common for certain ties in the final standings to persist after applying the B-index. Of course, the lack of discrimination is even more pronounced for the median.

Instead, the F-index is either an integer number or an integer number plus a fraction of the type $\frac{i}{2^{n-1}}$ where $i = 1, \ldots, 2^{n-1} - 1$. Thus the F-index very effectively discriminates ties, although naturally some may exceptionally persist.

The number of pairs of tied players in the final standings of the 2021 rapid world chess championship [16], who also tied for B or for B_{-1} was over 40 and 5 pairs remained tied for both B and B_{-1}. The number of pairs of tied players in the final standings of the 2021 women rapid world chess championship [15], who also tied for B or B_{-1} was over 30 and 4 pairs remained tied for both B and B_{-1}. This example illustrates the lack of discrimination of B and its variants, which is avoided with the F-index and any of its variants.

5.5   Near Independence from Extreme Opponents' Scores

Outliers are frequent in tournaments where players of very different levels compete and the number of rounds is not small. Extreme opponents' scores (outliers, but not necessarily) appear:

- *below* for the best ranked players in the final standings,
- *above* for the weakest ranked players in the final standings,
- *below or above* for the medium ranked players in the final standings.

According to Tukey's test for outliers a number is an outlier if it does not belong to the acceptable range given by the interval $(Q1 - 1.5 \cdot IQR, Q3 + 1.5 \cdot IQR)$. As the number of rounds is usually small, the coefficient 1.5 should be lowered, but a precise definition of an outlier is not too crucial here.

The weighted coefficients of extreme opponents' scores for f are small in comparison with the central weighted coefficients, so the incidence of extreme scores is minimal when F or any of its variants are used. On the other hand, the dependency on opponents' extreme scores of the B-index and its variants is high.

5.6   Consistency of Its Variants

Let x and y be two tied competitors after the last round. If $B(x) - B(y) > 0$ and $B(x) - B(y) < x_1 - y_1$, then $B_{-1}(x) - B_{-1}(y) < 0$. In words, if $B(x) - B(y) > 0$, $B(x)$ and $B(y)$ do not differ too much, x_1 is an outlier but y_1 is not; then B and B_{-1} reverse the Buchholz tie-breaker of the two players. Thus, extreme low scores easily change the orderings of tied players when using any pair of the indices: B, B_{-1}, B_{-1}^{-1}, B_{-2}^{-1} or B_{-2} as first and second tie-breaking criteria. This means that the performances of the worst opponents of x and y are decisive in deciding which of them is ranked first. The same also applies for the best opponents of x and y if, for instance, B, B_{-1}^{-1} or B_{-2}^{-1} are applied.

A *reversal of the players x and y* for the pair of indices, let's say, B and B_{-1} (or any other pair of indices) arises when

$$(B(x) - B(y)) \cdot (B_{-1}(x) - B_{-1}(y)) < 0.$$

This means that B and B_{-1} order x and y oppositely for the two indices. As B and all of its variants are based on the same criterion of being a 'weighted sum' of the opponents' scores, we regard reversals as a strong weakness of a method. We claim that any pair of Buchholz methods witnesses many reversals. For instance, B_{-1} and B, the first and second tie-breaking criteria for the 2021 rapid world chess championship show: 27 reversals, i.e., 27 pairs of players who were tied in the final standings would had been ranked oppositely if B had been the first tie-breaking criterion instead of B_{-1}. The number of reversals for the women's 2021 rapid world chess championship was 16. These two competitions had 150 and 100 players respectively and 13 and 11 rounds respectively. Barely any reversals were observed for F and F_{-1} in the two competitions.

Indeed, the F-index and its variants hardly present reversals. Mainly because they are very weakly dependent on extreme scores, see previous subsection. As an example, we may compare the coefficients $c_1^n = c_n^n = \frac{1}{n}$ and $q_1^n = q_n^n = \frac{1}{2^{n-1}}$ to see that the relative incidence of outliers or (if any) or extreme scores for the F-index with respect to the B-index is $\frac{n}{2^{n-1}}$, which is quite small for a standard number of rounds (usually from 8 to 11 in classic chess, 11 to 13 in rapid chess, or 11 to 21 in blitz).

5.7 Responsiveness

If one player is well above another in the final standings, it is expected (due to the Swiss pairing system) that the tiebreaker score obtained will also be higher for the first player. In other words, there must be a good significant positive correlation between the score obtained in the final classification and the score of the tie-breaking method used.

Some positive correlation is reached with almost all tie-breaking methods after the last round, including the Buchholz method and its variants. As the number of rounds increases, the correlation coefficient for B improves although it does so very slowly. However, the linear correlation coefficient is considerably lower for the Buchholz index and variants than for the F index and its variants.

For the first two rounds Buchholz's method and the F-method coincide, Buchholz's method does not respond well for the first rounds, say from the third to the sixth, in which the correlation coefficient is even negative or close to zero. On the contrary, the correlation coefficient applied to F and its variants is not negative from the third round and increases with the number of rounds in a greater way. The F-method responds much better because it almost ignores the opponents' scores which are very high or very small, so it responds very well from the fourth round onwards. The linear correlation coefficient between the scores in the final classification in the rapid 2021 chess world championship and B_{-1} and B are both close to 0.72 while for F_{-1} and F they are 7–8 hundredths greater.

5.8   Regularity

Any player usually finishes the tournament having played against a majority of opponents who did a performance not too dissimilar to his/her performance. The F-index gives great importance to opponents' central scores, and is only minimally affected by opponents' extreme scores. The scores of opponents whose final standings are considerably different are undervalued by the F-index, but they are not for the B-index. In addition, the F-index is not affected by extraordinarily good or bad results from opponents, while B is decisively affected in many cases.

5.9   Representativeness

All opponents' scores are used in the F-index, only one is discarded for F_{-1}, two for F_{-1}^{-1}, three for F_{-2}^{-1}. This is analogous to what occurs for the B-index.

5.10   Computational Simplicity

The main argument that favors the Buchholz index over the F-index is its simplicity of calculation, maybe an important property in the early past century. However, the F-index is not much more complex to compute since it is an OWA with very recognizable coefficients. In case there is any doubt, we present two very simple ways to calculate it.

Recursive method to determine the weights q_i^n:
Starting from the well–known formula

$$\binom{n-1}{i-1} = \binom{n-2}{i-1} + \binom{n-2}{i-2},$$

dividing both sides of this equality by 2^{n-1}, and taking into account the definition (4), we obtain

$$q_i^n = \frac{q_i^{n-1} + q_{i-1}^{n-1}}{2}.$$

In this way we can derive the weight q_i^n from the weights q_i^{n-1} and q_{i-1}^{n-1}. Thus, starting for $n = 2$ (then, $q_1^2 = q_2^2 = 1/2$) we can recursively find the weights for any arbitrary number n of rounds.

Method to find the F-index by iterative computation of arithmetic means
We start by considering the opponent's scores, $x_1 \leq \cdots \leq x_n$. Then, compute the arithmetic mean of the $n - 1$ pairs of consecutive scores. Next, compute the arithmetic mean of the $n - 2$ pairs of consecutive numbers obtained in the previous step. Continue this process to get a single number. It is trivial to show that the resulting number is f and therefore $F = f \cdot n$. Table 6 shows an example of such an iterative calculation.

Table 6. Recursive method for the F-index by arithmetic means.

1	3	5	6	6	6.5	6.5	7
2	4	5.5	6	6.25	6.5	6.75	
3	4.75	5.75	6.125	6.375	6.625		
3.875	5.25	5.9375	6.25	6.5			
4.5625	5.59375	6.09375	6.375				
5.078125	5.84375	6.234375					
5.4609375	6.0390625						
5.75							

Thus, the F-index is $F = 8 \cdot 5.75 = 46$.

6   Conclusion

Buchholz's method and some of its variants are by far the most used method to break ties in the final standings in open chess tournaments and other sports. B and B_{-1} are the first and second criteria to break ties in the rapid and blitz chess world championships that took place in December, 2021.

In this article we point out four important shortcomings of the Buchholz method: it is tremendously dependent on extreme opponents' scores, it discriminates little, is inconsistent in its variants, and is poorly correlated with the points of competitors in each round. The tie-breaks in the first places are the most important since they decide prizes. The outliers of the first classified competitors correspond to the worst scores of their opponents, which decisively influence the tiebreaker if the Buchholz method is used, something tremendously unfair.

As an alternative tie-breaking method also based on weighted averages of opponents' scores, we propose the F-index, which is hardly affected by outliers, highly discriminates, is highly consistent in its variants and well correlated with the points that obtain competitors in each round. Furthermore, its coefficients regarded as an ordered weighted average are based on the binomial distribution whose continuous approximation is the normal distribution.

We do think that FIDE in the case of chess (and respective federations which apply the B-index as a tie-breaker system) should adopt the F-method instead of the B-method promptly.

As more particular suggestions we recommend to:

- apply the F_{-1}-index, as a first tiebreaker criterion, for open tournaments with a reduced number of rounds (less than 9), F_{-2} (i.e., the F-index obtained after discarding the two lowest opponents' scores) for open tournaments with a number of rounds between 10 and 13, and F_{-3} (i.e., the F-index obtained after discarding the three lowest opponents' scores) for open tournaments with a number of rounds greater than 13. This is based on the arguments provided in Sects. 4 and 5 and because tie-breaks are much more important in the first positions. Moreover, some few withdrawals are common in most tournaments so that the use of F_{-1}, F_{-2} or F_{-3} counteract their potential incidence;

- avoid applying two criteria of the same nature as a first and second tie-breaker criteria. This still happens today with B_{-1} and B as the first and second criteria recommended by FIDE, see [5], and particularly applied in the rapid and blitz chess world championships that took place in December 2021. The use of F or any of its variants as a first tie-breaker criterion almost guarantees that ties do not persist. Thus, the incidence of the second tie-breaker method is minimal.

- As indicated in the first item, we recommend to use F_{-2} as a first tiebreaker criterion for the next rapid chess world championships and to use F_{-3} as the first tiebreaker criterion for the next blitz chess world championships.

Acknowledgements. This research is part of the I+D+i project PID2019-104987GB-I00 supported by MCIN/AEI/10.13039/501100011033/

The author greatly appreciates the detailed comments of the two referees that have contributed to improve the revised version of this article. He also acknowledges the comments made on this article by Jordi Magem, Chess Grandmaster and FIDE Senior Trainer; Vladimir Zaiats, Mathematician and International Chess Arbiter; Josep M. Barón, Mathematician and FIDE Chess Master; and Juli Pérez, Mathematician and National Chess Master.

References

1. Standard AGA Tournament Protocols. American Go Association. https://www.usgo.org/standard-aga-tournament-protocols
2. A.E. Elo. '8.4 Logistic Probability as a Rating Basis', The Rating of Chessplayers, Past & Present. Bronx NY 10453: ISHI Press International (2008). ISBN 978-0-923891-27-5
3. EGF Tournament System Rules. European Go Federation. https://www.eurogofed.org/egf/tourrules.htm
4. Regulations for the FIDE Open World rapid & blitz championships. International Chess Federation (2021). https://www.fide.com/
5. FIDE Handbook, Appendix C, Section 11.5.3, 2021. International Chess Federation, 2018, come into force 2019
6. Freixas, J., Parker, C.: Manipulation in games with multiple levels of output. J. Math. Econ. **61**, 144–151 (2015)
7. Gibbard, A.: Manipulation of voting schemes: a general result. Econometrica **41**, 587–601 (1973)
8. Golombek, H.: Golombek's Encyclopedia of Chess, Crown (1977). ISBN 0-517-53146-1
9. Moulin, H.: On strategy-proofness and single peakedness. Econometrica **35**(4), 437–455 (1980)
10. Satterthwaite, M.A.: Strategy-proofness and Arrow's conditions: existence and correspondence theorems for voting procedures and social welfare functions. J. Econ. Theory **10**(2), 187–217 (1975)
11. What is the Swiss System? Chess.about.com (2013). https://www.thesprucecrafts.com/the-swiss-system-611537

12. 125 years Swiss System. en.chessbase.com (2014). https://en.chessbase.com/post/125-years-swiss-system
13. Swiss Pairing. Sensei's Library. Nadunmi. https://senseis.xmp.net/?SwissPairing
14. Tukey, J.W.: Exploratory Data Analysis. Addison-Wesley, Reading (1977)
15. Women World Rapid Chess Championship 2021 chess-results.com (2021). https://chess-results.com/tnr600853.aspx?lan=1
16. World Rapid Chess Championship 2021 chess-results.com (2021). https://chess-results.com/tnr600852.aspx?lan=1
17. Yager, R.R.: On ordered weighted averaging aggregation operators in multicriteria decision making. IEEE Trans. Syst. Man Cybern. **18**, 183–190 (1988)
18. Yager, R.R., Kacprzyk, J.: The Ordered Weighted Averaging Operators, Theory and Applications. Kluwer Academic Publishers (1997)

Constructing Varied and Attractive Shortlists from Databases: A Group Decision Approach

David M. Ramsey[1(✉)] and Aleksander Mariański[2]

[1] Department of Computer Science and Systems Engineering, Faculty of Computer Science and Telecommunications, Wrocław University of Science and Technology, Wrocław, Poland
david.ramsey@pwr.edu.pl
[2] Department of Applied Computer Science, Faculty of Computer Science and Telecommunications, Wrocław University of Science and Technology, Wrocław, Poland
aleksander.marianski@pwr.edu.pl

Abstract. Thanks to the Internet, basic information can be found about a very large number of offers at very little cost. Many sites give basic information about real estate offers, including price, size, location and number of rooms. Information of this kind is sufficient to assess whether an offer is potentially attractive or not, but does not suffice in making an ultimate decision. The number of real estate offers in a city may be very large. In such a case, it can be beneficial to use an automatic procedure to first eliminate offers that do not satisfy the basic criteria of an individual or family and then construct a shortlist of varied and potentially attractive offers. This article recalls an algorithm that derives such a shortlist for an individual searcher. The novelty of this article lies in adapting this algorithm to scenarios in which a group decision is made. A practical example based on real estate offers in Warsaw is used to illustrate the algorithm.

1 Introduction

This paper proposes a method of decision support in cases when a small set of decision makers (DMs) are searching for a unique valuable good and a large number of offers are available. In such cases, it is unfeasible for the DMs to closely inspect all of these offers before making their final decision. Consider a family who are looking for a new home in a large city. Very often, the first step in the search procedure uses data from the Internet or an intermediary source to define a shortlist of offers that should be physically viewed. Basic information on offers, e.g. location, price, and floorspace, can be found easily. In the field of decision support, online filtering algorithms are available for removing offers that do not satisfy the DMs' basic search criteria, e.g. maximum price, maximum distance from city centre, minimum floorspace (see Guillet *et al.* (2020)). One

© Springer-Verlag GmbH Germany, part of Springer Nature 2022
N. T. Nguyen et al. (Eds.): Transactions on Computational Collective Intelligence XXXVII, LNCS 13750, pp. 21–52, 2022.
https://doi.org/10.1007/978-3-662-66597-8_2

way of determining a shortlist of k offers to view would to be use an online ranking algorithm and select the first k offers according to this ranking. Offers with multiple attributes may be ranked on the basis of those attributes judged to be most important in determining the attractiveness of an offer (see Rubenstein and Salant (2006) and Mandler et al. (2012)). Kimya (2018) presents a similar approach according to which offers are successively eliminated on the basis of a sequence of criteria of ever decreasing importance. Such ranking procedures can be very useful to DMs, but can also direct DMs in a particular, not always favourable, direction (see e.g. Ursu (2018)).

As Stojić et al. (2020) and Analytis et al. (2019) note, DMs can gain by investigating novel options. This is particularly true when the information contained in a decision problem is particularly rich (see Caplin et al. (2019), Billinger et al. (2021)). For example, when an individual is moving to a new city, there may be a large number of suitable real estate offers (at least according to initial information) in the near vicinity of his/her workplace. However, on closer inspection, this DM might find this quarter of the city very unattractive to live in. Hence, in order to assess the value of a shortlist, one should not only look at the potential attractiveness of the offers on the shortlist (based on the information available), but also at the variety of offers on the shortlist. Based on these considerations, the authors propose a method for selecting shortlists of potentially attractive offers based on both the individual assessments of the attractiveness of offers and the overall variety of offers placed on the shortlist. Ramsey and Mariański (2022) present an algorithm that selects shortlists on the basis of information from a database. The novelty of the work presented in this chapter lies in the fact that this approach is applied within the framework of a group decision problem.

The use of shortlists in such search procedures is a commonly used heuristic due to the cognitive limitations and time constraints faced by DMs. Viewing each property that meets predetermined conditions based on size, location and price may involve prohibitive search costs. However, overly restricting the set of offers that are to be considered may lead to purchasing a relatively unattractive offer. In practice, heuristics should be adapted to both the limitations of DMs and the way in which information can be accessed during search (see Simon (1955; 1956), Todd and Gigerenzer (2000), as well Bobadilla-Suarez and Love (2018)). When the number of offers is large, shortlists are useful when DMs can obtain some information about the potential attractiveness of an offer with little effort (e.g. via the Internet), but gaining precise information about an offer's attractiveness is relatively costly (e.g. travel and/or physical inspection are required). In such cases, exhaustive search is excessively costly and/or the cognitive abilities of DMs are insufficient to process all the information necessary (see Masatlioglu et al. (2012) and Lleras et al. (2017)).

Although a reasonably large amount of research on the theoretical properties of such shortlists has been carried out, little research has considered optimization models investigating such aspects as the number of offers that should be included in a shortlist, or how a shortlist should be constructed on the basis of multivariate data. Ramsey (2019) presents an optimization model for an individual DM searching for a valuable resource using a short list. This model assumes that there are two rounds of search. In the first round, offers are ranked on the basis of an initial signal. This signal is unidimensional, but one may interpret such signals as a measure of attractiveness based on multiple traits. In the second round of search, the DM closely inspects the k most attractive offers (according to the initial information). The assessments of the offers on this shortlist are updated on the basis of the information gained in the second round. The DM then selects the highest ranked offer. The costs of closely inspecting an offer (in the second round) are relatively high compared to the costs of observing the initial signal presenting an offer (in the first round). The goal of the analysis was to determine the optimal length of a shortlist on the basis of the relative costs of search in both rounds and amount of information contained in the initial signal. Constructing a shortlist that includes a moderate amount of offers (4–10 offers) was found to be a very robust procedure over a wide range of problems of this form.

Analytis (2014) presents a similar model that considers what might be interpreted as prioritizing items which are assessed to be potentially attractive based on initial information, rather than constructing a shortlist. During initial inspection (parallel search), offers are ranked according to an initial signal. During the second round of inspection, the DM closely observes offers in sequence according to the rank of an offer ascribed in the first round. The DM stops when the value of an offer exceeds the expected reward from future search. Rather than determining the optimal size of a shortlist (or an optimal procedure), this article considers how a shortlist should be formed given its required size. As argued above, an algorithm constructing such shortlists should not only consider the potential attractiveness of offers on the shortlist, but also their variety.

Classical models of group decision making (GDM) assume that each of the DMs involved gives a score to each of the offers based on a full set of data about the offers. The attractiveness of an offer to the group as a whole is then defined as an average (possibly weighted) of these scores (see Taha 2017). This paper considers a problem in which a number of numerical traits defining an offer (e.g. location, price, floor space) are available. The goal of the group is to choose a relatively small number of offers for further investigation from a very large set of offers. Hence, a large degree of automation at this stage of the decision process is desirable, due to the limitations of DMs in processing large data sets. Once the number of offers considered has been reduced, the DMs themselves may directly take additional traits of each offer (possibility qualitative) into consideration and/or decide whether to physically observe an offer. The offers placed on any shortlist should be generally attractive to the group members and relatively diverse. Hence, one can define a score for a particular shortlist as a weighted average of the mean measure of attractiveness of offers on the shortlist and the mean distance between these offers (a measure of their diversity according to the traits observed). One issue to solve when using such an approach is defining what the weights of attractiveness and diversity should be. For this reason, a data driven approach is used that successively increases the weight ascribed to diversity until the shortlist selected shows approximately the same diversity as the set of offers that satisfy the hard criteria of the DMs. It can be seen that such a procedure can be easily automized and also deals with the problem of balancing the attractiveness and diversity of offers on the shortlist.

Another approach to GDM is to use a voting procedure. Elkind *et al.* (2017) consider the properties of such voting procedures for choosing a committee from a set of candidates. Diss *et al.* (2020) carry out a comparison of such voting procedures. Such procedures are interesting from the point of view of this article, since a set of winners is chosen. However, they seem impractical in the framework considered here, due to the large number of offers (analogous to candidates in a voting procedure) and resulting need for automatization. Bock *et al.* (1998) describe an approach to choosing a committee. Each DM has a single vote. The result of the vote minimizes the distance between the vector describing the proportion of votes for each candidate and the power of each member of the committee (assumed to be the reciprocal of the size of the committee). This distance ensures that a diversity of opinions are represented on the committee, even though the method does not explicitly take into account the difference between the candidates. From this point of view, their paper is of particular relevance to the problem considered here. On the other hand, even when only one DM is selecting a shortlist, the question of the diversity of offers on the shortlist remains important. Hence, the distance measure used in this paper measures the distance between offers themselves on the basis of the observed values of their traits.

GDM can also be based on aggregating the rankings or pairwise comparisons carried out by individual DMs (see Cook 2006). D'Ambrosio *et al.* (2019) and Aledo *et al.* present methods for the automatic aggregation of rankings. Such an aggregate ranking can then be used to select a shortlist, for example by selecting the top k ranked offers overall. One drawback of this approach lies in the fact that this approach does not intrinsically take into account the diversity of the offers placed on the shortlist. Also, when there are a large number of offers assessed according to a set of criteria, in order to automize the ranking process it seems most natural to base such a ranking on a numerical assessment of the attractiveness of an offer to a DM according to his/her criteria regarding the observed traits.

By assumption, DMs give an honest assessment of the attractiveness of each offer. One important aspect of GDM processes is the robustness of a process in the face of dishonesty. When a process is robust, it pays the DMs to give honest assessments of the attractiveness of the offers (see Taylor and Pacelli (2008)). On the other hand, when DMs are able to communicate or possess information on the preferences of others, even such procedures can be manipulated (see Gibbard (1973), Kontek and Sosnowska (2020)). The problem of dishonesty does not seem to be of great importance in the specific problem considered here. This is due to the fact that it is assumed that the group of DMs is a household, or a similar group, the members of which share some common goals or criteria (e.g. regarding the size and price of a flat). A number of criteria might be individual (e.g. distance to work when household members work in different places). One problem might lie in the fact that there might be outliers in the group of decision makers (e.g. when several of the DMs work in the city centre, but one works in the suburbs). In this case, some procedure could be used to ensure that the shortlist contains an appropriate number of offers that are attractive to an outlying DM. Garcia-Zamora *et al.* (2021) consider procedures for appropriately scaling the assessments (rankings) made by a set of DMs in such situations.

This article takes a different approach to GDM in the framework of searching for a valuable resource. It is assumed that the group is formed by a family or household. The search criteria are split into two categories: group and individual. These criteria are set before the search procedure is initiated. Group criteria are determined by the group as a whole. For example, households will often have a joint financial account. Similarly, the size of a household will determine the minimum number of rooms and size of the property. Thus the maximum price of a property and the minimum dimensions will be interpreted as group criteria. On the other hand, members of the household will often work or study in different places. Each would prefer to live reasonably close to their workplace. Hence, we may treat the maximum distance from ones workplace as a criterion specific to an individual. In general, the choice of individual specific criteria should be made to avoid possible conflict or manipulation. This means that assessment according to an individual specific criterion should be clear to each of the other members of the group. Family members will generally know where the other members work. Also, based on information regarding the location of a property, objective measures of distance from workplaces (or journey time) are available. Hence, distance from ones workplace to a property can be treated as an individually specific criterion without automatically provoking conflict or manipulation. Finally, it is crucial that a procedure constructing a shortlist for a group should treat each of the individuals fairly.

As stated above, the algorithm uses multivariate data from the Internet to construct a shortlist that aims to maximize a weighted average of measures of the attractiveness of the offers and their variety (the mean of a standardized distance measure). Various methods for assessing the attractiveness of offers based on a set of traits (assumed to be continuous) are available. The simplest of these is Simple Additive Weighting (SAW, see e.g. Taha (2017)). Firstly, the attractiveness of an offer according to each of the individual traits is measured on a scale from 0 to 1. Each of the traits is assessed on the basis of a single criterion which states one of the following: a) the maximum acceptable value of the trait, b) the minimum acceptable value of the trait, or c) the admissible range of values of the trait. The overall attractiveness of an offer is then calculated as a weighted average of these individual attractiveness measures. Another commonly used approach is the TOPSIS procedure (Technique for Order of Preference by Similarity to Ideal Solution, see Yoon and Hwang (1995)). This process assesses each offer on the basis of standardized measures of distance from the "ideal" offer and the "anti-ideal".

The importance of the criteria can be described in both of these procedures using weights. These weights can be set by the DMs by allocating points to each criterion such that the sum of these points is 100. Another approach is to allocate each of the criteria a direct rating between 0 and 100 and then to normalize these ratings so that they sum to 1 (or 100). Bottomley *et al.* (2000) find that DMs find the direct rating easier and more effective than point allocation. Another approach is the Analytic Hierarchy Procedure (AHP, see Saaty (1990)), which can be applied to determine appropriate weights for the criteria via pairwise comparison of the relative importance of criteria. Riabacke *et al.* (2012) consider various procedures for ascribing weights to the criteria. For example, the swing procedure is based on the range of values of the traits observed for a given criterion. Suppose the i-th trait varies from $x_{i,min}$ to $x_{i,max}$. The criterion with the largest weight is defined to be the one for which a change in the observation from $x_{i,min}$ to $x_{i,max}$ would make the biggest impression on the DM. This criterion is then removed from consideration and the procedure repeated until a ranking of the importance of the criteria is obtained. The point allocation, direct rating and AHP procedures can be implemented without any knowledge of the data set. This is an advantage in the type of problem considered here, since it is assumed that there are a large number of offers and not all of these offers satisfy the hard constraints of the DMs. Implementation of the swing procedure for defining weights requires the initial filtering of data. In addition, the DMs might prefer the size of a flat to be in the middle of some interval. In such a case, the swing procedure should be adapted in order to ascribe an appropriate weight to a criterion based on the size of a flat. Another problem with the swing approach lies in the fact that the weights are defined according to the ranking of the importance of the criteria. Hence, such an approach can work badly when two criteria are of similar importance. Due to the nature of the problem, it is recommended that weights should be ascribed using a simple procedure that is independent of the data, e.g. direct rating or, when the number of criteria used is relatively small, AHP.

Kaliszewski and Podkopaev (2016) argue that decisions made by more complex approaches than SAW can be interpreted as decisions made using the SAW methodology for appropriately defined weights. Ramsey *et al.* (2022) define the standardized measure of distance used and show that shortlists formed using SAW and TOPSIS are very similar. In this article, the SAW approach is used.

Once the measures of attractiveness and distance between offers have been determined, the objective function to be maximized can be defined. This objective function is a weighted sum of the attractiveness of the offers and the distance between them. Any solution to this decision problem (a shortlist) can be defined by the set of offers placed on the shortlist. Hence, we can define a set of binary decision variables $u_1, u_2, \ldots, u_N$, where N is the number of offers considered. We define u_i such that $u_i = 1$ when the i-th offer is placed on the shortlist, otherwise $u_i = 0$. It follows that the sum of attractiveness measures of the offers placed on the shortlist is a linear function of the u_i. The sum of the distances between the offers on the shortlist is given by a linear combination of terms involving products of the form $u_i u_j$. Hence, the optimization problem to be solved is a binary quadratic programming (QP) problem. The set of feasible solutions is the set of shortlists of the required length, k. It should be noted that the problem of constructing a shortlist is very similar to the knapsack problem (see Martello and Toth (1990)). In the classical knapsack problem, a set of objects must be chosen so as to maximize the value of the contents of a "knapsack" subject to the capacity constraints.

QP problems with continuous variables are relatively easy problems to solve computationally (see Murty and Fu (1988)). When some of the variables take discrete values, the computational complexity of the solution of the resulting quadratic program often becomes much greater. Since the number of decision variables in our model will be generally large (often hundreds or thousands) and we wish to determine shortlists in a relatively short time (within a couple of minutes using a standard laptop), this article presents a method of generating "near-optimal" shortlists according to the optimization criterion. One of the problems often involved in QP is to find a relatively good feasible solution. This problem is considered in, for example, Fischetti *et al.* (2005), Bertacco *et al.* (2007) and Acherberg and Berthold *et al.* (2007). Various heuristics have recently been developed for solving QP problems. Some are applicable to fairly general QP problems (e.g. Takapoui *et al.* (2020), as well as Guignard and Ahlatcioglu (2021)), while others are adapted to specific (often practical) problems (e.g. Blackburn *et al.* (2019)). In the context of our paper, the heuristic presented in Dahmani and Hifi (2021) for binary quadratic knapsack problems is of particular interest.

Section 2 presents the general form of the QP problem to be solved. Section 3 describes the measures of attractiveness and diversity, together with an algorithm to find a very good solution of the appropriate QP problem for an individual DM. The adaptation of the algorithm to group decision making is considered in Sect. 4. Section 5 presents a toy example that illustrates how this adapted algorithm works. Section 6 presents the results of a computational study that investigates the robustness of the new algorithm using data regarding real estate offers in Warsaw. Finally, a conclusion and directions for future research are given in Sect. 7.

2 A Model of the Mathematical Problem Faced by an Individual Decision Maker

The aim is to construct a shortlist of k offers, where k is specified by the DM, such that the offers on the shortlist are both attractive and varied. This choice is based on an objective function defined to be a weighted average of the attractiveness of offers (here defined using SAW) and the diversity of offers, based on the mean of a standardized distance measure. The weight assigned to the diversity of offers is denoted by α. It is assumed that a shortlist defined in this way is used as a guide to choose offers that should be viewed in real life.

Low values of α place a high weight on the initial assessment of the attractiveness of offers. However, as previously argued, these offers may not be sufficiently differentiated for a DM to appropriately explore the range of offers. On the other hand, high values of α place too small a weight on the potential attractiveness of offers. For example, one might wish that the diversity of offers on the shortlist should be similar to the diversity of offers satisfying the basic requirements of the DM. This criterion ensures that the offers on the shortlist give the DM an appropriate range of offers. One possible approach is to select a robust value of α so that the diversity of offers on the shortlist is similar to the diversity of offers satisfying the basic requirements of the DM whatever the structure of the data and the requirements of the DM. Previous work (see Ramsey and Mariański (2022)) indicates that $\alpha = 0.2$ is relatively robust. Alternatively, the choice of α may be adapted to the data by allowing α to vary over a set of values. For example, shortlists can be formed using successively greater values of α. This procedure will give shortlists of ever increasing diversity. The process is stopped when the diversity of offers on the shortlist becomes greater than the diversity of offers satisfying the basic constraints. In this case, unless the shortlist based on the k highest ranked offers, corresponding to $\alpha = 0$, is adjudged to be relatively more varied than the set of offers satisfying the hard constraints, then the algorithm presents the penultimate shortlist formed to the DM.

Now we consider the mathematical problem to be solved for a fixed value of α. Suppose that N offers satisfy the basic constraints of the DM. Denote the attractiveness of offer i by a_i and the standardized measure of distance between offers i and j by $d_{i,j}$. These two measures are defined on the basis of the data available, as will be described in Sect. 3. The decision variable u_i, for $1 \leq i \leq N$, indicates whether offer i is placed on the shortlist, i.e. $u_i = 1$ if and only if offer i is chosen to be on the short list, otherwise $u_i = 0$.

Since $0.5k(k - 1)$ pairs of objects can be chosen from a set of k objects, the problem to be solved is $\max V(\mathbf{u})$, where $\mathbf{u} = (u_1, u_2, \ldots, u_N)$ and

$$V(\mathbf{u}) = \frac{1-\alpha}{k} \left(\sum_{i=1}^{N} u_i a_i \right) + \frac{2\alpha}{k(k-1)} \left(\sum_{1 \leq i < j \leq N} u_i u_j d_{i,j} \right), \qquad (1)$$

subject to the following conditions: i) $u_i \in \{0, 1\}$, ii) $\sum_{i=1}^{N} u_i = k$. Note that the second condition states that k offers should be placed on the shortlist.

When $\alpha = 0$, i.e. no weight is placed on the diversity of offers, this problem is a binary linear programming problem whose solution is very simple. In this case, the optimal shortlist contains the k offers with the largest measures of attractiveness based on the initial data. Whenever $\alpha > 0$, this is a binary quadratic programming problem which does not possess a simple general solution. Note that the number of feasible solutions to this problem (the number of possible shortlists) is

$$_NC_k = \frac{N!}{k!(N-k)!}.$$

One may solve this problem by exhaustive search or using an algorithm adapted to binary quadratic programs. However, when the number of decision variables, N is relatively large (in the problems considered N is often in the range from 100 to several thousand), such solution procedures are overly complex for the nature of the problem considered. In practice, a DM wishes to obtain a shortlist of attractive offers within a couple of minutes. Such a shortlist need not be optimal in terms of the programming problem described above, but must contain a diverse range of attractive offers. Hence, we need a relatively fast algorithm that guarantees a good solution. The following section presents a greedy algorithm specifically adapted to the form of the problem (as described above it is a binary quadratic knapsack problem, see Dahmani and Hifi (2021)).

3   The Greedy Algorithm for Shortlist Formation

The algorithm constructs shortlists using multivariate data, which include continuous variables, from a large database. The DM specifies the number of offers to be placed on the shortlist, together with a set of hard criteria that must be satisfied. Note that some of these hard criteria can be based on discrete and/or qualitative traits. The hard criteria are used to exclude offers that are unsuitable for the DM. The filtering of offers is discussed in Sect. 5. On the other hand, it is assumed that only continuous traits are used to measure the attractiveness and diversity of offers. The traits used to assess diversity do not have to coincide with the traits used to measure attractiveness. However, the required information must be available in the database. As previously discussed in Sect. 2, the algorithm aims to maximize a weighted average of the mean attractiveness and the diversity of the offers placed on the shortlist. We define these measures in the following two subsections.

3.1   Definition of the Attractiveness Measure

As stated earlier, we use the SAW procedure to assess the potential attractiveness of offers using information from a database. Suppose that the hard criteria of the DM are satisfied by N offers and M criteria are used to initially assess the attractiveness of offers (each of these criteria is based on a single quantitative trait). Each criterion is classified as a goal, incentive or disincentive. In the case of incentives, larger values of the corresponding trait are more attractive. In the case of disincentives, smaller values of the corresponding trait are more attractive. In the case of a goal, the DM specifies a preferred value of the corresponding trait, together with an acceptable level of variation on either side of this value.

Let $x_{i,j}$ be the observation for the i-th offer of the j-th trait used to define attractiveness. Each such observation is associated with a component measure of attractiveness $r_{i,j}$ belonging to the interval $[0, 1]$. If the j-th trait corresponds to an incentive, then

$$r_{i,j} = \frac{x_{i,j} - x_{min,j}}{x_{max,j} - x_{min,j}}, \qquad (2)$$

where $x_{min,j}$ and $x_{max,j}$ denote the minimum and maximum values, respectively, of the j-th trait among the set of offers satisfying the hard constraints. If the j-th trait corresponds to a disincentive, then

$$r_{i,j} = \frac{x_{max,j} - x_{i,j}}{x_{max,j} - x_{min,j}}. \qquad (3)$$

Suppose that the j-th trait corresponds to a goal and $x_{pref,j}$ is the preferred value of this trait. Denote the maximum deviation from this preferred value, among the offers satisfying the hard constraints, by $x_{maxd,j}$. In this case, define

$$r_{i,j} = \frac{x_{maxd,j} - |x_{i,j} - x_{pref,j}|}{x_{maxd,j}}. \tag{4}$$

Denote the weight of the criterion associated with the j-th trait by w_j. For the purposes of this paper, it is assumed that these weights are fixed. In practice, such weights can be defined directly, or indirectly by comparing the importance of criteria pairwise and then applying the Analytic Hierarchy Process (AHP, see Saaty (1990)).

Note that the value $r_{i,j}$ is a standardized measure of the attractiveness of offer i based on trait j. Using SAW, the overall attractiveness of offer i based on the information from the database is given by a_i, where

$$a_i = \sum_{j=1}^{M} w_j r_{i,j}. \tag{5}$$

3.2   Definition of the Diversity Measure

Assume that the diversity of a set of offers is measured using K continuous traits. These traits are not necessarily the same as those used to measure attractiveness. For example, suppose that one variable used to measure the attractiveness of a property is its distance from the city centre. The diversity of a set of offers should be defined according to the physical distance between pairs of properties and not according to "differences between distances from the city centre" (if two properties are the same distance from the city centre, they might be a relatively large distance from each other). However, all of the variables involved in defining the attractiveness and diversity of offers must be available from the database. It thus suffices that the location of each property is defined on the basis of two positional coordinates, e.g., distance east and distance north of the city centre.

Let $y_{i,j}$ be the observation for the i-th offer of the j-th trait used to define the distance between offers. Firstly, each of these variables is scaled to the interval $[0, 1]$ as in Eq. (2), i.e. define

$$s_{i,j} = \frac{y_{i,j} - y_{min,j}}{y_{max,j} - y_{min,j}}. \tag{6}$$

In order to define the distance between the i-th and m-th offers, we derive the Euclidean distance between the vectors $\mathbf{s_i}$ and $\mathbf{s_m}$, where $\mathbf{s_i} = (s_{i,1}, s_{i,2}, \ldots, s_{i,K})$. Denote this by $d_{i,m}$, i.e.

$$d_{i,m} = \sqrt{(s_{i,1} - s_{m,1})^2 + (s_{i,2} - s_{m,2})^2 + \ldots + (s_{i,K} - s_{m,K})^2}. \tag{7}$$

Even though the individual components of the vector $\mathbf{s_i}$ are standardized to the interval $[0, 1]$, these distances are not standardized. The maximum possible distance is $\sqrt{K}$. Hence, dividing $d_{i,m}$ by $\sqrt{K}$ we obtain a standardized measure of distance.

3.3 Constructing a Shortlist with a Fixed Weight Ascribed to Diversity

Suppose that the weight ascribed to the diversity of a shortlist in the objective function is α. Define the score of a set of offers S, $v(S)$, by $v(S) = (1-\alpha)\bar{a}_S + \alpha\bar{d}_S$, where $\bar{a}_S$ denotes the mean attractiveness of the offers in S and $\bar{d}_S$ denotes the mean of the standardized distances between pairs of offers in S. Consider the following greedy algorithm, which constructs a shortlist of k offers sequentially:

1. Let $c = 1$. The offer assessed to be the most attractive is the first to be placed on the shortlist.
2. Add an offer to the shortlist from the set of offers not yet placed on it to maximize the score, $v(S)$, of the resulting shortlist, S, This set is of size $c+1$.
3. Let $c = c + 1$. If $c = k$, then stop, otherwise return to step 2.

Hence, at each stage of the greedy algorithm an offer is added to the shortlist in such a way as to maximize the appropriate weighted average of attractiveness and diversity.

Note that a solution of the quadratic programming problem with objective function given in Eq. (1) is feasible if and only if k offers are selected. Hence, this algorithm constructs a feasible solution. Suppose that $\alpha = 0$, i.e. no weight is ascribed to diversity. In this case, at each step the greedy algorithm adds an offer with the highest attractiveness score of those not yet placed on the shortlist. Thus the shortlist constructed contains k offers assessed to be the most attractive. Hence, the mean attractiveness of the offers on the shortlist (in this case, the objective function) is maximized. This result also follows from the principles of dynamic programming, since the value of the objective function can be represented as a multiple of the sum of gains made at each step of the greedy algorithm (the gain at each step is the value of the offer added).

On the other hand, if $\alpha > 0$, then the value of the objective function cannot be defined as a multiple of the sum of the gains made at each step of the greedy algorithm. Hence, the shortlist constructed in this way is not necessarily an optimal solution of the quadratic program. However, at each stage of the algorithm, a function of a similar form to the objective function is maximized. Hence, it is expected that the solution constructed will be close to optimal, especially when α is relatively small. This is confirmed by the simulations carried out in Ramsey and Mariański (2022), who also consider the computational complexity of the algorithm.

3.4 Data Driven Choice of the Parameter α

As discussed above, it may be beneficial to choose an appropriate value of α, the weight ascribed to diversity, based on an adaptive procedure. Using such a procedure, α is successively increased until a stopping criterion is satisfied. As α increases, the diversity of the offers placed on the short list will increase. On the other hand, the mean measure of attractiveness of these offers will decrease.

Hence, a data driven value of α finds a suitable compromise between the diversity of offers on the shortlist and their mean attractiveness. In this article, it is assumed that the value of α selected ensures that the diversity of the offers placed on the shortlist will be very similar to the diversity of the offers that satisfy the hard constraints of the DM. Results from Ramsey and Mariański (2022) indicate that such a procedure results in shortlists which contain the majority of offers ranked amongst the top k using initial information, together with a set of "wild cards", which are relatively attractive and ensure that a diverse range of offers is selected for further consideration.

4   Adapting the Algorithm to Group Decision Making

One desirable trait of an algorithm constructing shortlists for a group of DMs is that the algorithm should treat the parties involved in a fair manner. For example, when a family is looking for a property, it seems reasonable that the adult members of a family are treated symmetrically. Similarly, the children should be treated symmetrically. As described above, the individuals involved in the decision process will have both common and personal interests. It is assumed that choice criteria which are group dependent or could potentially lead to conflict (especially when the basis for assessment is unclear) are negotiated before the search procedure is initiated. These criteria are treated as group criteria.

As described above, the location of a property relative to an individual's workplace can be assessed according to an individual specific criterion. Due to the spatial distribution of the offers with respect to the workplaces of members of the family, treating the distances to individual workplaces as common criteria each with the same weight for assessing the attractiveness of an offer might lead to a shortlist of offers which are on average much closer to one workplace than the others (see Ramsey and Mariański (2022)). For these reasons, preferences based on distance to ones workplace should be treated as personal and a procedure for balancing the personal preferences of the DMs could be used. It should be noted that the maximum acceptable distance of the property from the workplace of any of the members of the family may be defined by the family as a whole.

If there are a number of traits that define personal preferences, the individuals involved in a group decision process of this form may place different relative weights on the criteria used to assess attractiveness according to these traits. However, in order to treat the DMs in a fair manner, the overall weight of the personal criteria relative to the overall weight of the common criteria should be fixed.

For the purposes of this paper, it is assumed that the adult DMs set the common constraints and that the individual preferences of all parties involved in the decision are treated symmetrically. Denote the number of decision makers by J. The procedure used to define the overall attractiveness of an offer is as follows:

1. The attractiveness of an offer to each DM is calculated as a weighted average of the attractiveness measures according to each criterion. Note that each individual ascribes the same weight to the common criteria.

2. The distributions of the attractiveness measures are adjusted such that the mean and standard deviation of the assessments corresponding to any single DM is equal to the overall mean and overall standard deviation of the assessments, respectively.

3. The overall measure of attractiveness of an offer is defined to be the mean of the adjusted measures of attractiveness ascribed to it.

In order to do this, define $\overline{a}^{(j)}$ to be the mean of the attractiveness measures according to DMj and $\overline{a}$ to be the mean of all the attractiveness measures. Also, let

$$\sigma_j^2 = \frac{1}{N} \sum_{i=1}^{N} (a_i^{(j)} - \overline{a}^{(j)})^2 \tag{8}$$

denote the variance of the attractiveness measures according to DMj and set

$$\sigma^2 = \frac{1}{J} \sum_{j=1}^{J} \sigma_j^2 \tag{9}$$

to be the overall variance of the attractiveness measures.

We then define the adjusted attractiveness score of offer i according to DMj, $\tilde{a}_i^{(j)}$ by

$$\tilde{a}_i^{(j)} = \overline{a} + \frac{\sigma(a_i^{(j)} - \overline{a}^{(j)})}{\sigma_j}. \tag{10}$$

After such a transformation, the mean and standard deviation of the attractiveness scores according to each DM are equal to $\overline{a}$ and σ, respectively. One possible advantage of deriving attractiveness scores for each of the DMs lies in the fact that the output could highlight offers that are particularly attractive to individual DMs (or construct shortlists for individual DMs).

The definition of the standardized distance between offers is the same as in the algorithm for a single DM. This procedure will be described on the basis of a simple example in the following section.

5   A Simple Example

Suppose that a young couple are looking for a property. Their budget is 500 000PLN (approx. \$110 000) and they require a property with at least 2 rooms and a floorspace of at least $30 \, \text{m}^2$. The property can be at most 10km from either of their workplaces. Price and distance are treated as disincentives, while floorspace is treated as an incentive. Price and floorspace correspond to common criteria, while the distance to ones workplace corresponds to an individual specific criterion. Data regarding real estate offers were taken from the site otodom.pl on 18th August, 2021. The group criteria are given an overall weight of 0.6, with price being ascribed a weight of 0.2 and floorspace a weight of 0.4. The individual specific criterion (distance to work) is given a weight of 0.4. Suppose that the goal is to suggest a shortlist of three properties to view given the set of offers described in Table 1, where D_i gives the distance to the workplace of the i-th decision maker in kilometers. The final two columns give the coordinates of the location of the offers with respect to the workplace of the first DM (number of kilometers east and north). These coordinates are used in determining the standardized distance between offers.

Table 1. Offers of Warsaw properties: These example data are taken from real estate offers on the website otodom.pl (accessed on 18th August, 2021). D_i denotes distance to the workplace of individual i. East and North give the positional coordinates of the offers with respect to the workplace of individual 1.

Offer	Price (PLN)	Space (m²)	Rooms	D_1 (km)	D_2 (km)	East (km)	North (km)
1	363 200	30	2	8.99	5.58	−7.9263	4.2447
2	482 344	31.2	1	1.88	6.44	1.3500	1.3078
3	449 990	32.2	2	2.75	5.31	1.0361	2.5519
4	487 000	37.51	2	6.77	2.05	−0.7189	6.7320
5	519 000	38	2	13.26	6.40	−5.6735	11.9846
6	400 000	30.89	2	3.93	6.53	−3.9321	−0.1145
7	473 144	39.76	2	1.11	6.14	0.4142	1.0279
8	430 000	36.5	2	6.98	2.95	−5.1932	4.6673

Firstly, the offers are filtered using the hard constraints. Offer 2 is removed, since there is only one room. Offer 5 is removed, since the price is too high (also, it is too far from the workplace of DM1). After this initial filtering, we calculate the attractiveness of the offers according to the following traits: price, space and distance to work (for each DM). The attractiveness according to floorspace, together with the standardized coordinates, are calculated using Eq. (2), while the measures of attractiveness according to price and distance are calculated using Eq. (3). The overall measure of the attractiveness of offer i to DMj, $a_i^{(j)}$ is then calculated based on the weighted average

$$a_i^{(j)} = 0.2r_{i,1} + 0.4r_{i,2} + 0.4r_{i,3}^{(j)}, \tag{11}$$

where $r_{i,1}$ and $r_{i,2}$ are the common measures of attractiveness for price and floorspace, respectively and $r_{i,3}^{(j)}$ is the measure of attractiveness according to the distance from the workplace of DMj.

The standardized measures of attractiveness and overall assessments made by the individual DMs, together with the standardized positional coordinates, are summarized in Table 2. The assessment of the attractiveness an offer by DMj is denoted by $a^{(j)}$

The measures of attractiveness according to the decision makers are then adjusted using Eq. (10). The overall attractiveness of an offer is then defined to be the mean of the adjusted attractive scores (Table 3).

Table 2. Standardized values of attractiveness and positional coordinates. $a^{(j)}$ gives the assessment of the attractiveness of an offer by DMj.

Offer	Price	Size	D_1	D_2	$a^{(1)}$	$a^{(2)}$	East	North
1	1.0000	0.0000	0.0000	0.2121	0.2000	0.2848	0.0000	0.6367
3	0.2989	0.2254	0.7919	0.2723	0.4667	0.2589	1.0000	0.3895
4	0.0000	0.7695	0.2817	1.0000	0.4205	0.7078	0.8042	1.0000
6	0.7027	0.0912	0.6421	0.0000	0.4339	0.1770	0.4457	0.0000
7	0.1119	1.0000	1.0000	0.0871	0.8224	0.4572	0.9306	0.1669
8	0.4604	0.6660	0.2551	0.7991	0.4605	0.6781	0.3050	0.6984

Table 3. Adjustment of the attractiveness scores, together with the overall attractiveness of an offer to the group as a whole.

Offer	$\tilde{a}^{(1)}$	$\tilde{a}^{(2)}$	a
1	0.1634	0.3127	0.2381
3	0.4467	0.2882	0.3674
4	0.3976	0.7123	0.5549
6	0.4118	0.2108	0.3113
7	0.8244	0.4756	0.6500
8	0.4401	0.6843	0.5622

The standardized distance between two offers is calculated as one half of the Euclidean distance between the standardized vectors describing an offer (price, floorspace and positional coordinates). Note that the standardizing factor, $\frac{1}{\sqrt{K}}$ where K is the number of traits used to calculate the distance measure, ensures that the standardized distance lies between zero and one (similarly to the attractiveness measures). The matrix of standardized distances between the offers is given in Table 4.

Table 4. Standardized distances between the offers.

	Offer 3	Offer 4	Offer 6	Offer 7	Offer 8
Offer 1	0.6331	0.7699	0.4185	0.8479	0.4459
Offer 3		0.4462	0.4000	0.4151	0.4469
Offer 4			0.7215	0.4404	0.3751
Offer 6				0.5996	0.4735
Offer 7					0.4762

Now we construct a shortlist according to the algorithm described in Sect. 3. The weight ascribed to diversity is assumed to be $\alpha = 0.2$. In the first step, the offer with the highest overall measure of attractiveness, Offer 7, is placed on the shortlist. In the second step, we consider all the shortlists of length 2 which include Offer 7. The necessary calculations are described in Table 5. The final column (score) gives the weighted average of the distance between the offers and their mean attractiveness. Since adding Offer 8 maximizes the weighted average of attractiveness and diversity, this offer is placed on the shortlist.

Table 5. Calculations required for the second step of the algorithm. The score is the weighted average of the mean attractiveness (weight 0.8) and the distance between offers (weight 0.2).

Offer added	Attractiveness measures	Mean Attractiveness	Distance	Score
1	{0.6500, 0.2381}	0.4440	0.8479	0.5248
3	{0.6500, 0.3674}	0.5087	0.4151	0.4900
4	{0.6500, 0.5549}	0.6025	0.4404	0.5700
6	{0.6500, 0.3113}	0.4806	0.5996	0.5044
8	{0.6500, 0.5622}	0.6061	0.4762	0.5801

In the third step, we consider all the shortlists of length 3 which include Offers 7 and 8. The necessary calculations are described in Table 6. Since adding Offer 4 maximizes the weighted average of attractiveness and diversity, this offer is placed on the shortlist. This completes the algorithm.

Table 6. Calculations required for the third step of the algorithm. The score is the weighted average of the mean attractiveness (weight 0.8) and the mean distance between offers (weight 0.2).

Offer added	Attractiveness measures	Mean attractiveness	Distance measures	Mean distance	Score
1	{0.6500, 0.5622, 0.2381}	0.4834	{0.4762, 0.8479, 0.4559}	0.5933	0.5054
3	{0.6500, 0.5622, 0.3674}	0.5265	{0.4762, 0.4151, 0.4469}	0.4461	0.5104
4	{0.6500, 0.5622, 0.5549}	0.5890	{0.4762, 0.4404, 0.3751}	0.4306	0.5573
6	{0.6500, 0.5622, 0.3113}	0.5078	{0.4762, 0.5996, 0.4735}	0.5164	0.5095

Note that we can derive shortlists for the individual DMs based on the adjusted attractiveness scores. Using the analogous procedure, the shortlist based on DM1's preferences (in order of selection) is Offer 7, Offer 6 and Offer 4. The shortlist based on DM2's preferences (in order of selection) is Offer 4, Offer 8 and Offer 7. Hence, the shortlist constructed for DM2 is the same as the shortlist determined for both DMs. In the shortlist constructed for DM1, Offer 6 replaces Offer 8. It should be noted that Offers 4 and 8 look particularly attractive to DM2 (they lie close to DM2's workplace), while being of reasonable attractiveness to DM1. On the other hand, based on the information from the Internet, Offer 7 is clearly the most attractive offer to DM1, while being of reasonable attractiveness to DM2. As a result, these three offers are significantly more attractive than other offers based on the joint assessment of the two DMs using this initial information.

It should be noted that the greedy algorithm can be also applied using unadjusted measures of attractiveness. This is considered in the computational study described in the following section.

6   Computational Study

The data used for the computational study describe 8 309 offers of real estate in Warsaw (taken from the otodom.pl on 18th August, 2021). The data used are: floorspace (m^2), price (in PLN), longitude and latitude (used to calculate the distance e.g. to ones workplace) and number of rooms (not including kitchen or bathrooms). The number of rooms was only used in the initial filtering based on the hard constraints of the DMs. It should be noted that if other data are available on offers, then they can be appropriately used in the procedure for constructing a shortlist.

The goal was to propose a shortlist of 30 properties for a set of 100 scenarios. These scenarios are constructed by combining five sets of hard constraints regarding the size and price of a property, ten combinations of two different workplaces and two different weights for the weight of the factor "distance from workplace", $w_3 = 0.2$ and $w_3 = 0.4$ (the individual specific factor of choice). Floorspace was given twice as large a weight as price, such that the sum of these two weights was $1 - w_3$. The maximum acceptable distance to ones workplace was fixed to be 15km. The algorithm was implemented for values of α starting at 0 and increasing by 0.01 successively until the diversity of the offers on the shortlist exceeded the diversity of the offers satisfying the hard constraints. The shortlist outputted by the algorithm was the one corresponding to the final value of α for which the diversity of the offers on the shortlist did not exceed the diversity of offers satisfying the hard constraints, or the top k ranked offers (the shortlist corresponding to $\alpha = 0$) when there was no such shortlist.

The sets of constraints regarding the size and price of a property are described in Table 7. The ten combinations of workplaces are described in Table 8. The number of offers that satisfy the hard constraints, as well as their relative diversity, for the 50 combinations of hard constraints and workplaces are given in Table 9.

Warsaw, the capital of Poland, lies on a plain on the banks of the Vistula river. The distribution of the spatial location of offers relative to the city centre and according to the budget of the DMs is illustrated in the Appendix (Figs. 1, 2, 3, 4 and 5). The river flows from the south-eastern side of the city towards the north-west, passing slightly to the east of the city centre. Its path corresponds to the diagonal from bottom right towards top left on the scatterplots in Figs. 1, 2, 3, 4, and 5 where there are very few offers. In particular, there are very few offers in the south-east of the city, where there is a large amount of greenland

Table 7. Sets of hard constraints used for the scenarios.

Set	Minimum floorspace (m^2)	Maximum price (PLN)	Minimum no. of rooms
1	30	500 000	2
2	40	650 000	2
3	50	750 000	2
4	60	900 000	3
5	70	1 000 000	3

Table 8. Combinations of workplaces used for the scenarios. Centre denotes Warsaw city centre, taken to be the Palace of Culture. North, South, East and West denote points 8km north, south, east and west, respectively, of the city centre.

Combination	Workplace 1	Workplace 2	Combination	Workplace 1	Workplace 2
1	Centre	South	6	South	North
2	Centre	West	7	South	East
3	Centre	North	8	West	North
4	Centre	East	9	West	East
5	South	West	10	North	East

Table 9. Number of offers satisfying the hard constraints for each scenario and the mean standardized distance between them. Set gives the index denoting the set of hard constraints used (from Table 7), combination gives the index denoting the pair of workplaces used (from Table 8).

Set	Combination	N	Dist.	Set	Combination	N	Dist.	Set	Combination	N	Dist.
1	1	1002	0.2280	2	8	2329	0.2618	4	5	1083	0.2574
1	2	1269	0.2510	2	9	1786	0.2568	4	6	1091	0.2526
1	3	1533	0.2783	2	10	2104	0.2556	4	7	1009	0.2561
1	4	1192	0.2681	3	1	1590	0.2317	4	8	1295	0.2693
1	5	914	0.2359	3	2	1873	0.2485	4	9	1018	0.2634
1	6	962	0.2571	3	3	2155	0.2615	4	10	1154	0.2637
1	7	760	0.2531	3	4	1841	0.2473	5	1	698	0.2721
1	8	1257	0.2720	3	5	1446	0.2505	5	2	736	0.2845
1	9	892	0.2711	3	6	1454	0.2580	5	3	806	0.2916
1	10	1154	0.2822	3	7	1329	0.2422	5	4	761	0.2904
2	1	2016	0.2292	3	8	1795	0.2655	5	5	597	0.2771
2	2	2409	0.2432	3	9	1430	0.2584	5	6	595	0.2703
2	3	2731	0.2579	3	10	1707	0.2612	5	7	631	0.2800
2	4	2231	0.2439	4	1	1222	0.2498	5	8	677	0.2935
2	5	1864	0.2460	4	2	1369	0.2591	5	9	593	0.2873
2	6	1885	0.2537	4	3	1510	0.2636	5	10	658	0.2927
2	7	1617	0.2433	4	4	1285	0.2601	–	–	–	–

surrounding the river. There is a high density of offers in the outer western and northern suburbs. In the east of the city, the pattern of residential buildings is different. In particular, there is a large area of residential properties lying close to the city centre, but on the opposite bank of the river. This area contains Saska Kępa, an attractive residential area. The western suburbs lie close to the Kampinoski National Park, a popular area for recreation. For these reasons, there is a relatively high density of offers for those with a large budget in the east and west, while a relatively large number of offers for those with a low budget are found in the northern suburbs. Overall, there are relatively few offers in the south of the city. Offers of large properties (at least $70\,m^2$, see Fig. 5) tend to be more dispersed in space. For this reason, the mean standardized distance between offers acceptable to a couple with a budget of one million PLN is significantly greater than the mean standardized distance between offers acceptable to couples with a lower budget. The mean standardized distance between offers acceptable to a couple in each of the ten scenarios corresponding to a budget of one million PLN are all within the top 14 of the mean standardized distances between offers in the 50 scenarios considered.

Although there are very few offers in the strict centre of the city (the commercial/administrative district), the vast majority of offers are within 15km of the city centre. Hence, the number of offers with acceptable locations is greatest for those working in the centre. The number of offers with acceptable locations according to the workplace of a DM is given in Table 10.

Table 10. Number of offers with acceptable location according to the workplace of a DM.

Centre	8202
North	7730
West	7400
East	7273
South	6870

We now statistically analyze the relation of this non-homogeneous distribution of offers with the locations of the DMs workplaces, the weight given to location and the hard constraints. The explanatory variables in this analysis are the following:

1. The weight ascribed to distance to work (the individual specific factor).
2. Location of the DMs' workplaces (including the distance between them).
3. The number of offers satisfying the hard constraints.
4. The budget.

Note that due to the strict correlation between the budget and the required floorspace, we do not need to additionally treat required floorpace as an explanatory variable. The dependent variables in this analysis are as follows:

1. The weight ascribed to diversity by the algorithm, α.
2. The mean overall ranks of offers on the shortlist (joint assessment), $\overline{R}_g$.
3. The maximum of the two mean ranks of offers on the shortlist as assessed by the individual DMs, $\overline{R}_{max} = \max[\overline{R}_1, \overline{R}_2]$, where $\overline{R}_i$ is the mean rank of offers on the shortlist according to DMi.
4. The absolute difference between the mean ranks ascribed to the offers on the shortlist by the individual DMs, $\overline{R}_{diff} = |\overline{R}_1 - \overline{R}_2|$.
5. The absolute difference between the mean distances from offers on the shortlist to a DMs workplace, $\overline{D}_{diff} = |\overline{D}_1 - \overline{D}_2|$, where $\overline{D}_i$ is the mean distance from offers on the shortlist to the workplace of DMi.

The patterns of change in α indicate how the algorithm adapts to the data and the coherence of the DMs preferences. Ideally both $\overline{R}_g$, and $\overline{R}_{max}$ should be low, i.e. the offers on the shortlist should be generally attractive both to the group as a whole and the DMs individually. Cases where the absolute difference between the means of the ranks ascribed to offers on the shortlist by the individual DMs, $\overline{R}_{diff}$, is large may indicate a conflict of interest between the DMs which the algorithm has not solved. However, when analyzing this parameter, one should take into account the fact that $\overline{R}_{diff}$ is expected to be positively correlated with the number of offers satisfying the hard constraints. For this reason, a more robust assessment of the level of conflict between the DMs can be obtained in this case by looking at the absolute difference between the mean distances of the offers on the shortlist to the two workplaces of the DMs, denoted by $\overline{D}_{diff}$. Note that a rank of 1 is ascribed to the most attractive offer and a rank of N to the least attractive offer. It follows that an increase in the mean rank of offers on the shortlist corresponds to a decrease in their general attractiveness.

In addition, in order to analyze the effect of the adjustment of the attractiveness scores in balancing the level of conflict between the DMs, the algorithm was also applied without any adjustment of the attractiveness scores.

6.1 Effect of the Weight Given to Location

Since two values of the weight parameter were used for each of the 50 combinations of hard constraints and workplaces, we treat the results obtained as two dependent samples of size 50. Since the distribution of the differences between the dependent variables in paired experiments is not normal, we apply a non-parametric test, the median test. Table 11 indicates the number of times a dependent variable i) decreased, ii) did not change, iii) increased when the weight ascribed to location increased from 0.2 to 0.4. Using the median test, it is assumed that when the weight given to location has no statistical effect on a variable, then the probability of an increase is equal to the probability of a decrease. Under this assumption, when there are n changes, the number of increases has a Binomial distribution with parameters n and 0.5 (practically speaking, the pairs for which no change is observed are removed for the purpose of analysis).

First, it should be noted that the weight ascribed to diversity by the algorithm, α, is generally lower than in analogous problems where there is only one DM. This is expected, since the difference between the DM's preferences should lead to a relatively high level of variety in the offers that are attractive to both of them. However, from this point of view, it is strange that as the weight ascribed to distance from ones workplace, w_3, increases (i.e. individual preferences become more important), α also tends to increase (35 increases, compared to one decrease). It should be noted that there is a very high correlation between floorspace and price. Hence, the location of a property is very significant in describing the variety of offers available. As w_3 increases, there is more selection pressure on the location of a property which counteracts the diversity resulting from the DMs having different preferences. The results indicate that as w_3 increases, the geographical spread of highly ranked offers becomes more concentrated around a corridor between the two workplaces and thus the data driven algorithm counteracts this by placing a higher weight on the value of diversity. In general, the nature of the effect of the weight of individual specific criteria on α will depend on the nature of these criteria and the joint distribution of the data.

Given the relation between w_3 and α, it is unsurprising that as w_3 increases the mean overall rank, R_g, of the offers placed on the shortlist also tends to increase (i.e. these offers are generally less attractive on the basis of initial information). However, these mean ranks are very close to the minimum (15.5), which indicates that the items placed on the shortlist are attractive to the pair of DMs. The absolute difference between the mean ranks ascribed by the two DMs to offers on the shortlist, $\overline{R}_{diff}$ and the maximum of these two mean ranks, $\overline{R}_{max}$ are increasing in w_3. However, the absolute difference between the mean distances from the offers on the list to the two workplaces is not significantly affected by this weight (it actually falls slightly as w_3 increases). This indicates that, in practical terms, the algorithm is relatively robust to changes in the weight of the individual specific factors.

Table 11. The effect of the weight ascribed to distance from workplace (the individual specific factor). N_+, N_- and N_0 give the number of scenarios for which an increase in w_3 leads to an increase, decrease and no change in the parameter of interest, respectively.

Parameter	Mean ($w_3 = 0.2$)	Mean ($w_3 = 0.4$)	N_+	N_-	N_0	p-value
α	0.0364	0.1216	35	1	14	1.08×10^{-9}
$\overline{R}_g$	16.33	21.83	35	2	13	1.02×10^{-8}
$\overline{R}_{max}$	55.70	225.46	50	0	0	1.78×10^{-15}
$\overline{R}_{diff}$	21.99	107.09	46	4	0	4.46×10^{-10}
$\overline{D}_{diff}$	2.057	1.628	19	31	0	0.1189

6.2   Effect of the Location of the DMs' Workplaces

First, we consider the effect of the distance between the DMs' workplaces. Note that this distance (either 8, $8\sqrt{2}$ or 16 km) depends on the specific location of these workplaces (e.g. this distance is 8 if and only if one of the DMs works in the city centre). Hence, it is also important to assess the effect of the specific locations of the workplaces. Since there are three possible distances, the appropriate variant of the median test is used. Due to the strong influence of w_3, the data are split into two groups according the value of w_3. Table 12 gives results. The p-values are calculated using Fisher's exact test.

It can be seen that the weight given to diversity is decreasing in the distance between the two workplaces. As this distance increases, the preferences of the DMs become less coherent. This means that the offers that are ranked highly overall become naturally more diverse. Hence, the maximization procedure does not need to place a high weight on diversity. As a result, the mean overall ranking of offers decreases as the distance between workplaces increases. The absolute difference between the mean distances of offers on the shortlist to the two workplaces is increasing in the distance between the two workplaces. However, such a change is somewhat expected (since the mean distances to the two workplaces naturally increases) and the pattern of these changes is not statistically significant. Hence, increasing the distance between the workplaces of the DMs does not lead to an increasing level of conflict between the DMs regarding the generation of the shortlist. When $w_3 = 0.2$, the changes in the values of the dependent parameters exhibit a similar pattern.

Now we investigate the relation between the geographical locations of the workplaces and the mean ranks ascribed individually by the DMs to the offers placed on the shortlist. The absolute differences in these ranks are most visible when distance to work has a large weight ($w_3 = 0.4$). In general, the offers on the shortlist are slightly more attractive to a DM working in the centre of town than to their partner working in the north, south or west. This is particularly visible when the DMs are looking for a relatively small property. This seems to be due to the fact that a larger number of offers will be relatively close to the centre of the city than to a point more on the outskirts. Rather more surprisingly, when $w_3 = 0.4$, a DM working in the east tends to find offers on the shortlist more attractive than a partner working in the west or north. This may be due to the spatial distribution of offers resulting from the position of the river. As a result, there will be a relatively small collection of acceptable offers that are very attractive to the DM working in the east, while the majority of offers will be closer to their partner's workplace. This means that the attractiveness scores ascribed by the DM working in the east will be adjusted upwards and a relatively small group of these adjusted scores will then be particularly large. In such cases, when $w_3 = 0.4$, the mean distance of an offer to the workplace in the east is clearly lower than the mean distance of an offer to the workplace in the north or west.

Table 12. The effect of the distance between the workplaces. The fractions in brackets give the number of observations strictly greater than the overall median, together with the size of a group. Note that several observations can be equal to the median, which means that less than half of the observations are greater than the median.

$w_3 = 0.2$			
Parameter	Mean $(d = 8)$	Mean $(d = 8\sqrt{2})$	Mean $(d = 16)$	p-value
α	0.0380 (9/20)	0.0530 (11/20)	0.0000 (0/10)	0.007736
$\overline{R}_g$	16.40 (3/20)	16.68 (7/20)	15.50 (0/10)	0.2128
$\overline{R}_{max}$	38.71 (5/20)	61.06 (12/20)	78.96 (8/10)	0.009711
$\overline{R}_{diff}$	12.86 (7/20)	22.65 (11/20)	38.91 (7/10)	0.2026
$\overline{D}_{diff}$	1.647 (8/20)	2.8765 (14/20)	1.24 (3/10)	0.0587

$w_3 = 0.4$			
Parameter	Mean $(d = 8)$	Mean $(d = 8\sqrt{2})$	Mean $(d = 16)$	p-value
α	0.1715 (13/20)	0.1265 (12/20)	0.012 (0/10)	0.001135
$\overline{R}_g$	25.48 (13/20)	21.25 (12/20)	15.67 (0/10)	0.001135
$\overline{R}_{max}$	195.35 (8/20)	221.74 (9/20)	293.13 (8/10)	0.1292
$\overline{R}_{diff}$	106.80 (9/20)	78.92 (9/20)	164.02 (7/10)	0.4094
$\overline{D}_{diff}$	1.25 (8/20)	1.59 (11/20)	2.47 (6/10)	0.6133

6.3   Effect of the Number of Offers Satisfying the Hard Constraints

Since the dependent variables do not have normal distributions, Kendall's test of correlation was used. The weight of the distance to work factor was fixed for each test. Table 13 gives results of the analysis for $w_3 = 0.4$.

It can be seen that there is no significant correlation between the number of offers satisfying the hard constraints, N, and each of the following variables: a) the weight ascribed to diversity, α, b) the mean of the overall ranks of the offers on the shortlist, c) the absolute difference between the mean distances of offers to the two workplaces. These results indicate that the algorithm selects highly ranked offers regardless of the number of offers satisfying the constraints. The significant increases in the maximum of the mean ranks ascribed by the individual DMs and the absolute difference between these mean ranks might indicate that the degree of conflict increases when the weight, w_3, of the individual criterion and the number of offers both increase. However, the relative difference between these mean ranks (obtained by dividing by N) is independent of N and the relative value of the maximum of these mean ranks is actually decreasing in N. These results indicate that, in practice, the level of conflict between the DMs is relatively independent of the number of offers satisfying the hard constraints. This is confirmed by the lack of any significant effect (a small negative correlation) between the number of offers and the mean distances from offers on the shortlist to the two workplaces.

Table 13. Estimators of Kendall's coefficient of correlation between the number of offers satisfying the hard constraints and the dependent parameters.

Parameter	$w_3 = 0.2$		$w_3 = 0.4$	
	r	p-value	r	p-value
α	−0.1095	0.3106	0.0161	0.8725
$\overline{R}_g$	−0.1256	0.2490	−0.0524	0.6005
$\overline{R}_{max}$	−0.1486	0.1279	0.2956	0.00246
$\overline{R}_{diff}$	−0.1038	0.2880	0.3071	0.00166
$\overline{D}_{diff}$	0.03516	0.7190	−0.1357	0.1649

6.4   Effect of the Budget of the DMs

As can be seen from Table 9, the largest number of acceptable offers are available to DMs with a budget of 650 000PLN who are looking for a property of at least $40\,m^2$. The smallest number of offers are available to DMs with a budget of one million PLN who are looking for a property of at least $70\,m^2$. On the other hand, the relative diversity of the offers available to those with a budget of one million PLN is greatest. One of the reasons for this may lie in the fact that offers of small to medium sized properties are often concentrated in estates containing blocks of very similar sized and priced flats. A summary of the mean number of acceptable flats and their relative diversity is given in Table 14.

Table 14. The number of acceptable offers and their relative diversity according to the budget of the DMs.

Budget (thou. PLN)	500	650	750	900	1 000
Mean no. of acceptable offers	1093.5	2049.5	1662	1203.6	675.2
Mean standardized distance	0.2391	0.2492	0.2596	0.2679	0.2858

The relation between the budget of the DM and the dependent variables is summarized in Table 15. There is a positive relationship between the available budget and the weight ascribed to diversity by the algorithm. This may result from the higher diversity of offers acceptable to those with a larger budget. This could mean that a higher weight needs to be ascribed to diversity to ensure that the shortlist has sufficient diversity. However, this is unclear, since the offers ranked most highly by DMs with a large budget should also have a relatively high diversity compared to those with a lower budget.

Since more weight is ascribed to diversity as the budget increases, it is natural that the mean overall rank of the offers placed on the shortlist is also increasing in the budget. The pattern of the changes in the maximum of the mean ranks ascribed by individual DMs and the absolute difference between these mean ranks naturally follows the pattern in the number of acceptable offers (larger values of these two variables are associated with larger numbers of acceptable offers). On the other hand, there is no significant relation between the budget of the DMs and the absolute difference between the mean distances of offers on the shortlist to the workplaces of the DMs. This suggests that the level of conflict between the DMs is not affected by the common constraints.

Table 15. The relation between the budget and the dependent parameters when $w_3 = 0.4$. The fractions in brackets give the number of observations above the overall median, together with the size of a group.

$w_3 = 0.2$						
Budget	500 000	650 000	750 000	900 000	1 000 000	p-value
α	0.021 (2/10)	0.035 (3/10)	0.015 (3/10)	0.033 (5/10)	0.078 (7/10)	0.1855
$\overline{R}_g$	17.10 (2/10)	15.8 (3/10)	15.51 (1/10)	16.11 (5/10)	17.13 (6/10)	0.1314
$\overline{R}_{max}$	71.92 (7/10)	55.22 (5/10)	35.86 (2/10)	57.54 (4/10)	57.96 (7/10)	0.1446
$\overline{R}_{diff}$	38.39 (6/10)	23.66 (5/10)	6.09 (2/10)	19.50 (6/10)	22.28 (6/10)	0.3423
$\overline{D}_{diff}$	2.486 (7/10)	2.556 (7/10)	1.703 (4/10)	1.763 (3/10)	1.779 (4/10)	0.3090
$w_3 = 0.4$						
Budget	500 000	650 000	750 000	900 000	1 000 000	p-value
α	0.035 (1/10)	0.111 (5/10)	0.08 (3/10)	0.194 (8/10)	0.188 (8/10)	0.004261
$\overline{R}_g$	16.20 (1/10)	18.53 (5/10)	18.15 (3/10)	28.98 (8/10)	27.28 (8/10)	0.004261
$\overline{R}_{max}$	216.65 (6/10)	295.26 (7/10)	242.53 (5/10)	231.54 (6/10)	141.35 (1/10)	0.06854
$\overline{R}_{diff}$	116.48 (6/10)	156.40 (7/10)	133.79 (6/10)	90.08 (5/10)	38.72 (1/10)	0.06854
$\overline{D}_{diff}$	2.01 (8/10)	1.51 (5/10)	1.66 (4/10)	1.52 (4/10)	1.45 (4/10)	0.3423

6.5   Effect of Adjusting the Attractiveness Measures

The algorithm was also implemented without adjusting the attractiveness for each of the 100 scenarios. A pairwise comparison of the absolute difference between the mean distances from the offers on the shortlist to the two workplaces, $\overline{D}_{diff}$ was carried out. In 36 out of the 100 scenarios, $\overline{D}_{diff}$ was greater when the adjustment procedure was implemented. In 39 out of the 100 scenarios, $\overline{D}_{diff}$ was lower when the adjustment procedure was implemented. In the remaining 25 cases, there was no change in $\overline{D}_{diff}$. These results indicate that there is no systematic improvement in balancing the differing preferences of the DMs by using the adjustment procedure. Both procedures give shortlists of offers that are relatively attractive to both DMs. It may be concluded that the process of standardizing the variables used to assess attractiveness suffices to balance the interests of the DMs to an appropriate degree.

7   Conclusions and Future Work

This paper has presented an algorithm for constructing shortlists of potentially attractive offers, to a group of DMs, from a large database. It is assumed that the data available are sufficient to indicate whether an offer is potentially attractive to the group, but insufficient to make a final decision. For example, such a database might contain basic information about real estate offers in a city. The choice criteria of the DMs are split into two categories, common and individual. For example, when a family is looking for a new home, the price and dimensions of a property correspond to common criteria, while the distance from ones workplace corresponds to an individual criterion. A set of hard criteria is defined in order to filter out unacceptable offers. The choice criteria are then used to assess the potential attractiveness of an offer on the basis of the information from the database. In this article, attractiveness is assessed by each of the DMs using the SAW approach. A procedure has been presented for adjusting these attractiveness scores ensuring that the mean and variance of the scores ascribed by the DMs are the same for each DM. A standardized measure of the diversity of offers satisfying the hard constraints has been defined.

Shortlists are constructed by maximizing a weighted average of the mean attractiveness of offers placed on the shortlist and their diversity. Mean attractiveness and diversity are given weights of $1 - \alpha$ and α, respectively. These assumptions mean that shortlist formation is based on solving a binary quadratic programming problem. Due to the large number of variables involved in practical problems of this kind, a greedy algorithm is used to find a very good solution of the optimization problem corresponding to a given value of α. According to this algorithm, offers are successively added to the shortlist so as to maximize in each step a function of a similar form to the objective function of the QP problem. The choice of an appropriate value of α is unclear, thus a data driven approach is applied. Based on this approach, the value of α is successively increased over a relatively dense set of values until the diversity of offers on the shortlist is very similar to the diversity of the offers that satisfy the hard constraints. Hence, the overall procedure aims to maximize the mean attractiveness of the offers on the shortlist under the condition that the level of diversity in the offers is preserved. A simple example was given to illustrate this procedure. Finally, a computational study was carried out based on 100 scenarios describing the preferences of a pair of DMs jointly looking for a new home in Warsaw and using data regarding 8 309 real estate offers advertised in the summer of 2021. The goal of this study was to investigate the robustness of this algorithm.

It should be noted that when there is a single DM and a data driven procedure is used to select an appropriate value of α, then the computational complexity of the algorithm is largely defined by the calculation of the matrix of standardized distances between offers (see Ramsey and Mariański (2022)). The adaptation of the algorithm to multiple DMs only additionally involves the calculation and adjustment of attractiveness scores. Hence, computational time is very similar to the algorithm for one DM. Each of the shortlists for the 100 scenarios were generated on a laptop with a 1.4GH Intel Core i5 processor within two minutes.

The results of this study indicate that as the difference between the "ideal solutions" of the two DMs increases (in this example, the physical distance between their workplaces increase), the algorithm places a lower weight on the diversity measure. This is unsurprising, since decreasing the coherence of the preferences of the DMs will increase the diversity of offers that are jointly assessed as being attractive. In general, diversity is ascribed a lower weight by the algorithm when there are two DMs than when there is a single DM. However, this relation is not entirely simple. For example, one might expect that when the weight of the individual specific criteria is increased that the weight ascribed to diversity is likely to decrease. However, due to the nature of the individual specific criterion in the example presented, as its weight, w_3, increases the selection pressure on the location of a property increases. Thus as w_3 increases, the offers assessed to be most attractive lie in a corridor between the DMs workplaces. Due to the high correlation between price and floorspace, the variation in location is very important in determining the diversity of offers. Hence, in this case, increasing the weight of the individual specific criterion actually increases the weight ascribed to diversity by the algorithm.

The distribution of the offers, in particular with respect to the locations of the DMs workplaces, is related to the attractiveness of the offers on the shortlist to the individual DMs. For example, the properties on the shortlist tend to be more attractive to a DM working in the centre of the city than to a partner working outside of the city centre. This is unsurprising, since there are generally more offers acceptable to a DM working in the city centre. On the other hand, the results indicate that the algorithm for constructing a shortlist selects offers that are jointly attractive to both DMs. The procedure for equalizing the attractiveness scores ascribed by the DMs has no significant effect on the balance between the preferences of the DMs in selecting a shortlist. Hence, it appears that the procedure for defining a standardized attractiveness measure enables a reasonable balance to be found between the preferences of the DMs. However, a question remains as to whether a more advanced method of balancing these preferences could find a better compromise between the DMs' preferences without decreasing the overall attractiveness of the offers placed on the shortlist.

The computational study considered scenarios in which there were two DMs who were treated symmetrically. The distance to a DMs workplace was defined using the standard Euclidean distance. These assumptions mean that there a several possible directions for future research. For example, instead of using the Euclidean distance, one could use mean journey time to work to define distance. One might also consider asymmetries between the DMs. For example, it might be the case that only one of the DMs drives and thus it is preferable that a property lies close to the other DM's workplace. One might also consider problems in which there are a larger number of DMs. In this case, one of the DMs might have preferences that can be regarded as outlying with respect to the preferences of the other DMs. Future research should look at how such a problem should be dealt with. With regard to families looking for a new home, this will obviously lead to other asymmetries between the DMs. For example, the workplace of adults is specific, while the school attended by a child may depend on the home selected. Hence, a much richer set of information is required to derive an algorithm that can take into account the specific requirements of families.

The weight ascribed by the algorithm to the diversity of offers, α, is defined using a stopping rule ensuring that the diversity of offers on the shortlist is similar to the diversity of offers satisfying the hard constraints. One could use other stopping rules to select an appropriate value of α. For example, one might demand that a certain proportion of the k offers on a shortlist should be amongst the k offers ranked as the most attractive. This proportion will be typically high (70–80%). By successively increasing the value of α from 0, this proportion will decrease from 1. This process is halted when the proportion of offers ranked in the top k falls to the appropriate value.

Consideration of the factors described above could enable the implementation of a general algorithm to derive shortlists of potentially attractive properties for a wide range of groups of DMs.

Acknowledgements. This research was funded by Polish National Science Centre grant number 2018/29/B/HS4/02857, "Logistics, Trade and Consumer Decisions in the Age of the Internet".

Appendix: Spatial Distribution of Real Estate Offers

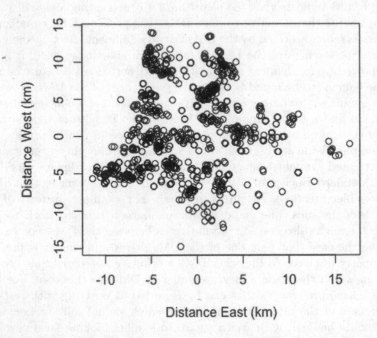

Fig. 1. Spatial distribution (relative to the city centre) of real estate offers satisfying the first set of constraints regarding price (at most 500 000PLN), floorspace (at least $30\,\mathrm{m}^2$) and number of rooms (at least two). There are 1602 such offers.

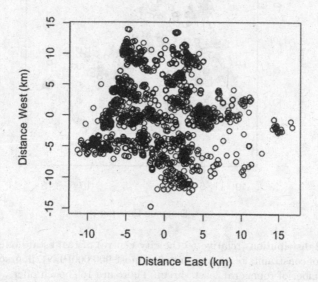

Fig. 2. Spatial distribution (relative to the city centre) of real estate offers satisfying the second set of constraints regarding price (at most 650 000PLN), floorspace (at least 40 m²) and number of rooms (at least two). There are 2927 such offers.

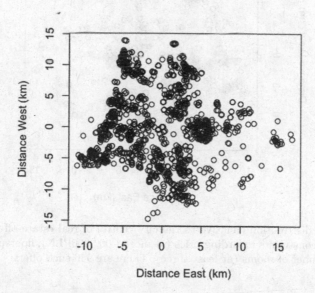

Fig. 3. Spatial distribution (relative to the city centre) of real estate offers satisfying the third set of constraints regarding price (at most 750 000PLN), floorspace (at least 50 m²) and number of rooms (at least two). There are 2360 such offers.

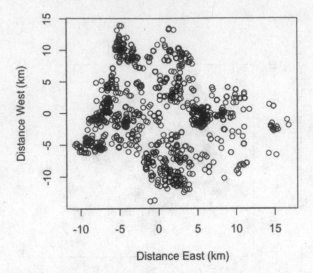

Fig. 4. Spatial distribution (relative to the city centre) of real estate offers satisfying the fourth set of constraints regarding price (at most 900 000PLN), floorspace (at least $60 \, m^2$) and number of rooms (at least three). There are 1693 such offers.

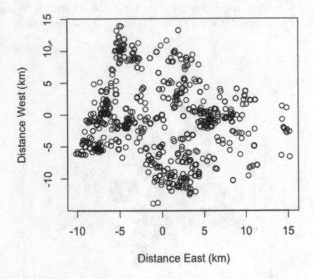

Fig. 5. Spatial distribution (relative to the city centre) of real estate offers satisfying the fifth set of constraints regarding price (at most 1 000 000PLN), floorspace (at least $70 \, m^2$) and number of rooms (at least three). There are 946 such offers.

References

Achterberg, T., Berthold, T.: Improving the feasibility pump. Discret. Optim. **4**(1), 77–86 (2007)

Aledo, J.A., Gámez, J.A., Rosete, A.: A highly scalable algorithm for weak rankings aggregation. Inf. Sci. **570**, 144–171 (2021)

Analytis, P.P., Kothiyal, A., Katsikopoulos, K.: Multi-attribute utility models as cognitive search engines. Judgm. Decis. Mak. **95**, 403–419 (2014)

Analytis, P.P., Wu, C.M., Gelastopoulos, A.: Make-or-break: chasing risky goals or settling for safe rewards? Cogn. Sci. **43**(7), e12743 (2019)

Bertacco, L., Fischetti, M., Lodi, A.: A feasibility pump heuristic for general mixed-integer problems. Discret. Optim. **4**(1), 63–76 (2007)

Billinger, S., Srikanth, K., Stieglitz, N., Schumacher, T.R.: Exploration and exploitation in complex search tasks: how feedback influences whether and where human agents search. Strateg. Manag. J. **42**(2), 361–385 (2021)

Blackburn, L., Young, A., Rogers, P., Hedengren, J., Powell, K.: Dynamic optimization of a district energy system with storage using a novel mixed-integer quadratic programming algorithm. Optim. Eng. **20**(2), 575–603 (2019)

Bobadilla-Suarez, S., Love, B.C.: Fast or frugal, but not both: decision heuristics under time pressure. J. Exp. Psychol. Learn. Mem. Cogn. **44**(1), 24 (2018)

Bock, H.H., Day, W.H., McMorris, F.R.: Consensus rules for committee elections. Math. Soc. Sci. **35**(3), 219–232 (1998)

Bottomley, P.A., Doyle, J.R., Green, R.H.: Testing the reliability of weight elicitation methods: direct rating versus point allocation. J. Mark. Res. **37**(4), 508–513 (2000)

Caplin, A., Dean, M., Leahy, J.: Rational inattention, optimal consideration sets, and stochastic choice. Rev. Econ. Stud. **86**(3), 1061–1094 (2019)

Cook, W.D.: Distance-based and ad hoc consensus models in ordinal preference ranking. Eur. J. Oper. Res. **172**(2), 369–385 (2006)

Dahmani, I., Hifi, M.: A modified descent method-based heuristic for binary quadratic knapsack problems with conflict graphs. Ann. Oper. Res. **298**(1), 125–147 (2021)

D'Ambrosio, A., Iorio, C., Staiano, M., Siciliano, R.: Median constrained bucket order rank aggregation. Comput. Stat. **34**(2), 787–802 (2019)

Diss, M., Kamwa, E., Tlidi, A.: On some k-scoring rules for committee elections: agreement and Condorcet Principle. Revue d'economie politique **130**(5), 699–725 (2020)

Elkind, E., Faliszewski, P., Skowron, P., Slinko, A.: Properties of multiwinner voting rules. Soc. Choice Welfare **48**(3), 599–632 (2017)

Fischetti, M., Glover, F., Lodi, A.: The feasibility pump. Math. Program. **104**(1), 91–104 (2005)

García-Zamora, D., Labella, Á., Rodríguez, R.M., Martínez, L.: Nonlinear preferences in group decision-making. Extreme values amplifications and extreme values reductions. Int. J. Intell. Syst. **36**(11), 6581–6612 (2021)

Gibbard, A.: Manipulation of voting schemes. A general result. Econometrica **41**, 587–601 (1973)

Guignard, M., Ahlatcioglu, A.: The convex hull heuristic for nonlinear integer programming problems with linear constraints and application to quadratic 0–1 problems. J. Heuristics **27**(1), 251–265 (2021)

Guillet, B.D., Mattila, A., Gao, L.: The effects of choice set size and information filtering mechanisms on online hotel booking. Int. J. Hosp. Manag. **87**, 102379 (2020)

Kaliszewski, I., Podkopaev, D.: Simple additive weighting? A metamodel for multiple criteria decision analysis methods. Expert Syst. Appl. **54**, 155–161 (2016)

Kimya, M.: Choice, consideration sets, and attribute filters. Am. Econ. J.: Microecon. **10**(4), 223–247 (2018)

Kontek, K., Sosnowska, H.: Specific tastes or cliques of jurors? How to reduce the level of manipulation in group decisions? Group Decis. Negot. **29**(6), 1057–1084 (2020)

Lleras, J.S., Masatlioglu, Y., Nakajima, D., Ozbay, E.Y.: When more is less: limited consideration. J. Econ. Theory **170**, 70–85 (2017)

Mandler, M., Manzini, P., Mariotti, M.: A million answers to twenty questions: choosing by checklist. J. Econ. Theory **147**(1), 71–92 (2012)

Martello, S., Toth, P.: Knapsack Problems: Algorithms and Computer Implementations. Wiley, Hoboken (1990)

Masatlioglu, Y., Nakajima, D., Ozbay, E.Y.: Revealed attention. Am. Econ. Rev. **102**(5), 2183–2205 (2012)

Murty, K.G., Yu, F.T.: Linear Complementarity, Linear and Nonlinear Programming, vol. 3. Heldermann, Berlin (1988)

Otodom.pl. www.otodom.pl/. Accessed 18 Aug 2021

Ramsey, D.M.: Optimal Selection from a set of offers using a short list. Multiple Criteria Decis. Making **14**, 75–92 (2019)

Ramsey, D.M., Mariański, A., Szczurowski, L., Kędziora, M.: On creating shortlists from a large database of offers. Acta Academica Karviniensia (2022, to appear)

Ramsey, D.M., Mariański, A.: An Algorithm for Creating Shortlists of Differentiated and Attractive Offers from Large Databases. Submitted to Computers and Operations Research (2022)

Riabacke, M., Danielson, M., Ekenberg, L.: State-of-the-art prescriptive criteria weight elicitation. Advances in Decision Sciences (2012)

Rubinstein, A., Salant, Y.: A model of choice from lists. Theor. Econ. **1**(1), 3–17 (2006)

Saaty, T.L.: How to make a decision: the analytic hierarchy process. Eur. J. Oper. Res. **48**(1), 9–26 (1990)

Simon, H.A.: A behavioral model of rational choice. Q. J. Econ. **69**(1), 99–118 (1955)

Simon, H.A.: Rational choice and the structure of the environment. Psychol. Rev. **63**(2), 129 (1956)

Stojić, H., Schulz, E., Analytis, P., Speekenbrink, M.: It's new, but is it good? How generalization and uncertainty guide the exploration of novel options. J. Exp. Psychol.: Gen. **149**(10), 1878 (2020)

Takapoui, R., Moehle, N., Boyd, S., Bemporad, A.: A simple effective heuristic for embedded mixed-integer quadratic programming. Int. J. Control **93**(1), 2–12 (2020)

Taha, H.A.: Operations Research: An Introduction. Pearson Education Limited, London (2017)

Taylor, A.D., Pacelli, A.M.: Mathematics and Politics: Strategy, Voting, Power, and Proof. Springer, Berlin (2008)

Todd, P.M., Gigerenzer, G.: Précis of simple heuristics that make us smart. Behav. Brain Sci. **23**(5), 727–741 (2000)

Ursu, R.M.: The power of rankings: quantifying the effect of rankings on online consumer search and purchase decisions. Mark. Sci. **37**(4), 530–552 (2018)

Yoon, K.P., Hwang, C.L.: Multiple Attribute Decision Making: An Introduction. (Series: Quantitative Applications in the Social Sciences, vol. 104). Sage Publications, Thousand Oaks (1995)

Algorithms for Measuring Indirect Control in Corporate Networks and Effects of Divestment

Jochen Staudacher[1]([⊠])[iD], Linus Olsson[1], and Izabella Stach[2][iD]

[1] Fakultät Informatik, Hochschule Kempten,
Bahnhofstr. 61, 87435 Kempten, Germany
jochen.staudacher@hs-kempten.de, linus.m.olsson@stud.hs-kempten.de
[2] AGH University of Science and Technology,
Al. Mickiewicza 30, 30-059 Kraków, Poland
istach@agh.edu.pl

Abstract. This paper discusses algorithms for measuring indirect control in complex corporate shareholding networks and investigates the importance of mutual connections in the network in the sense of shareholdings of one firm in another. Our algorithms rely on the concept of power indices from cooperative game theory. We focus on a variant of the implicit power index by Stach and Mercik based on the absolute Banzhaf index. We extend this algorithm by determining the number of regressions in an adaptive network-dependent manner taking into account the maximal length of a path to each controlled company in the network and by a model for the float, i.e., the set of unidentified small shareholders. We compare our method with existing algorithms and discuss the importance of linkages by investigating divestment of shares for a theoretical network with 21 players.

Keywords: Cooperative game theory · Power indices · Corporate shareholding structures · Direct and indirect control · Banzhaf index

1 Introduction

Measuring the power of firms in corporate shareholding networks is challenging as such networks can be large and as cross-shareholdings, cycles and complex ownership chains can turn an analysis of the power structure into a complex problem [11,17,18,34]. This article studies a game-theoretical approach using power indices [10]. We model shareholders as players in a simple game, i.e., a TU cooperative game in which a coalition is either winning or losing. We employ power indices for measuring the power of the firms in that simple game whereas the simple game itself is interpreted as a voting situation in a stock company [47].

This article puts its focus on so-called implicit power indices [40,42] and extends a previous article by the authors [54] in the same series. We improve the

© Springer-Verlag GmbH Germany, part of Springer Nature 2022
N. T. Nguyen et al. (Eds.): Transactions on Computational Collective Intelligence XXXVII,
LNCS 13750, pp. 53–74, 2022.
https://doi.org/10.1007/978-3-662-66597-8_3

algorithms from [54] by determining the number of regressions in an adaptive network-dependent way, i.e., we set the number of regressions for a controlled company equal to the number of arcs in a path of maximal length from another controlled company to that company. This paper puts the modified implicit power index π^β [50,54] based on the absolute Banzhaf index [7] at the center of the investigations. We point out how the float, i.e., the set of unidentified small shareholders, can be incorporated into this algorithm in a straightforward and computationally inexpensive manner and thus present and discuss the first implicit power index for incomplete shareholding networks.

Furthermore, this work analyzes how the power structure within a network changes when a shareholder decides to divest. We discuss algorithms and software for the following question: How does the power structure within a network change if a firm decides to sell parts or all of its shareholdings in a company either to another firm in the network or to the float? By addressing this question, we extend and complement a recent study by Stach and Mercik (2021) [49] which investigates the importance of linkages in corporate networks.

The article is structured as follows: Sect. 2 introduces some notation, concepts and definitions from cooperative game theory. Section 3 is the centerpiece of methodological innovation of this paper. It motivates the problem of indirect control in shareholding networks with an example with 21 players, introduces approaches for measuring indirect control and points out how we integrate the float in computations of the implicit index π^β based on the Banzhaf index [50,54]. Section 4 discusses computational and software aspects for algorithms for measuring indirect control and emphasizes the favourable computational properties of the implicit index π^β. Section 5 discusses different instances of divestment for our network with 21 players and interprets the results. Section 6 summarizes our conclusions and provides an outlook to open research questions.

2   Preliminaries on Cooperative Game Theory and Power Indices

This section serves as a preface for some definitions and theoretical background we use later in our article.

2.1   Cooperative Game Theory and Simple Games

Cooperative game theory [16] studies the outcomes and benefits which players can achieve by joining coalitions.

In the following paragraph, we briefly review the terminology for the definition of a TU cooperative game, i.e., a cooperative game with transferable utility. Let $N = \{1, ..., n\}$ be a finite set of n players. A group of players $S \subseteq N$ is referred to as a coalition, whereas 2^N denotes the set of all subsets of N. The *empty coalition* is expressed by $\emptyset$ and the *grand coalition* is denoted by N. The notation $|S|$ stands for the cardinality of a coalition S, i.e., the number of its members, hence $|N| = n$. An n-person TU cooperative game is characterized as a pair (N, v) where $v : 2^N \rightarrow \mathbb{R}$ is the so-called *characteristic function* which assigns a real value to all coalitions $S \in 2^N$ and follows the postulate $v(\emptyset) = 0$. We call a cooperative game *monotone* if for all coalitions $S, T \in 2^N$ the relation $S \subseteq T$ implies $v(S) \leq v(T)$.

A cooperative game is called *simple* if it is monotone and $v(S) = 0$ or $v(S) = 1$ for each coalition $S \subseteq N$. For a simple game v, coalitions for which $v(S) = 1$ are named *winning coalitions* and coalitions with $v(S) = 0$ *losing coalitions*. A player i is referred to as a *critical player* (also known as a decisive player or swing player) in a winning coalition S if $v(S\backslash\{i\}) = 0$, i.e., the winning coalition S turns into a losing one if player i departs. A player i who is never critical for any coalition $S \in 2^N$, i.e., $v(S \cup i) - v(S) = 0$, is called a *null player*. A player i is called a *dictator* if $v(S) = 1$ whenever $i \in S$ and $v(S) = 0$ otherwise. The set of coalitions for which player $i \in N$ is critical is expressed by $C_i = \{S \subseteq N : i \in S \wedge v(S) = 1 \wedge v(S\backslash\{i\}) = 0\}$ and $Cr(S)$ denotes the set of critical players for a coalition $S \in 2^N$. We refer to a coalition S with at least one critical player, i.e., $|Cr(S)| > 0$, as a *vulnerable* coalition. A coalition S is called *minimal winning* if S consists entirely of critical players.

Weighted voting games (also known as weighted majority games or weighted games) are probably the most important subclass of simple games to model voting situations. Weighted voting games are characterized by n non-negative real weights $w_i, i = 1, \ldots, n$, and a non-negative real quota q, normally $\frac{1}{2}\sum_{i=1}^n w_i < q < \sum_{i=1}^n w_i$. Frequently, they are specified in the form $W = [q; w_1, \ldots, w_n]$. The corresponding characteristic function $v : 2^N \rightarrow \{0, 1\}$ takes the value $v(S) = 1$ for winning coalitions S, i.e., $w(S) = \sum_{i \in S} w_i \geq q$, and $v(S) = 0$ otherwise, implying that S is a losing coalition. In Sects. 3, 4 and 5 we employ weighted voting games to define voting situations in stock companies.

2.2 Power Indices

In general, a *power index* f is a function receiving a simple n-person cooperative game specified by its player set N and its characteristic function v as its input and delivering a unique real-valued vector $f(v) = (f_1(v), \ldots, f_n(v))$ as its output. In the following, we only introduce those three power indices which we use in Sects. 3, 4 and 5. Likewise, we restrict our presentation to only four properties of power indices. For a detailed discussion of power indices and their properties, we recommend the overview article by Bertini, Freixas, Gambarelli and Stach (2013) [10].

A power index f is called *efficient* if for all simple games (N, v) (apart from the null game) there holds $\sum_{i=1}^n f_i(v) = v(N) = 1$. A power index f satisfies the *null player property* if $f_i(v) = 0$ for every simple game v and each null player i in (N, v). A power index f maintains the *null-player removable property* if the power measures for all non-null players are unaffected by the removal of any null players from any simple game. In the more general context of TU cooperative games, this is also known as the NPO (Null Player Out) property, see Derks and Haller (1999) [21].

Finally, we define the *donation property* for a power index f applied to a weighted voting game W along the lines of [10]. Consider a pair of weighted voting games $W = [q; w_1, \ldots, w_n]$ and $W' = [q; w'_1, \ldots, w'_n]$ on the same set of players N with identical quota q and weight sum, i.e., $w(N) = \sum_{i \in N} w_i = \sum_{i \in N} w'_i = w'(N)$. Let us assume that W represents the initial distribution of weights and W' follows from it by a single redistribution, i.e. there is a single donor i with $w_i > w'_i$ giving away some weight to a single recipient j with with $w_j < w'_j$. The idea behind the donation property is that that the donor i must not gain power. A power index f satisfies the donation property if in the above configuration with a sole donor i and a sole recipient j, there holds $f_i(W) \geq f_i(W')$.

Let us define three power indices frequently used in the context of indirect control, i.e., the Banzhaf, Johnston and Shapley-Shubik index and their variants. Let v be a simple n-player game and let $\eta_i(v) = |C_i|$ stand for the number of coalitions for which player i is critical and $\eta_i(v, c)$ for the number of coalitions of cardinality c for which i is a critical player.

a) The *(absolute) Banzhaf index* [7,12] of player i is defined as

$$\beta_i(v) = \frac{\eta_i(v)}{2^{n-1}}.$$

The *relative Banzhaf index* [12]

$$\beta'_i(v) = \frac{\eta_i(v)}{\sum_{k=1}^{n} \eta_k(v)}$$

is frequently used as an efficient counterpart, i.e., $\sum_{i=1}^{n} \beta'_i(v) = v(N) = 1$. Sometimes the number $\eta_i(v)$ itself is referred to as the *raw Banzhaf index* of player i, see e.g., [16], p. 118.

b) The *Johnston index* [27] of player i is defined as

$$\gamma_i(v) = \frac{\sum_{i \in Cr(S)} \frac{1}{|Cr(S)|}}{\sum_{k=1}^{n} \sum_{k \in Cr(S)} \frac{1}{|Cr(S)|}}$$

if i is not a null player in (N, v) and $\gamma_i(v) = 0$ otherwise. Correspondingly, the *raw Johnston index* of player i is given as

$$\gamma_i^{raw}(v) = \sum_{i \in Cr(S)} \frac{1}{|Cr(S)|}$$

if i is not a null player in (N, v) and $\gamma_i^{raw}(v) = 0$ otherwise. It loses the efficiency and null-player removable properties of the Johnston index.

c) The *Shapley-Shubik index* [45,46] of player i is defined as

$$\sigma_i = \sum_{c=1}^{n} \frac{\eta_i(v, c)}{c \binom{n}{c}}.$$

The Shapley-Shubik index is derived from the Shapley value, which was originally defined by Shapley (1953) [44] and is the most widely employed solution concept in cooperative game theory. For a synopsis of theoretical and applied results on the Shapley value we refer to Algaba, Fragnelli and Sánchez-Soriano (2020) [4]. We finally stress that all power indices presented in this subsection satisfy the null player property whereas only the absolute Banzhaf index and the Shapley-Shubik index fulfill the donation property [10].

3   Algorithms for Indirect Control in Corporate Shareholding Networks

This section motivates the problem of indirect control with a shareholding network with 21 entities, introduces existing methods for measuring control power and presents a novel approach of an implicit index with network-dependent regressions and a model for the float.

3.1   Modelling of Corporate Shareholding Networks and an Illustrative Example

We model corporate networks as weighted directed graphs [17]. A very brief introduction to some definitions from graph theory along the lines of the textbook by Bang-Jensen and Gutin (2008) [6] and the article by Crama and Leruth (2007) [17] is adequate. The set of vertices V in the directed graph represents the firms in the corporate network whereas the set of arcs $A \subseteq V \times V$ illustrates the linkages between the firms. For each arc $(i, j) \in A$ the weight $w_{i,j}$ symbolizes the fraction of share ownership of firm i in firm j. For an arc $(i, j) \in A$, we call i a predecessor of j, while j is a successor of i. A path is a sequence of vertices $(i_1, ..., i_k)$ with $(i_p, i_{p+1}) \in A$ for $p = 1, ..., k-1$ such that all vertices $i_1, ..., i_{k-1}$ are different. A path is referred to as a cycle if $i_1 = i_k$. Thus cross-shareholdings between firms lead to cycles in the directed graph.

For each $j \in V$, we denote the set of predecessors of firm j by V_j. Whenever $V_j = \emptyset$, we call firm j an *investor*, i.e., firm j acts as an uncontrolled entity in our network. In any other case, i.e., $V_j \neq \emptyset$, we call firm j a *company* implying that it is owned by shareholders and treated as a controlled entity [50]. Following the notation used in [50,54], N^C stands for the set of companies while N^I is the set of investors in a corporate network.

We readopt the theoretical shareholding network with 10 companies (numbered from 1 to 10) and 11 investors (numbered from 11 to 21) introduced in [54]. We display our network as a directed graph in Fig. 1. As explained before, the weights on the arcs represent the voting rights of a firm in a company. For the sake of clarity, Table 1 also lists direct ownership relations for our example.

Note that our corporate network in Fig. 1 is complete in the sense that for all companies $c \in N^C$ there holds $\sum_{s \in V_c} w_{s,c} = 1$ meaning that we know the complete ownership structure. For real-world examples gathering comprehensive data about the ownership structure for all the firms involved in the corporate

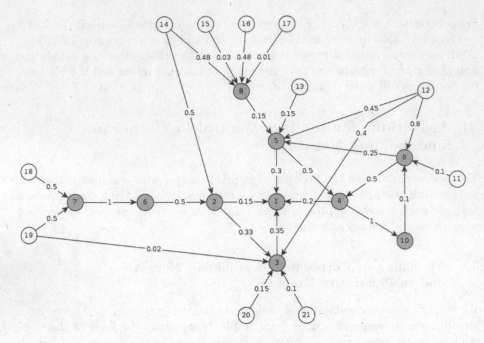

Fig. 1. A theoretical shareholding network with 21 players.

network is not always possible, as in many cases a fraction of shareholders of a firm may simply be unknown. This set of unidentified shareholders is generally denoted as the *float* [17,18,36]. A number of reasons for the occurence of incomplete networks are summarized by Crama and Leruth (2013) [18]. One major cause is that according to the transparency requirements in most countries, only shareholders that own more than 3% or 5% of the shares must be identified. As a consequence, we also look into models for the float and define it for each company $c \in N^C$ as $fl_c = 1 - \sum_{s \in V_c} w_{s,c}$.

For each company $c \in N^C$ in a network we can specify a weighted voting game modelling direct control exerted by its shareholders. We regard each shareholder $s \in V_c$, i.e., each individual predecessor of company c, as a player with the weight $w_{s,c}$ corresponding to the arc $(s,c) \in A$. For simplicity, we always assume that the quota is 50% plus one share throughout this paper.

Our theoretical 21-player example network displays various different features [54]. We recall that investor 12 holds more than 50 percent of the voting rights in company 9 and thus exerts complete control over that company. Investors 11 and 17 are obviously null players with no direct or indirect control in any company within the network. We observe investors wielding indirect control in companies in which they do not hold any shares, e.g., investors 18 and 19 exerting influence in companies 6 and 2 via company 7, as well as loops, e.g., for companies 4, 9 and 10.

Table 1. Direct ownership relationships for our theoretical example with 21 players.

Company firm	1	2	3	4	5	6	7	8	9	10
1										
2	15%		33%							
3	35%									
4	20%									100%
5	30%			50%						
6		50%								
7						100%				
8					15%					
9				50%	25%					
10									10%	
11									10%	
12			40%		45%				80%	
13					15%					
14		50%						48%		
15								3%		
16								48%		
17								1%		
18							50%			
19		2%					50%			
20		15%								
21		10%								

3.2 The Approach by Crama-Leruth

In two papers, Crama and Leruth (2007, 2013) [17,18] propose a method for evaluating the power of each investor in each company in a network. Their idea is also discussed and explained in detail in the article by Bertini, Mercik and Stach (2016) [11]. We give a brief overview focussing on acyclic networks.

The approach by Crama-Leruth [17,18] relies on a simple game v modelled as a Boolean function $\phi_v : \{0,1\}^n \to \{0,1\}$ with $n = |N^I|$. The variables of ϕ_v correspond to the votes of the individual firms in the corporate network and are summarised in a vector $X = (x_1, x_2, ..., x_n) \in \{0,1\}^n$. In a decision process, if firm i votes "yes" then $x_i = 1$ and if firm i votes "no" then $x_i = 0$. Thus,

$$\phi_{v(X)} = \begin{cases} 1, & \text{if } v(\{i : x_i = 1\}) = 1. \\ 0, & \text{otherwise.} \end{cases}$$

Let g_j denote the weighted voting game for direct control of company $j \in N^C$ as introduced at the end of Subsect. 3.1. Subsequently, for acyclic graphs the indirect game v_j can be defined recursively for any firm j and all $X = (x_1, x_2, ..., x_n) \in \{0,1\}^n$ as follows:

$$v_j(X) = \begin{cases} x_j, & \text{if } j \in N^I. \\ g_j(v_{i_1}(X), v_{i_2}(X), ..., v_{i_k}(X)) & \text{otherwise.} \end{cases} \tag{1}$$

Here $i_1, i_2, ..., i_k$ are the direct shareholders of the company $j \in N^C$. However, in graphs with cycles the above recursive definition cannot be applied. Therefore Crama and Leruth [17] suggest an iterative procedure called MIX to handle cycles and estimate the values of games which are not perfectly defined, i.e., in those situations when the votes of the companies cannot be immediately derived from the votes of the investors. The procedure then attempts to find a stable voting pattern by generating sequences of votes. A voting pattern $X \in \{0,1\}^{|N^I \cup N^C|}$ is called stable if $x_j = g_j(X)$ for any firm j. If a stable pattern can not be reached the expected value for the game is estimated by averaging over all the values the game can take in the sequence of votes. Finally, Crama and Leruth [17] compute the Z index as an estimate of the Banzhaf index for corporate networks with indirect control. The Z index measures the voting power for an investor $j \in N^I$ in a target company $c \in N^C$ and is given by

$$Z_c(j) = \frac{1}{2^{n-1}} \left(\sum_{X \in \{0,1\}^n : x_j = 1} v_c(X) - \sum_{X \in \{0,1\}^n : x_j = 0} v_c(X) \right) \tag{2}$$

The three steps of the algorithm for the Crama-Leruth approach are visualized in Fig. 2.

Under the presence of a float the indirect game v_j for a company $j \in N^C$, is extended as follows

$$v_j(X) = g_j(v_{i_1}(X), v_{i_2}(X), ..., v_{i_k}(X)) = \begin{cases} 1, & \text{if } \sum_{m=1}^{k} w_{i_m, j} \cdot v_{i_m}(X) + fl_j \cdot \phi_j \geq q. \\ 0, & \text{if } \sum_{m=1}^{k} w_{i_m, j} \cdot v_{i_m}(X) + fl_j \cdot \phi_j < q. \end{cases}$$

Here ϕ_j is a random variable which takes values between 0 and 1 and thus represents the fraction of the float that votes"yes" or 1. Therefore the distribution of this random variable corresponds to the voting behaviour of the float, resulting in different possibilities to model the float. A simple model is the monolithic float, where the entire float votes the same way. However, this model does not reflect the fact that the small shareholders have different interests and therefore will vote independently. A very straightforward way to incorporate this aspect is to model the float as the sum of m small shareholders where each shareholder has the same amount of voting rights. Then $f_j = \frac{B(m,p)}{m}$, where B stands for a binomial distribution. As all float models discussed in this article estimate the Banzhaf index and as the Banzhaf index depends on a probability of $\frac{1}{2}$ for each player to vote either 0 or 1, we restrict our attention to a binomial model of the float with probability $p = \frac{1}{2}$. For a discussion of other models for the float we refer to Levy (2011) [35].

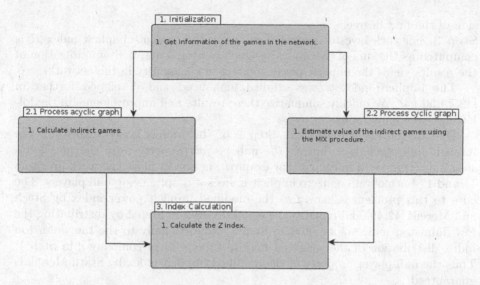

Fig. 2. Visualization of the algorithm for the Crama-Leruth approach.

3.3   The Implicit Index by Mercik-Łobos and Its Generalizations

Recent research on indirect control studies the voting power of both investors and companies. The method by Levy and Szafarz (2017) [36] is closely related to the approach by Crama and Leruth [17] and measures the voting power of all firms in the network rather than only investors. In a different fashion, the method by Karos and Peters (2015) [28] measures and ranks the influence of both companies and investors. Although the approaches by Karos and Peters (2015) [28] and Levy and Szafarz (2017) [36] are very worthwhile, the focus of this work are the so-called implicit power indices [40,42,50,54] which likewise measure voting power of both investors and companies.

Mercik and Łobos (2016) [40] proposed the original implicit index of power as a measure of reciprocal ownership by computing the raw Johnston index for the weighted majority games for direct control of individual companies. Their intention was to estimate the powers of both investors and companies in a network and to address cyclic structures in a simple and straightforward way.

We denote the set of investors of company $c \in N^C$ by N_c^I, whereas N_c^C stands for the companies, i.e., the controlled entities, that are shareholders of company c. The following three-step algorithm calculates the original implicit power index π by Mercik-Łobos.

Step 1. For each company c the raw Johnston index γ_i^{raw} is computed for the associated weighted voting game v_c for each shareholder i of c. In this step only the direct ownership of the immediate shareholders matters.

Step 2. For each non-individual shareholder, i.e., each shareholding-company, $\tilde{c} \in N_c^C$ the corresponding raw Johnston index computed in Step 1 is divided equally among all investors of $\tilde{c}$. Mercik and Łobos (2016) [40] call this a regression of the first degree.

Step 3. For each investor and each company the absolute implicit index Π is computed as the sum of the values assigned in Step 1 and 2. Standardization of the results yields the implicit power index π of each entity in the network.

The implicit index π was studied, enhanced and developed further in [42,49,50,54]. We quickly summarize these results and improvements in the following three paragraphs.

Due to the equal division in Step 2 of the Mercik-Łobos algorithm, the implicit index π fails to inherit the null player property from the raw Johnston index employed in Step 1. For example, in our 21-player network investors 11 and 17 both obtain nonzero implicit indices π despite being null players. The cure to this problem is known as the modified implicit power index by Stach and Mercik [42,49] and replaces the equal division in Step 2 by distributing the raw Johnston indices computed in Step 1 proportionally to the raw Johnston index distribution of the weighted majority game v_c of company c in Step 1. Thus the null player property of the modified implicit index by Stach-Mercik is guaranteed.

Mercik and Łobos (2016) [40] advocate for only one regression in Step 2 of the algorithm for their implicit power index π. In [54] we point out that for networks where certain shareholder-companies of a company only have controlled entities, i.e., companies, as their shareholders additional regressions are beneficial. For example, in our 21-player network example an additional regression is necessary in the case of the weighted voting game for company 2 for otherwise the indirect control in company 2 exercised by investors 18 and 19 would be neglected.

In Subsect. 2.2 we pointed out that the raw Johnston index lacks the null player removable probably. The article [54] establishes that the modified implicit index by Stach-Mercik briefly introduced in the penultimate paragraph inherits this problem from the raw Johnston index. The paper [54] regards the (modified) implicit indices as a general algorithmic framework by replacing the raw Johnston index with various other power indices, see Fig. 3 for a visualization. The study goes well beyond the power indices introduced in Subsect. 2.2 and also investigates different variants of both the Public Good index [25,26] and the Deegan-Packel index [20], two concepts based on minimal winning coalitions. In brief, the study [54] presents strong arguments for replacing the raw Johnston index within the Stach-Mercik framework by the absolute Banzhaf index enforcing an idea that was first proposed by Stach, Mercik and Bertini (2020) [50] and called the implicit index π^β.

The modified implicit power index π^β based on the absolute Banzhaf index satisfies the null-player property and the null investor removable property [54]. We wish to contribute an additional argument for π^β not mentioned in [54], namely, the absolute Banzhaf index satisfies the donation property whereas the various variants of the Johnston, Deegan-Packel and Public Good indices as well as the relative Banzhaf index do not [10]. The donation property is desirable in the context of indirect control as it guarantees that a firm which sells shares in another firm in the network can not increase its power in the network through

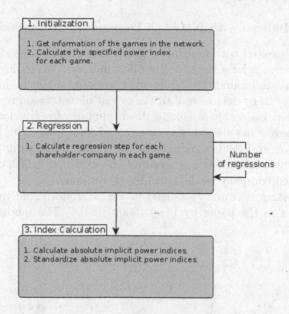

Fig. 3. Visualization of the algorithm for computing implicit indices.

that sale [49]. Within our framework of generalized implicit indices π^β will be our focus in the rest of the article. We formalize it below. For each investor $i \in N^I$ the implicit power index π^β is given by

$$\pi_i^\beta = \frac{\Pi'_\beta}{\sum_{r \in N^I} \Pi_r^\beta}$$

with the absolute implicit index Π_i^β defined by

$$\Pi_i^\beta = \sum_{c \in N^C} \left(\beta_i(v_c) + \sum_{\substack{k \in N_i^C \\ i \in N_k^I}} \left(\beta_k(v_c) \frac{\beta_i(v_k)}{\sum_{l \in N_k^I} \beta_l(v_k)} \right) \right).$$

For each company $c \in N^C$ the implicit power index π^β is given by

$$\pi_c^\beta = \frac{\Pi_c^\beta}{\sum_{r \in N^C} \Pi_r^\beta}$$

with the absolute implicit index Π_c^β defined by

$$\Pi_c^\beta = \sum_{i \in N_c^I} \beta_i(v_c) + \sum_{k \in N_c^C} \sum_{i \in N_k^I} \left(\beta_k(v_c) \frac{\beta_i(v_k)}{\sum_{l \in N_k^I} \beta_l(v_k)} \right).$$

The first and third steps of the calculations of the Mercik-Łobos index and the modified implicit index π^β are identical.

3.4   Implicit Indices with Network-Dependent Regressions

In [54] we experimented with multiple regressions within the second step of the algorithmic framework for generalized implicit indices. We employed fixed numbers of regressions and found that while one regression might be insufficient, too many regressions can be detrimental to the extent of distorted investor rankings. We concluded that rather than using a fixed number of regressions throughout the algorithm, regressions should be used in an adaptive way. This paper answers this open question and studies regressions for a controlled company depending on the concrete network taking into account the maximal length of a path from another controlled company to the considered company.

The shareholding network visualized in Fig. 4 is motivated by smaller, but similar, examples in the paper by Levy (2009) [34]. The method by Crama-

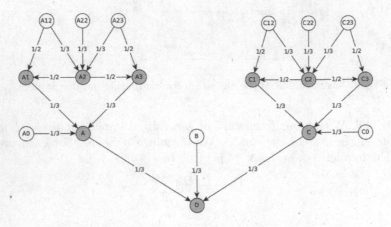

Fig. 4. A shareholding network with 18 firms.

Leruth [17, 18] introduced in Subsect. 3.2 measures non-zero indices of control power for investors A12, A22, A23, C12, C22 and C23 in company D. An implicit index can only detect this indirect control power with at least 3 regressions. However, more than 3 regressions are never warranted [54].

Thus we suggest to make the number of regressions in Step 2 of the implicit index algorithm depicted in Fig. 3 network-dependent for each shareholder-company, i.e., the number of regressions equals the number of arcs in a path of maximal length from another controlled company to the considered company. Formally, if the considered company is called c and there is a directed path $(c_1, c_2, ..., c_{k-1}, c)$ of maximal length k, then we need $k-1$ regressions. Our definition includes the case $c_1 = c$, i.e., a path of maximal length may be a cycle.

For the shareholding network in Fig. 4 our definition implies that we need no regressions for companies A2 and C2, one regression for companies A1, A3, C1 and C3, two regressions for companies A and C and three regressions for company D.

For our 21-player network from 1 we need no regressions for companies 7 and 8 as these are entirely controlled by investors. For company 6 only one regression is needed, for company 2 we need two regressions whereas for companies 1 and 3 three regressions are required. For companies 4, 5, 9 and 10 four regressions are called for, reflecting the cycle (5,4,10,9,5) as well as the path (8,5,4,10,9) for company 9.

3.5   The Implicit Index π^β with a Model for the Float

The implicit index π^β presented at the end of Subsect. 3.3 relies on computing absolute Banzhaf indices for weighted voting games for direct control of companies. Thus it allows for incorporating a binomial float with $p = \frac{1}{2}$ in a simple and straightforward manner using a result by Dubey and Shapley (1979) [22]. For an oceanic float, i.e., for an infinite number of unknown shareholders with each of them holding a vanishingly small fraction of the shares of a company $c \in N^C$ and each of them voting either 0 or 1 with probability $p = \frac{1}{2}$, the Banzhaf indices of the m known shareholders of company c can be approximated by the Banzhaf indices of the modified weighted voting game

$$[q - 0.5fl_c; w_{1,c}, \ldots, w_{m,c}], \tag{3}$$

i.e., for a weighted game specified by the quota $\tilde{q} = q - 0.5fl_c$ and the weights of the m known shareholders in which fl_c denotes the total weight of the float. This model was affirmed in empirical studies by Leech (2013) [33]. However, we emphasize that results for incomplete shareholding networks should be interpreted with more care than results for complete shareholding networks and refer to [17, 18, 34–36] for details.

4   Software Aspects

We use the R programming environment [56] for implementing the framework of generalized implicit indices and other approaches for estimating indirect control. R is very well-suited for rapid prototyping and the R ecosystem thrives on the idea of R packages [57], i.e., official extensions of the R environment for specific purposes contributed by users, quality-checked and made available by CRAN, the Comprehensive R Archive Network, in one central repository [56].

Our software for measuring indirect control in corporate networks makes extensive usage of the R packages igraph [19] for working with graphs and CoopGame [52] for TU cooperative games. The R package igraph implements an R interface to an established C++ library with the identical name making a comprehensive set of tools for creating, manipulating analyzing networks available to R users [19]. Our code uses igraph for creating directed graphs of corporate shareholding networks, for checking them for cycles and for finding the maximal length of a path to a node in order to implement the idea from Subsect. 3.4. The R package CoopGame [52] consists of a large collection of functions for

TU cooperative games, including power indices. However, CoopGame [52] provides reference implementations based on the characteristic function of a TU cooperative game and thus storage requirements grow exponentially in the number of players.

The implicit index π^β requires computations of absolute Banzhaf indices for weighted voting games. The problem of computing power indices for large weighted voting games was investigated extensively by Leech in [31–33]. These articles also discuss approximations and an ocean of small players. The most popular approach for power index computation uses generating functions, see [2,3]. For our Banzhaf index computations we employ the publicly available C++ software EPIC for weighted voting games [53, 55]. EPIC is based on the paradigm of dynamic programming which is strongly related to the approach based on generating functions. Even though computing Banzhaf indices for weighted voting games is NP-hard [38], EPIC allows for the efficient computation of large problem instances without any need to store the complete characteristic function of the simple game, implying that there is no need to use the functionality from CoopGame for weighted voting games. Instead, we rely on package Rcpp [23] for seamless integration of efficient C++ implementations of power indices for weighted majority games from EPIC [53,55] enabling us to handle the 21-player example in fractions of seconds. Following Subsect. 3.4 the functions for computing implicit indices described in [54] obtain an additional Boolean argument specifying whether regressions should be network dependent or not.

Our implementation of the algorithm for the Crama-Leruth approach depicted in Fig. 2 uses the concept of bit matrices provided by CoopGame and generates all possible voting patterns of the investors. In the acyclic case, the algorithm iterates through the rows of the bit matrix and processes each game with the current investor voting pattern using a recursive function corresponding to Eq. (1). Finally, we know the characteristic function of the corresponding indirect game for each company j and all investor voting patterns enabling us to compute the Z index (2).

5   Measuring the Effects of Divestment and the Power of Linkages

The recent article by Stach and Mercik (2021) [49] presents a novel approach for measuring the power of linkages in corporate networks and considers desirable properties of indirect control measures, including properties concerning the addition or elimination of links. The article [49] also discusses an instance of an elimination of a link of an investor holding 90% of shares in a company by analyzing the resulting changes in minimal winning coalitions and vulnerable coalitions. This section extends and complements the investigations in [49,50]. We study transformations of the power structure within a network when a shareholder decides to divest. Concretely, we address the question how the power structure within a network is altered if a firm decides to sell parts or all of its shareholdings in a company either to another firm in the network or to the float and look at a number of instances for our 21-player network shown in Fig. 1.

5.1   A Model for Measuring the Power of Linkages

For a corporate network M^L with a set of links L and a set of firms N we define the power of a link $l \in L$ for any firm $i \in N$ in the network along the lines of [50] as

$$\triangle_l^i(M^L) = f_i(M^L) - f_i(M^{L \setminus \{l\}}) \tag{4}$$

where f_i denotes the control power of firm i in the network, which can be computed using, e.g., one of the implicit power indices from Subsect. 3.3. Hence, the power of a link in the network for a firm i equals the difference between the power attributed to firm i before and after removing or modifying the link [50]. The removal or modification of a link l increases the control power of firm i when $\triangle_l^i(M^L) < 0$, while the control power decreases when $\triangle_l^i(M^L) > 0$.

The power of a linkage can be computed via the three-step algorithm visu-

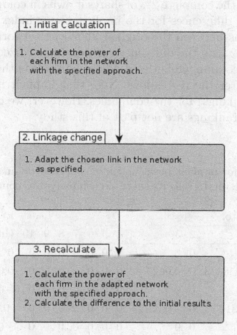

Fig. 5. Visualization of the algorithm for computing the power of a linkage.

alized in Fig. 5. The corresponding function has five parameters. One parameter specifies the corporate network. Further, users need to specify the approach for estimating the control power of the firms in the network. A third parameter specifies the link to be modified (with a link consisting of a firm and a company in which that firm owns shares). A fourth parameter specifies the amount of shares to be sold. The last parameter specifies the entity to which that amount of shares is sold and defaults to the float.

5.2 Investigating Divestment for a Corporate Network with 21 Firms

In this subsection we study the effects of investors selling parts or all of their shares on the control power in our corporate network with 21 firms. We consistently employ the implicit index π^β with network-dependent regressions for measuring control power in Eq. (4). We remark that the implicit indices provide a number for measuring the power of a firm within the whole network whereas the approach by Crama-Leruth measures only the power of investors in companies. It is straightforward to aggregate the power of all investors for the Crama-Leruth approach in the same way as for the implicit indices. Yet, in our experiments we focus on the implicit index π^β using the approach by Crama-Leruth only for validation purposes as outlined in the following paragraphs.

Let us discuss one example in detail and explain our methodology. Assume that investor 19 sells the complete 2% of shares it owns in company 3 to company 2. Table 2 shows the differences for the implicit power index π^β with network-dependent regressions between the original 21-player network and the network after the sale. Table 2 lists the differences of the standardized indices π^β of the investors in the last column while the middle columns lists the differences in the values aggregated after the regressions. Note that implicit indices also deliver results (and thus rankings) for the companies. However, we do not list them in Table 2 as company rankings are not part of this study.

Table 2. Differences for implicit power index π^β between original 21-player network and network after investor 19 sells its shares in company 3 to company 2.

Investor	Investor										π^β
	1	2	3	4	5	6	7	8	9	10	(Investor)
11	0	0	0	0	0	0	0	0	0	0	0
12	0.01458333	0	0.0625	0	0	0	0	0	0	0	0.0024839685
13	0	0	0	0	0	0	0	0	0	0	−0.0001977993
14	−0.03125	0	−0.03125	0	0	0	0	0	0	0	-0.0044687990
15	0	0	0	0	0	0	0	0	0	0	−0.0003223396
16	0	0	0	0	0	0	0	0	0	0	−0.0003223396
17	0	0	0	0	0	0	0	0	0	0	0
18	0	0	0	0	0	0	0	0	0	0	−0.0008791080
19	0.025	0	0.0625	0	0	0	0	0	0	0	0.0044644035
20	−0.03125	0	−0.0625	0	0	0	0	0	0	0	−0.0059120013
21	0.02291667	0	0.0625	0	0	0	0	0	0	0	0.0051540148

Let us compare the results from Table 2 with the results from the method by Crama-Leruth. We list the differences for the Z indices by Crama-Leruth in Table 3.

Table 3. Differences for the Crama-Leruth approach between original 21-player network and network after investor 19 sells its shares in company 3 to company 2.

Investors	Companies									
	1	2	3	4	5	6	7	8	9	10
11	0	0	0	0	0	0	0	0	0	0
12	0.09375	0	0.09375	0	0	0	0	0	0	0
13	0	0	0	0	0	0	0	0	0	0
14	−0.03125	0	−0.03125	0	0	0	0	0	0	0
15	0	0	0	0	0	0	0	0	0	0
16	0	0	0	0	0	0	0	0	0	0
17	0	0	0	0	0	0	0	0	0	0
18	−0.03125	0	−0.03125	0	0	0	0	0	0	0
19	0.09375	0	0.09375	0	0	0	0	0	0	0
20	−0.09375	0	−0.09375	0	0	0	0	0	0	0
21	0.09375	0	0.09375	0	0	0	0	0	0	0

After the sale investors 12 and 21 can no longer form a minimal winning coalition with investor 19. Tables 2 and 3 verify that not only investor 19 but also investors 21 and 12 lose control in companies 1 and 3. On the other hand, Tables 2 and 3 confirm that investors 20, 14 and 18 gain control in the network indirectly via company 2. Comparing Tables 2 and 3 in detail for investor 18, we see increases of the Z indices of investor 18 in companies 1 and 3 after the sale in Table 3 whereas the implicit index π^β with network-dependent regressions aggregates the identical numbers for investor 18 in companies 1 and 3 before and after the sale. Thus the increased influence of investor 18 in the network after the sale is reflected in Table 2 only via the larger implicit index π^β_{18}.

Table 4 reports three experiments of investors selling their shares. Each time we compare the results for sales to another firm in the network with sales to the float. The implicit index π^β with network-dependent regressions is chosen to calculate the power of the firms in the network before and after the adaption of a link. Once the impact of a sale has been determined for each investor, the results are grouped and ranked. The extracted rankings, illustrating the decrease or increase in control power for the firms, are given in ascending order with the top position of the rankings denoting the firm that loses or gains the most control power, respectively. The symbol $\equiv$ stands for a tie. Firms with neither an increase or a decrease in control power, i.e., $\triangle^i_l(M^L) = 0$, are excluded from the rankings.

Let us discuss the divestments in Table 4 in more detail. We already elaborated on the case that investor 19 sells its shares owned in company 3 to company 2. However, the picture changes as soon as the 2% of shares investor 19 holds in company 3 go to the float. In that case investors 12 and 21 become a minimal

Table 4. Linkage power calculations in the network with 21 firms using the implicit power index π^β with network-dependent regressions. The rankings illustrate the decrease or increase in control power for the investors after the sale.

Link	Amount	Sold to	Investors losing	Investors gaining
(19, 3)	0.02	2	21, 19, 12	20, 14, 18, 15 ≡ 16, 13
(19, 3)	0.02	float	20, 19, 14	12, 21, 18, 15 ≡ 16, 13
(12, 3)	0.4	2	12, 20, 21	14, 18, 19, 15 ≡ 16, 13
(12, 3)	0.4	float	12, 20, 21	14, 18, 19, 15 ≡ 16, 13
(16, 8)	0.02	17	15 ≡ 16	14 ≡ 17
(16, 8)	0.02	float	15 ≡ 16	14 ≡ 17

winning coalition for the modified weighted voting game Eq. (3) for company 3 and hence also gain control in company 1. On the other hand, investors 19 and 20 are losing control power in companies 1 and 3.

Another scenario for company 3 is the sale of the shares held by investor 12 to company 2. Consequently, company 2 can solely control company 3 and investors 20 and 21 turn into null players exerting no control in any company in the network. Studying the individual numbers for the power of investors in companies for the implicit index π^β as well as for the approach by Crama-Leruth unanimously explains that while investor 19 loses any control power in company 3 that loss is compensated through additional control power in company 1 exerted via company 2. Once the shares of investor 12 in company 3 go to the float, the picture does not change even though company 2 is no longer a dictator in the modified weighted voting game Eq. (3) for company 3.

In our last scenario, when investor 16 sells two percent of its shares held in company 8 either to investor 17 or to the float, one can observe that only the distribution of power among the direct investors of company 8 changes. In both cases investor 17 ceases to be a null player.

6   Conclusions and Further Developments

This paper extends a previous study of the framework of implicit power indices for measuring indirect control in complex corporate shareholding networks [54] by introducing network-dependent regressions setting the number of regressions for a controlled company equal to the number of arcs in a path of maximal length from another controlled company to that company. Motivated by results from [50,54] and by the fact that the absolute Banzhaf index satifies the donation property [10] we focus on the implicit index π^β based on the absolute Banzhaf index. We point out how a binomial float can be incorporated into π^β in a straightforward and computationally inexpensive way and thus present a first implicit power index for incomplete corporate networks. We use the implicit index π^β in a study of the effects of divestment on indirect control in a theoretical shareholding network with 21 entities. The observations for the implicit index

π^β coincide with those from the more sophisticated approach by Crama-Leruth [17,18] which we use for comparison throughout the article.

The implicit index π^β relies on the computation of the absolute Banzhaf index for weighted voting games. Using efficient software exploiting the compact representation of weighted voting games [53] allows us to compute large corporate network structures quickly and with comparably very low requirements for memory storage. Nevertheless, we regard more efficient implementations of the methods by Crama-Leruth [17,18] and Levy-Szafarz [36] a very worthwhile subject of research. For these two strongly related methods, we need to compute power indices for simple games which, in general, can no longer be represented as weighted voting games. We intend to investigate both generating functions along the lines of [2,3] and a recent approach based on relational algebra called quasi-ordered binary decision diagrams [8,9,13,14]. Likewise, we strive to provide a fast implementation of the Karos-Peters method [28]. The solution concept by Karos-Peters [28] derives its attractivity from its axiomatic characterization and requires computations of Shapley-Shubik indices for a series of simple games characterized by their sets of minimal winning coalitions. For the latter purpose we plan to analyze, implement and compare the methods by Lange and Kóczy (2013) [30] and by Kirsch and Langner (2010) [29] which both describe procedures for computing Shapley-Shubik indices directly from the minimal winning coalitions of a simple game.

We think it will be profitable to research the relations of the methods discussed in this paper and studies of the influence of nodes in networks via cooperative games on communication structures as introduced by Myerson (1977) [43]. We highlight algorithms for computing the Myerson value for weighted voting games [24] as well as the more general approach for computing the Myerson value for cooperative games restricted by a combinatorial structure [1]. In addition, a game theoretical approach following the concepts of the arc game and the position value for communication situations introduced in [15] could be beneficial.

In future studies we also wish to investigate precoalitions in corporate networks. The recent article [39] considers different connections among firms, like personal connections of the managements, and their effect on company valuation. We strive to extend these ideas to the problem of indirect control in complex shareholding networks using the sub-coalitional approach by Stach (2017) [48] or power indices with precoalitions [5,37,41]. The integration of the latter into our framework of generalized implicit indices will be facilitated by the algorithms for computing certain power indices with precoalitions for weighted voting games introduced in [51,55].

Acknowledgements. The first author thanks the funding of the Bavarian State Ministry of Science and Arts. The third author's contribution to the article was funded under subvention funds for the AGH University of Science and Technology in Krakow, Poland. The authors thank two anonymous reviewers for their careful reading of the manuscript and their helpful comments and suggestions.

Conflict of Interest. The authors declare no conflicts of interest.

References

1. Algaba, E., Bilbao, J., Fernández, J., Jiménez, N., López, J.: Algorithms for computing the Myerson value by dividends. In: Moore, K.B. (ed.) Discrete Mathematics Research Progress, pp. 1–13. Nova Science Publishers (2007)
2. Algaba, E., Bilbao, J.M., Fernández Garcıa, J.R.: The distribution of power in the European constitution. Eur. J. Oper. Res. **176**(3), 1752–1766 (2007). https://doi.org/10.1016/j.ejor.2005.12.002
3. Algaba, E., Bilbao, J.M., Fernández Garcıa, J.R., López, J.: Computing power indices in weighted multiple majority games. Math. Soc. Sci. **46**(1), 63–80 (2003). https://doi.org/10.1016/S0165-4896(02)00086-0
4. Algaba, E., Fragnelli, V., Sánchez-Soriano, J.: Handbook of the Shapley value. CRC Press, Boca Raton (2020). https://doi.org/10.1201/9781351241410
5. Alonso-Meijide, J.M., Bowles, C., Holler, M.J., Napel, S.: Monotonicity of power in games with a priori unions. Theor. Decis. **66**(1), 17–37 (2009). https://doi.org/10.1007/s11238-008-9114-2
6. Bang-Jensen, J., Gutin, G.Z.: Digraphs: theory, algorithms and applications. Springer Science & Business Media, Berlin (2008)
7. Banzhaf, J.F.: Weighted voting doesn't work: a mathematical analysis. Rutgers L. Rev. **19**, 317–343 (1965)
8. Berghammer, R., Bolus, S.: On the use of binary decision diagrams for solving problems on simple games. Eur. J. Oper. Res. **222**(3), 529–541 (2012)
9. Berghammer, R., Bolus, S., Rusinowska, A., De Swart, H.: A relation-algebraic approach to simple games. Eur. J. Oper. Res. **210**(1), 68–80 (2011)
10. Bertini, C., Freixas, J., Gambarelli, G., Stach, I.: Comparing power indices. Int. Game Theory Rev. **15**(02), 1340004 (2013)
11. Bertini, C., Mercik, J., Stach, I.: Indirect control and power. Oper. Res. Decisions **26**(2), 7–30 (2016). https://doi.org/10.5277/ord160202
12. Bertini, C., Stach, I.: Banzhaf voting power measure. In: Dowding, K. (ed.) Encyclopedia of Power, SAGE Publications, pp. 54–55. Sage Publications (2011)
13. Bolus, S.: Power indices of simple games and vector-weighted majority games by means of binary decision diagrams. Eur. J. Oper. Res. **210**(2), 258–272 (2011)
14. Bolus, S.: A QOBDD-based approach to simple games. Ph.D. thesis, Christian-Albrechts Universität Kiel (2012)
15. Borm, P., Owen, G., Tijs, S.: On the position value for communication situations. SIAM J. Discret. Math. **5**(3), 305–320 (1992)
16. Chakravarty, S.R., Mitra, M., Sarkar, P.: A Course on Cooperative Game Theory. Cambridge University Press, Cambridge (2015)
17. Crama, Y., Leruth, L.: Control and voting power in corporate networks: concepts and computational aspects. Eur. J. Oper. Res. **178**(3), 879–893 (2007). https://doi.org/10.1016/j.ejor.2006.02.020
18. Crama, Y., Leruth, L.: Power indices and the measurement of control in corporate structures. Int. Game Theory Rev. **15**(03), 1340017 (2013). https://doi.org/10.1142/S0219198913400173
19. Csardi, G., Nepusz, T., et al.: The igraph software package for complex network research. Int. J. complex syst. **1695**(5), 1–9 (2006). https://igraph.org/
20. Deegan, J., Packel, E.: A new index of power for simple n-person games. Int. J. Game Theory **7**(2), 113–123 (1978)
21. Derks, J., Haller, H.: Null players out? linear values for games with variable supports. Int. Game Theory Rev. **1**(03n04), 301–314 (1999)

22. Dubey, P., Shapley, L.S.: Mathematical properties of the Banzhaf power index. Math. Oper. Res. **4**(2), 99–131 (1979)
23. Eddelbuettel, D., et al.: RCPP: seamless R and C++ integration. J. Stat. Softw. **40**(8), 1–18 (2011)
24. Fernández, J.R., Algaba, E., Bilbao, J.M., Jiménez, A., Jiménez, N., López, J.J.: Generating functions for computing the Myerson value. Ann. Oper. Res. **109**(1), 143–158 (2002). https://doi.org/10.1023/A:1016348001805
25. Holler, M.J.: Forming coalitions and measuring voting power. Polit. Stud. **30**(2), 262–271 (1982)
26. Holler, M.J., Packel, E.: Power, luck and the right index. Z. f. Nationalökonomie **43**(1), 21–29 (1983). https://doi.org/10.1007/BF01283881
27. Johnston, R.: On the measurement of power: some reactions to Laver. Environ. Plan. A **10**(8), 907–914 (1978). https://doi.org/10.1068/a100907
28. Karos, D., Peters, H.: Indirect control and power in mutual control structures. Games Econom. Behav. **92**, 150–165 (2015). https://doi.org/10.1016/j.geb.2015.06.003
29. Kirsch, W., Langner, J.: Power indices and minimal winning coalitions. Soc. Choice Welf. **34**(1), 33–46 (2010). https://doi.org/10.1007/s00355-009-0387-3
30. Lange, F., Kóczy, L.Á.: Power indices expressed in terms of minimal winning coalitions. Soc. Choice Welf. **41**(2), 281–292 (2013). https://doi.org/10.1007/s00355-012-0685-z
31. Leech, D.: Voting power in the governance of the international monetary fund. Ann. Oper. Res. **109**(1), 375–397 (2002). https://doi.org/10.1023/A:1016324824094
32. Leech, D.: Computing power indices for large voting games. Manage. Sci. **49**(6), 831–837 (2003)
33. Leech, D.: Power indices in large voting bodies. Public Choice **155**(1), 61–79 (2013)
34. Levy, M.: Control in pyramidal structures. Corp. Gov. Int. Rev. **17**(1), 77–89 (2009)
35. Levy, M.: The Banzhaf index in complete and incomplete shareholding structures: a new algorithm. Eur. J. Oper. Res. **215**(2), 411–421 (2011)
36. Levy, M., Szafarz, A.: Cross-ownership: a device for management entrenchment? Rev. Finan. **21**(4), 1675–1699 (2017). https://doi.org/10.1093/rof/rfw009
37. Malawski, M.: Counting power indices for games with a priori unions. In: Gambarelli, G. (ed.) Essays in Cooperative Games. Theory and Decision Library, vol. 36, pp. 125–140. Springer, Boston (2004). https://doi.org/10.1007/978-1-4020-2936-3_10
38. Matsui, Y., Matsui, T.: NP-completeness for calculating power indices of weighted majority games. Theoret. Comput. Sci. **263**(1–2), 305–310 (2001)
39. Mercik, J., Gładysz, B., Stach, I., Staudacher, J.: Shapley-based estimation of company value-concept, algorithms and parameters. Entropy **23**(12), 1598 (2021). https://doi.org/10.3390/e23121598
40. Mercik, J., Łobos, K.: Index of implicit power as a measure of reciprocal ownership. In: Nguyen, N.T., Kowalczyk, R., Mercik, J. (eds.) Transactions on Computational Collective Intelligence XXIII. LNCS, vol. 9760, pp. 128–140. Springer, Heidelberg (2016). https://doi.org/10.1007/978-3-662-52886-0_8
41. Mercik, J., Ramsey, D.M.: The effect of Brexit on the balance of power in the European union council: an approach based on pre-coalitions. In: Mercik, J. (ed.) Transactions on Computational Collective Intelligence XXVII. LNCS, vol. 10480, pp. 87–107. Springer, Cham (2017). https://doi.org/10.1007/978-3-319-70647-4_7
42. Mercik, J., Stach, I.: On measurement of control in corporate structures. In: Nguyen, N.T., Kowalczyk, R., Mercik, J., Motylska-Kuźma, A. (eds.) Transac-

tions on Computational Collective Intelligence XXXI. LNCS, vol. 11290, pp. 64–79. Springer, Heidelberg (2018). https://doi.org/10.1007/978-3-662-58464-4_7

43. Myerson, R.B.: Graphs and cooperation in games. Math. Oper. Res. **2**(3), 225–229 (1977)

44. Shapley, L.S.: A value for n-person games. In: Kuhn, H., Tucker, A. (eds.) Contributions to the Theory of Games II, pp. 307–317. Princeton University Press (1953). https://doi.org/10.1515/9781400881970-018

45. Shapley, L.S., Shubik, M.: A method for evaluating the distribution of power in a committee system. Am. Polit. Sci. Rev. **48**(3), 787–792 (1954). https://doi.org/10.2307/1951053

46. Stach, I.: Shapley-Shubik index. In: Dowding, K. (eds.) Encyclopedia of Power, pp. 603–606. Sage Publications (2011)

47. Stach, I.: Indirect control of corporations: analysis and simulations. Decis. Mak. Manuf. Serv. **11**(1–2), 31–51 (2017). https://doi.org/10.7494/dmms.2017.11.1-2.31

48. Stach, I.: Sub-coalitional approach to values. In: Mercik, J. (ed.) Transactions on Computational Collective Intelligence XXVII. LNCS, vol. 10480, pp. 74–86. Springer, Cham (2017). https://doi.org/10.1007/978-3-319-70647-4_6

49. Stach, I., Mercik, J.: Measurement of control power in corporate networks. Oper. Res. Decis. **31**(1), 97–121 (2021). https://doi.org/10.37190/ord210106

50. Stach, I., Mercik, J., Bertini, C.: Some propositions of approaches for measuring indirect control power of firms and mutual connections in corporate shareholding structures. In: Nguyen, N.T., Kowalczyk, R., Mercik, J., Motylska-Kuźma, A. (eds.) Transactions on Computational Collective Intelligence XXXV. LNCS, vol. 12330, pp. 116–132. Springer, Heidelberg (2020). https://doi.org/10.1007/978-3-662-62245-2_8

51. Staudacher, J.: Computing the public good index for weighted voting games with precoalitions using dynamic programming. In: Power & Responsibility: Interdisciplinary Perspectives for the 21st Century in Honor of Manfred J. Holler, p. 17. Springer, Berlin (2022)

52. Staudacher, J., Anwander, J.: Using the R package CoopGame for the analysis, solution and visualization of cooperative games with transferable utility, R Vignette (2021). https://cran.r-project.org/package=CoopGame

53. Staudacher, J., et al.: Computing power indices for weighted voting games via dynamic programming. Oper. Res. Decis. **31**(2), 123–145 (2021). https://doi.org/10.37190/ord210206

54. Staudacher, J., Olsson, L., Stach, I.: Implicit power indices for measuring indirect control in corporate structures. In: Nguyen, N.T., Kowalczyk, R., Motylska-Kuźma, A., Mercik, J. (eds.) Transactions on Computational Collective Intelligence XXXVI. LNCS, vol. 13010, pp. 73–93. Springer, Heidelberg (2021). https://doi.org/10.1007/978-3-662-64563-5_4

55. Staudacher, J., Wagner, F., Filipp, J.: Dynamic programming for computing power indices for weighted voting games with Precoalitions. Games **13**(1), 6 (2022). https://doi.org/10.3390/g13010006

56. The R Core team and others: R: A language and environment for statistical computing. Vienna, Austria (2021). https://www.r-project.org/

57. Wickham, H.: R packages: organize, test, document, and share your code. O'Reilly Media (2015). https://r-pkgs.org/

Lies, Damned Lies, and Crafty Questionnaire Design

Jarl K. Kampen[1] , Ynte K. Van Dam[2] , and Johannes (Joost) Platje[3(✉)]

[1] Wageningen University & Research, PSG/Biometris, Radix Building, W4.Fd.035,
Droevendaalsesteeg 1, 6708 PB Wageningen, The Netherlands
jarl.kampen@wur.nl

[2] Wageningen University and Research, SSG/MCB, P.O. Box 9101,
6700 HB Wageningen, The Netherlands
ynte.vandam@wur.nl

[3] WSB University in Wrocław, ul. Fabryczna 29-31, 53-609 Wrocław, Poland
johannes.platje@wsb.wroclaw.pl

Abstract. It is well-established in the literature that particular design features of questionnaires affect the distribution and association of collected data. We present a survey approach called Crafty Questionnaire Design (CQED), that allows predictability and replicability of outcomes, expected of the natural sciences, to be achieved in the social sciences. Two independent proof-of-principle experiments studying interpersonal and institutional trust of Polish and Mexican students (n = 1402), show that using different versions of a questionnaire offers predictably different outcomes. CQED promises a large gain in efficiency of research in terms of sample size required and number of replications needed. This knowledge can safeguard the social scientific researcher against unpleasant surprises and inconvenient results. Knowledge about the principles of CQED could also be a tool for editors as well as reviewers of social scientific journals to scrutinize the methodological soundness and improve the relevance of publications.

Keywords: Research methodology · Trust · Survey · Questionnaire · Peer review

1 Introduction

It is fairly widely acknowledged for at least the past three decades that the social sciences are in crisis (Kagan 2009; Kampen 2020; Legg and Stagaki 2002; Lopreato and Crippen 1999; Prus 1990). The main problem of the social sciences is arguably that it tries to be rigidly scientific without the availability of rigid scientific experiments. A major obstacle to the rigidity of social scientific experiments is the measurement unobservable variables. This concerns the social indicators to be controlled in experiments (Coleman 1969) as well as the hypothetical constructs and intervening variables that assumedly explain the workings of the black box that is the human mind (Hilgard 1958; MacCorquodale and

---

"For a man is angry at a libel because it is false, but at a satire because it is true." (G.K. Chesterton).

© Springer-Verlag GmbH Germany, part of Springer Nature 2022
N. T. Nguyen et al. (Eds.): Transactions on Computational Collective Intelligence XXXVII,
LNCS 13750, pp. 75–88, 2022.
https://doi.org/10.1007/978-3-662-66597-8_4

Meehl 1948). These measurements are inevitably dependent on self-reported surveys that are notoriously subject to bias (Gove and Geerken 1977). The acknowledged inadequacy of surveys easily results in harvesting more misinformation than information from one's respondents, which cannot be solved by larger samples or increased acuity in analysis (Blalock 1969; Hauser 1969). Routinely models are tested on datasets in which true variance is only a fraction of measurement error. Consequently empirical relations are not sufficiently predictable and generalisable beyond single topics and incidental micro applications, leaving the researcher in constant fear of non-results that falsify even the most plausible hypotheses. In the publish or perish world of modern academia social scientists are therefore hampered by the lack of dependable research models in sociology (Davis 1994) as well as psychology (Koch 1981, 1993). As long as journals are heavily biased towards confirmed hypotheses (Dickersin 1990) it is moot to state that contrary results are not failed experiments (Wigboldus and Dotsch 2016), because they will be a failed publication and for most researchers that equals another step away from tenure, promotion, budget or glory.

It has been forty years since Koch (1981) condemned the quest for 'scientificity' and the consequent 'epistemopathological emptiness' of the social sciences. Theory has been elevated from a way of understanding to the goal of research, and relevance has been exchanged for methodological rigidity in a 'cargo-cult' science that is devoid of meaning (Feynman 1974). The culprit then was the positivist search for simple truths fed by the radical denial that essential questions in life may be unanswerable. The vain quest for non-existent empirical truths in the intrinsic absence of replicability and predictability of outcomes has caused many questionable practices and undesirable results in applied social scientific research and the derailment of ambitious researchers who are desperate for positive results (Crocker and Cooper 2011; Sijtsma 2016). The culmination of these developments is the contemporary belief in statistics for the detection of scientific fraud (Barch and Yarkoni 2013; Masicampo and Lalande 2012; Simonsohn 2013; Simonsohn et al. 2014) in order to save the illusion of reproducible social science (Barch and Yarkoni 2013; Munafò et al. 2017). Because a critical assessment of the reasonable limits of social science apparently goes unheeded (Simmons et al. 2011), we take a more provocative approach and push quantitative research in the social sciences over the edge.

Replicability and predictability of outcomes, routinely expected of research in the natural sciences, can also be achieved in the social sciences if researchers start to rely on the available body of empirical evidence in the scientific literature on research methodology. At present, however, theoretical and empirical studies are diverging (Schmaus 1994). Applied social science and the study of social scientific research methods appear to be going separate ways. This is unfortunate, because lack of methodological knowledge in general and of surveys in particular has caused the inevitable exposure of scientific fraud by ambitious researchers desperate for positive results (Crocker and Cooper 2011). Each exposure is a blemish on social science that should and could have been avoided. For the well-informed social scientific researcher survey bias is not a nuisance but a tool in the box that can be used to obtain confirmatory social scientific evidence that is both verifiable and replicable. Never tamper with your data!

It is already well-established in the literature that particular design features of questionnaires affect the distribution and association of collected data (Bradburn and Sudman

2004; DeCastellarnau 2018; Rockwood et al. 1997; Sudman and Bradburn 1974). In this article, we will show that application of this knowledge can safeguard the social scientific researcher against unpleasant surprises and inconvenient results. We focus on questionnaires as the method of data collection because in empirical social science the quantitative survey remains the single most important tool for data collection (Savage and Burrows 2007). Survey design has always been a craft rather than a science, but designing a survey that enhances the likelihood of expedient results is turning craftmanship and skill into craftiness and cunning. The proposed method can be labelled Crafty Questionnaire Design (CQED). The range of applications of CQED is rapidly increasing. Research of which the outcomes can be confidently anticipated may provide a uniquely advantageous strategy for the survival of a social scientific research group. Particularly in the field of externally funded research (whether by government, governance or corporate commissioners) arriving at conclusions satisfying the commissioner is vital to obtain future financial grants. A senior researcher may design the questionnaire, whereas an independent junior researcher can be ordered to carry out the field research and analysis, and meanwhile the commissioner can be confident that the outcomes are in line with anticipations. Also PhD-students can apply CQED to avoid blundering into dead-end research in their contractually limited research time. Even tenured researchers may benefit from CQED (see Kezar and Gehrke 2014) to smoothen their career by boosting scientific productivity. Best of all CQED evades statistical detection methods.

In the next section, a brief review of survey bias in social scientific research methodology is given, and examples are provided how this knowledge could be applied to produce CQED. In Sect. 3 an application of CQED research is given, illustrating its effectivity in a split ballot experiment carried out in Poland and Mexico in 2019. The article ends with policy recommendations and a word of caution. It goes without saying that none of the procedures for anticipated outcome research outlined below, imply plain scientific fraud. In fact, most of the proposed procedures are routinely (wittingly or unwittingly) applied by contemporary practicing empirical social scientists.

2 Options in CQED Research Design

In most instances the dataset of the social scientist contains several variables that are as highly related to each other as they are to the variable that is labelled 'dependent'. Also, the real changes of this dependent variable more often than not are minute compared to the random measurement error in a survey (Blalock 1969). Added to this is the current beatification of large samples, which helps to raise the significance of the most tenuous relation between two variables disproportionally. Jointly this implies that any shift from random error to systematic error will dramatically improve the statistical significance of results.

The design of survey based research requires a myriad of weighty decisions (e.g., Brace 2013; Malhotra 2019), all of which leave their mark on the results (e.g., Aquilino 1994; Bowling 2005; Catania et al. 1986; De Leeuw and Collins 1997; Fowler Jr. et al. 1998; Grandcolas et al. 2003; Singer and Kohnke-Aguirre 1979; Tourangeau 2003). The conscientious researcher may be overwhelmed by the responsibility to provide a fair test of hypotheses, while others perceive as many ways to bend the results to their whims or wishes (Huff 1954; Steele 2005). Here we focus on two innocuous manipulations of Likert-type items: question order, and answer format.

2.1 Deciding on Question Order

Respondents use the information contained in preceding items when producing the answers for following items (Chan 1991). The more specific the content of a question and the more concrete the required response the less susceptible the question is to order effects (Dillman 1978; McFarland 1981). Vice versa, the more abstract the item content the more likely the response is influenced by the context. This context includes preceding items, explanations given by interviewers or given as text in the (e)mail questionnaire, answering instructions, information about the commissioner and conductor of the research, etc. Among the more notable effects of question order are changes of measures of central tendency (e.g., Benton and Daly 1991; Van De Walle and Van Ryzin 2011) and changes of associations (Krosnick and Alwin 1987). A well-known example concerns the contribution of marital satisfaction to general life-satisfaction, where pending the order of the items correlations can be as high as .67 or as low as .18 (Schwarz et al. 1991). The crafty social scientist may have to test various questionnaire designs to determine the context that optimally guides the respondent toward confirmatory results. As a rule of thumb, order questions from concrete to abstract to find convergence, and from abstract to concrete to allow for divergence between scores.

2.2 Deciding on Question Format

Question format can have decisive influence on response patterns (Bradburn and Sudman 2004; Christian and Dillman 2004; DeCastellarnau 2018; Schwarz 1999; Tourangeau et al. 2004, 2007). The degrees of freedom in framing questions is virtually unlimited since too many social scientists conducting or reviewing questionnaire based surveys have never in their career followed a course in questionnaire construction. Moreover, a metrology (a system of measurement; see e.g., Isaev 1993) of social scientific concepts does not exist (e.g., Fisher and Stenner 2011), nor is it likely that such a metrology is to be developed in the near future. The interested reader may consult Sudman and Bradburn (1974) for an early overview of question format issues. The following list, though far from exhaustive, already provides a palette of possibilities for the shrewd social scientist to choose from in the quest for confirmatory results.

Most obvious is the wording of items, statements and questions. Most readers will have come across convincing examples of suggestive wording during their career, which immediately shows the flaw of this approach – it is easily recognised and unmasked. A more subtle approach is to vary the polarity of Likert-type rating scales, because regardless of item content respondents use the left end of a scale rather than the right end (Krebs and Hoffmeyer-Zlotnik 2010), at least in languages that are written left to right. Thus, if in two subsequent waves of a survey, the commissioner anticipates an increase of an attitude, one would use right to left at the first, left to right at the second wave of the survey (and of course it would be rightfully claimed to have used the same response categories and range at both occasions). The choice of the number of scale points of the rating scales is reported by some to have no effect on inter-item correlations (e.g., Leung

2011) and by others to have some (Xu and Leung 2018) or even considerable effect (Chang 1994). To stay on the safe side, one would therefore offer 10-point rating scales to increase probability to find high correlations, and a 5-point rating scale to enhance finding low correlations.

Another well-known technique to exercise influence on the responses in questionnaires is by the selection of response categories (e.g., Rockwood et al. 1997; Schwarz 1999). Omitting vital categories (e.g., a neutral midpoint and/or 'not applicable/no opinion') is a rather blunt, yet effective strategy. As said, the varieties in question formatting are limitless, and will remain to be so, because there is no interest in developing a social scientific metrology in the social scientific community (Kampen and Tobi 2011).

3 An Application of CQED

3.1 Two Scenarios About Interpersonal Trust

A proof-of-principle experiment may illustrate the practical applications of CQED, by showing that a few simple steps may suffice to find what one seeks to prove. The topic of research is interpersonal trust, with the objects of trust divided in two sets. Set A probes after general institutional trust in 'people', 'clergy men', 'politicians', 'civil servants', and 'businessmen'. Set B probes after local trust in 'lecturers in our university', 'students at our university', 'class mates', and finally, oneself ('I'). It may be assumed that trust in set A will be lower than trust in set B (see Kampen et al. 2006; Van de Walle et al. 2005). Two contrasting scenarios will be created that correspond to two different hypotheses about the nature of interpersonal trust. The first scenario tests the hypothesis that trust is specific rather than diffuse. In this scenario the level of trust in set A cannot be explained by the level of trust in set B. Analytically, set A and set B will be easy to separate in Principal Components Analysis. In this scenario the commissioner further anticipates a low level of trust in set A and a high level of trust in set B. This will be called the "Low Scenario." The alternative scenario tests the hypothesis that trust is diffuse rather than specific. In the alternative scenario the level of trust in set A can be explained by the level of trust in set B. Analytically, set A and set B will be hard to separate in PCA. In this scenario the commissioner anticipates higher levels of trust in set A and high levels of trust in set B. We refer to this scenario as the "High Scenario". Our job in the following is to design independent studies that will confirm either (diametrically opposed) hypothesis.

3.2 Sample and Method

Data collection method is a questionnaire based survey (available at request from the corresponding author). Both scenarios require carefully selected design features. An overview of the manipulations in our crafty questionnaire design are in Table 1. A split-ballot experiment was conducted where students were given one of two versions of a paper-and-pencil questionnaire. One version corresponded to the "Low" and one version corresponded to the "High" scenario, with question order, location and format formatted as explained. Care was taken that the visual properties of the questionnaires were equal at first glance. Students in the class rooms would receive either version in their native language (Polish or Spanish) on a random basis. The experiment was replicated in two separate Polish institutions for higher education (WSB University in Wrocław (one group of students of logistics and one group of students of management) and Opole University (faculty of economics)) and one Mexican university (Universidad de Sonora). Data were collected from April to July 2019 in Poland, and from September to October 2019 in Mexico. Total sample size after listwise deletion amounted to n = 1410 (546 Mexican and 874 Polish students). After screening for obvious data entry errors (e.g., scores outside the possible range of the items) an effective sample size of n = 1402 (537 Mexican and 865 Polish) remained. Sample from Mexico had 31% female students, sample from Poland had 44% females students. Over 95% of students were between 17 and 27 years of age (mean 21.0, sd 3.45), with students from Mexico being on average somewhat younger (mean 19.1, sd 1.58) than students from Poland (mean 22.2, sd 3.7). For the sake of ease in making comparisons, all variables were rescaled such that they ranged from 0 to 10.

Table 1. Decisions in design of the questionnaires for each scenario

	Low scenario	High scenario
Organization of items	The trust items will be offered to respondents in two separate question batteries	The trust items will be offered to respondents in a single question battery
Location of items in questionnaire	Items probing after trust in set A are placed near the beginning and those about trust in set B near the end of the questionnaire	All items probing after trust are placed at the end of the questionnaire which contains a fairly large number of similarly stated items probing after agreement
Polarization	Response options for set A range from low trust (left) to high trust (right), and response options for set B range from high trust (left) to low trust (right)	Response options in both sets range from high trust (left) to low trust (right)
Item order	Institutions in set A will be ordered from least to most trusted institution, while in set B ordering will be from most to least trusted	Items are ordered from most trusted institutions to least trusted institutions (priming; see Kahneman 2011)
Resolution	The size of correlations is reduced by using low resolution scales for assessment, in this a case a 5-point scale	The size of correlations is amplified by using high resolution scales for assessment, in this a case an 11-point scale

3.3 Results and Discussion

Most expectations with respect to the recorded levels of trust as well as their correlations came true. Table 2 presents a summary of findings for the level of trust at aggregate level (students of all subsamples combined). It shows that the level of general trust in the High Scenario is significantly higher than in the Low Scenario (paired samples t-test, p < .001), which was one of the goals to be achieved. The average level of local trust is equal in both scenarios, but always significantly higher than general trust. The levels of trust for each institution within each version are displayed in Table 3. The WSB University in Wrocław management sample exhibits 'model' behaviour, as each general institution receives lower trust in the Low Scenario than in the High Scenario. In the other subsamples this pattern is broken by trust in clergymen and people in general, but is otherwise sufficiently consistent.

Table 2. Mean trust in Set A and Set B within aggregate data

	Set A	Set B	Paired sample	df	p
Low scenario	3.6	6.2	29.10	61	<.001
High scenario	4.1	6.2	19.69	686	<.001
Indept. sample t	5.64	.02			
df	1318.4	1348.2			
p	<.001	.98			

Table 3. Average trust for each institution within scenarios

	Poland: WSB Logistics		Poland: Opole		Poland: WSB Management		Mexico	
	Low	High	Low	High	Low	High	Low	High
Set A: general	3.3	↑4.2	3.9	↑4.3	3.2	↑4.6	3.7	3.9
People	4.3	4.7	4.5	4.8	4.0	↑4.9	4.2	4.5
Clergymen	3.4	3.0	3.9	↑3.1	3.1	↑4.0	4.4	↑2.6
Politicians	1.7	↑3.9	2.5	↑4.4	2.0	↑4.6	2.4	↑4.0
Civil servants	3.8	↑4.3	4.2	4.4	3.2	↑4.6	3.1	3.4
Businessmen	3.5	↑4.9	4.3	↑4.8	3.7	↑4.5	4.4	4.7
Set B: local	6.4	6.1	6.2	6.0	6.0	5.6	6.1	↑6.6
Lectures	6.7	6.5	5.9	5.9	6.3	↓5.5	6.1	6.5
Students	5.5	5.2	5.5	5.3	5.5	5.3	5.3	↑5.7
Classmates	6.4	↓5.6	6.2	↓5.5	5.9	5.3	5.7	5.8
I	7.0	7.1	7.2	7.1	6.2	6.1	7.3	↑8.6

↓ significantly lower than Low Scenario; ↑ significantly higher than Low Scenario (p < .05)

The specific character of interpersonal trust in the Low Scenario compared to the diffuse character of interpersonal trust in the High Scenario becomes entirely clear when the factor loadings are displayed in factor loading plots, both across the aggregated sample (Fig. 1) and for each subsample separately (Fig. 2). The pattern of clustering in the Low Scenario and dispersion in the High Scenario is visually confirmed (tables with factor loadings are not shown for saving space). Additional evidence for the difference between scenarios is a linear regression of average general trust in on trust in the various local institutions (Table 4). Though both regressions are significant ($p < .001$), the explained variance in the Low scenario ($R^2 = .04$) is negligible whereas in the High scenario ($R^2 = .25$) it can be reported as acceptable in social scientific studies.

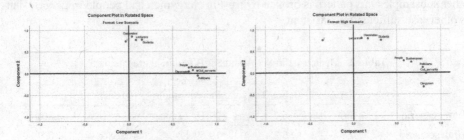

Fig. 1. Factor loading plots for each scenario across aggregated sample

Table 4. Regression of trust in set A on members of set B

Predictor	Low scenario			High scenario		
	ß	t	p	ß	T	P
Lecturers	.120	2.446	.015	.141	3.203	.001
Students	.115	2.181	.030	.306	6.767	<.001
Classmates	−.009	−0.153	.879	.124	2.759	.006
I	−.028	−0.600	,549	−.470	−11.841	<.001
Model test	$R^2_{(adj)} = .030$			$R^2_{(adj)} = .244$		
	$F_{(4,647)} = 5.958; p < .001$			$F_{(4, 682)} = 56.493; p = < .001$		

The results with respect to correlations even exceeded our expectations: the near orthogonal factor structure of general and local trust desired in the High Scenario is completely destroyed in the Low Scenario. Also in terms of the measures of central tendency, our questionnaire design returned the desired results. Fair enough, despite our efforts general trust remained significantly lower than local trust also in the High scenario, and this adds to the credibility of the overall study. The results of the present study comply with what may expected given the acknowledged political and economic context of Poland and Mexico (e.g., both are countries with strong catholic traditions), and our apparent failure to substantially increase general trust actually adds to the persuasiveness of the results: any study showing that trust in politicians, civil servants, businessmen and clergy exceeds trust in oneself or one's classmates would immediately be flagged as suspicious.

4 The Future of CQED

Seemingly innocuous design features of questionnaires affect the distribution and association of collected data, as is already well-established in the literature. Our goal was to apply this knowledge craftily in order to get the empirical outcomes we desired. Given the success of this enterprise in four independent samples, we are confident that CQED methodology may be refined to warrant confirmatory evidence of any research hypothesis. Therefore, CQED leads to a large gain in the efficiency of social scientific research in terms of e.g. sample size required and in the number of replications needed to corroborate the desired conceptual social scientific outcome by p-hacking. Eventually CQED will be fine-tuned to perfection and confirmation of hypotheses becomes certainty and social scientific research does not need to be carried out anymore, creating momentous potential to increase the cost efficiency within the scientific discipline even further.

On a final note, Eliza Cook (1852, p. 226) warned that "the habit of exaggeration in language should be guarded against; it misleads the credulous and offends the perceptive." To those readers who were initially appalled by the suggestions made in this essay, we offer our apologies even though you are in fact, our target audience. It is our sincere hope that on the basis of the condensed information supplied in this essay, you are enabled to further improve both your research and the reviews you make. Poe's law states that without a clear indication of the author's intent, it is impossible to tell the difference between an exaggerated parody and a sincere extreme opinion (Aikin 2013). We trust to have made fully clear our position regarding the strategy of seeking what needs to be demonstrated (CQED).

5 Recommendations to Take Away

The danger of false positive outcomes in social science and humanities is hard to overstate. The damage to scientific progress and the damage to the image of science are comparatively mild consequences. The damage to society caused by the implementation of ineffective or counterproductive policies based on false positive research outcomes is worse (Stroebe et al. 2012). In the past decade the awareness of questionable research practices promoting false positives is increasing, some would say better late than never.

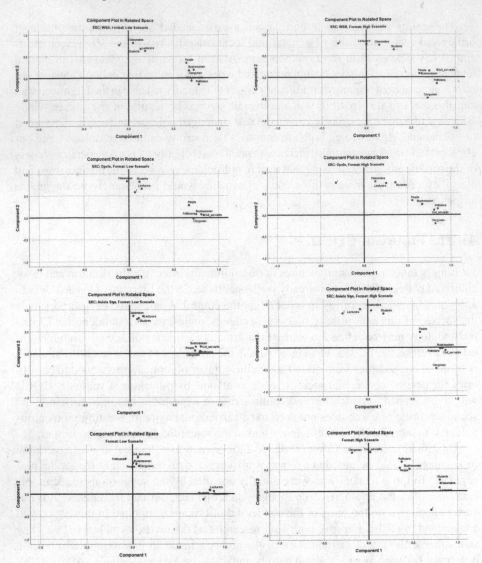

Fig. 2. Factor loading plots for each scenario in each subsample

The raised alertness has triggered a wave of statistical detection techniques that may detect the unwary and deter the unwitting. We have shown that those researchers who purposefully manipulate their results can easily avoid detection by drawing from a host of CQED techniques. That is why more should be done to counter the cultural factors that stimulate the pursuit of false positive results (Fox 1990).

We could point to the lingering positivism that makes commissioners, politicians, media and journals value imagined 'truths' more than honest doubts. We could point to an academic culture in which quantity of published papers outweighs quality. We could point to the observation that the vast majority of studies is performed to gain publication credits rather than understanding in a relevant phenomenon. But eventually all of this boils down to the positivist search for simple truths fed by the radical denial that some essential questions in life are unanswerable. In a universe of unanswerable questions the purpose of social science is not to find the truth but merely to expose the lies.

Acknowledgements. We express our gratitude to David Zepeda Quintana (University of Sonora, Hermosillo, Mexico) and Bartosz Fortuński (Opole University, Poland) for their support with the collection of the data.

References

Aikin, S.F.: Poe's law, group polarization, and argumentative failure in religious and political discourse. Soc. Semiot. **23**(3), 301–317 (2013). https://doi.org/10.1080/10350330.2012.719728

Aquilino, W.S.: Interview mode effects in surveys of drug and alcohol use: a field experiment. Public Opin. Q. **58**(2), 210–240 (1994). https://doi.org/10.1086/269419

Barch, D.M., Yarkoni, T.: Introduction to the special issue on reliability and replication in cognitive and affective neuroscience research. Cogn. Affect. Behav. Neurosci. **13**(4), 687–689 (2013). https://doi.org/10.3758/s13415-013-0201-7

Benton, J.E., Daly, J.L.: A question order effect in a local government survey. Public Opin. Q. **55**(4), 640–642 (1991). https://doi.org/10.1086/269285

Blalock, H.M.: Comment on Coleman's paper. In: Bierstedt, R. (ed.) A Design for Sociology: Scope, Objectives, and Methods, pp. 115–121. American Academy of Political and Social Science, Philadelphia (1969)

Bowling, A.: Mode of questionnaire administration can have serious effects on data quality. J. Public Health **27**(3), 281–291 (2005). https://doi.org/10.1093/pubmed/fdi031

Brace, I.: Questionnaire Design: How to Plan, Structure and Write Survey Material for Effective Market Research, 3rd edn. Kogan Page Limited, London (2013)

Bradburn, N.M., Sudman, S.: The current status of questionnaire research. In Biemer, P.P., Groves, R.M., Lyberg, L.E., Mathiowetz, N.A., Sudman, S. (eds.) Measurement Errors in Surveys, pp. 29–40. John Wiley & Sons, Inc., New York

Catania, J.A., McDermott, L.J., Pollack, L.M.: Questionnaire response bias and face-to-face interview sample bias in sexuality research. J. Sex Res. **22**(1), 52–72 (1986). https://doi.org/10.1080/00224498609551289

Chan, J.C.: Response-order effects in Likert-Type scales. Educ. Psychol. Meas. **51**(3), 531–540 (1991). https://doi.org/10.1177/0013164491513002

Chang, L.: A psychometric evaluation of 4-point and 6-point Likert-type scales in relation to reliability and validity. Appl. Psychol. Meas. **18**(3), 205–215 (1994). https://doi.org/10.1177/014662169401800302

Christian, L.M., Dillman, D.A.: The influence of graphical and symbolic language manipulations on responses to self-administered questions. Public Opin. Q. **68**(1), 57–80 (2004). https://doi.org/10.1093/poq/nfh004

Coleman, J.S.: The methods of sociology. In: Bierstedt R. (ed.) A Design for Sociology: Scope, Objectives, and Methods, pp. 86–114. American Academy of Political and Social Science, Philadelphia

Cook, E.: Exaggeration. Eliza Cook's J. **7**(171), 225–226 (1852)

Crocker, J., Cooper, M.L.: Addressing scientific fraud. Science **334**(6060), 1182 (2011). https://doi.org/10.1126/science.1216775

Davis, J.A.: What's wrong with sociology? Sociol. Forum **9**(2), 179–197 (1994). https://doi.org/10.1007/BF01476361

De Leeuw, E., Collins, M.: Data collection methods and survey quality: an overview. In: Lyberg, L.E., et al. (eds.) Survey Measurement and Process Quality, pp. 197–220 (1997)

DeCastellarnau, A.: A classification of response scale characteristics that affect data quality: a literature review. Qual. Quant. 1–37 (2018). https://doi.org/10.1007/s11135-017-0533-4

Dickersin, K.: The existence of publication bias and risk factors for its occurrence. JAMA: J. Am. Med. Assoc. **263**(10), 1385–1389 (1990). https://doi.org/10.1001/jama.1990.03440100097014

Dillman, D.A.: Mail and Telephone Surveys: The Total Design Method. Wiley, New York (1978)

Feynman, R.P.: Cargo cult science. Eng. Sci. **37**(7), 10–13 (1974)

Fisher Jr, W.P., Stenner, A.J.: Integrating qualitative and quantitative research approaches via the phenomenological method. Int. J. Mult. Res. Approaches **5**(1), 89–103 (2011). https://doi.org/10.5172/mra.2011.5.1.89

Fowler, F.J., Jr., Roman, A.M., Di, Z.X.: Mode effects in a survey of medicare prostate surgery patients. Public Opin. Q. **62**(1), 29–46 (1998). https://doi.org/10.1086/297829

Fox, M.F.: Fraud, ethics, and the disciplinary contexts of science and scholarship. Am. Sociol. **21**(1), 67–71 (1990). https://doi.org/10.1007/BF02691783

Gove, W.R., Geerken, M.R.: Response bias in surveys of mental health: an empirical investigation. Am. J. Sociol. **82**(6), 1289–1317 (1977). https://doi.org/10.1086/226466

Grandcolas, U., Rettie, R., Marusenko, K.: Web survey bias: sample or mode effect? J. Mark. Manag. **19**(5–6), 541–561 (2003). https://doi.org/10.1080/0267257X.2003.9728225

Hauser, P.M.: Comment on Coleman's paper. In: Bierstedt, R. (ed.) A Design for Sociology: Scope, Objectives, and Methods, pp. 122–128. American Academy of Political and Social Science, Philadelphia (1969)

Hilgard, E.R.: Intervening variables, hypothetical constructs, parameters, and constants. Am. J. Psychol. **71**(1), 238–246 (1958). https://doi.org/10.2307/1419211

Huff, D.: Norton, New York (1954)

Isaev, L.K.: The place of metrology in the science system: on postulates. Meas. Tech. **36**(8), 853–854 (1993). https://doi.org/10.1007/BF00983977

Kagan, J.: The Three Cultures: Natural Sciences, Social Sciences, and the Humanities in the 21st Century. Cambridge University Press, New York (2009)

Kampen, J.K.: A proposal for the demarcation of theory and knowledge: of language-dependent and language-independent reality. Metaphilosophy **51**(1), 97–110 (2020). https://doi.org/10.1111/meta.12398

Kampen, J.K., Tobi, H.: Social Scientific metrology as the mediator between sociology and socionomy: a cri de coeur for the systemizing of social indicators. In: Baird, C.M. (ed.) Social Indicators: Statistics, Trends and Policy Development, pp. 1–26. Nova Science Publishers, New York (2011)

Kampen, J.K., Van De Walle, S., Bouckaert, G.: Assessing the relation between satisfaction with public service delivery and trust in government the impact of the predisposition of citizens toward government on evalutations of its performance. Public Perform. Manag. Rev. **29**(4), 387–440 (2006). https://doi.org/10.1080/15309576.2006.11051881

Kezar, A., Gehrke, S.: Why are we hiring so many non-tenure-track faculty? Lib. Educ. **100**(1), n1 (2014)

Koch, S.: The nature and limits of psychological knowledge: lessons of a century qua "science." Am. Psychol. **36**(3), 257–269 (1981). https://doi.org/10.1037/0003-066X.36.3.257

Koch, S.: "Psychology" or "the psychological studies"? Am. Psychol. **48**(8), 902–904 (1993). https://doi.org/10.1037/0003-066X.48.8.902

Krebs, D., Hoffmeyer-Zlotnik, J.H.: Positive first or negative first? effects of the order of answering categories on response behavior. Methodol.: Eur. J. Res. Methods Behav. Soc. Sci. **6**(3), 118–127 (2010). https://doi.org/10.1027/1614-2241/a000013

Krosnick, J.A., Alwin, D.F.: An evaluation of a cognitive theory of response-order effects in survey measurement. Public Opin. Q. **51**(2), 201–219 (1987). https://doi.org/10.1086/269029

Legg, C., Stagaki, P.: How to be a postmodernist: a user's guide to postmodern rhetorical practices. J. Fam. Ther. **24**(4), 385–401 (2002). https://doi.org/10.1111/1467-6427.00226

Leung, S.O.: A comparison of psychometric properties and normality in 4-, 5-, 6-, and 11-point Likert scales. J. Soc. Serv. Res. **37**(4), 412–421 (2011). https://doi.org/10.1080/01488376.2011.580697

Lopreato, J., Crippen, T.: Crisis in Sociology: The Need for Darwin. Transaction, New Brunswick (1999)

MacCorquodale, K., Meehl, P.E.: On a distinction between hypothetical constructs and intervening variables. Psychol. Rev. **55**(2), 95–107 (1948). https://doi.org/10.1037/h0056029

Malhotra, N.K.: Marketing Research: An Applied Orientation, 7th edn. Pearson, Boston (2019)

Masicampo, E., Lalande, D.R.: A peculiar prevalence of p values just below. 05. Q. J. Exp. Psychol. **65**(11), 2271–2279 (2012)

McFarland, S.G.: Effects of question order on survey responses. Public Opin. Q. **45**(2), 208–215 (1981). https://doi.org/10.1086/268651

Munafò, M.R., et al.: A manifesto for reproducible science. Nat. Hum. Behav. **1**(1), 1–9 (2017)

Prus, R.: The interpretive challenge: the impending crisis in sociology. Can. J. Sociol./Cahiers canadiens de sociologie **15**(3), 355–363 (1990). https://doi.org/10.2307/3340924

Rockwood, T.H., Sangster, R.L., Dillman, D.A.: The effect of response categories on questionnaire answers: context and mode effects. Sociol. Methods Res. **26**(1), 118–140 (1997). https://doi.org/10.1177/0049124197026001004

Savage, M., Burrows, R.: The coming crisis of empirical sociology. Sociology **41**(5), 885–899 (2007). https://doi.org/10.1177/0038038507080443

Schmaus, W.: Durkheim's Philosophy of Science and the Sociology of Knowledge: Creating an Intellectual Niche. University of Chicago Press, Chicago (1994)

Schwarz, N.: Self-reports: how the questions shape the answers. Am. Psychol. **54**(2), 93–105 (1999). https://doi.org/10.1037//0003-066x.54.2.93

Schwarz, N., Strack, F., Mai, H.P.: Assimilation and contrast effects in part-whole question sequences: a conversational logic analysis. Public Opin. Q. **55**(1), 3–23 (1991). https://doi.org/10.1086/269239

Sijtsma, K.: Playing with data—or how to discourage questionable research practices and stimulate researchers to do things right. Psychometrika **81**(1), 1–15 (2016). https://doi.org/10.1007/s11336-015-9446-0

Simmons, J.P., Nelson, L.D., Simonsohn, U.: False-positive psychology: undisclosed flexibility in data collection and analysis allows presenting anything as significant. Psychol. Sci. **22**(11), 1359–1366 (2011)

Simonsohn, U.: Just post it: the lesson from two cases of fabricated data detected by statistics alone. Psychol. Sci. **24**(10), 1875–1888 (2013)

Simonsohn, U., Nelson, L.D., Simmons, J.P.: P-curve: a key to the file-drawer. J. Exp. Psychol. Gen. **143**(2), 534 (2014)

Singer, E., Kohnke-Aguirre, L.: Interviewer expectation effects: a replication and extension. Public Opin. Q. **43**(2), 245–260 (1979). https://doi.org/10.1086/268515

Steele, J.M.: Darrell Huff and fifty years of "how to lie with statistics." Stat. Sci. **20**(3), 205–209 (2005)

Stroebe, W., Postmes, T., Spears, R.: Scientific misconduct and the myth of self-correction in science. Perspect. Psychol. Sci. **7**(6), 670–688 (2012). https://doi.org/10.1177/1745691612460687

Sudman, S., Bradburn, N.M.: Response Effects in Surveys: A Review and Synthesis. Aldine Publ. Co., Chicago (1974)

Tourangeau, R.: Cognitive aspects of survey measurement and mismeasurement. Int. J. Public Opin. Res. **15**(1), 3–7 (2003). https://doi.org/10.1093/ijpor/15.1.3

Tourangeau, R., Couper, M.P., Conrad, F.: Spacing, position, and order: interpretive heuristics for visual features of survey questions. Public Opin. Q. **68**(3), 368–393 (2004). https://doi.org/10.1093/poq/nfh035

Tourangeau, R., Couper, M.P., Conrad, F.: Color, labels, and interpretive heuristics for response scales. Public Opin. Q. **71**(1), 91–112 (2007). https://doi.org/10.1093/poq/nfl046

Van de Walle, S., Kampen, J.K., Bouckaert, G.: Deep impact for high-impact agencies? assessing the role of bureaucratic encounters in evaluations of government. Public Perform. Manag. Rev. **28**(4), 532–549 (2005). https://doi.org/10.1080/15309576.2005.11051846

Van De Walle, S., Van Ryzin, G.G.: The order of questions in a survey on citizen satisfaction with public services: lessons from a split-ballot experiment. Public Adm. **89**(4), 1436–1450 (2011). https://doi.org/10.1111/j.1467-9299.2011.01922.x

Wigboldus, D.H.J., Dotsch, R.: Encourage playing with data and discourage questionable reporting practices. Psychometrika **81**(1), 27–32 (2016). https://doi.org/10.1007/s11336-015-9445-1

Xu, M.L., Leung, S.O.: Effects of varying numbers of Likert scale points on factor structure of the Rosenberg Self-Esteem Scale. Asian J. Soc. Psychol. **21**(3), 119–128 (2018). https://doi.org/10.1111/ajsp.12214

Solidarity Measures

Izabella Stach[1]([⊠]) [iD] and Cesarino Bertini[2] [iD]

[1] AGH University of Science and Technology, Al. Mickiewicza 30, 30-059 Krakow, Poland
istach@agh.edu.pl
[2] Department of Economics, University of Bergamo, Via dei Caniana, 2, 24127 Bergamo, Italy
cesarino.bertini@unibg.it

Abstract. This paper regards some measures for sharing (public) goods or budgets among members with different participation quotas in a binary decision-making process. The main characteristic of such measures is that they should have elements of solidarity with those who have a weak quota of participation in the process. These measures seem appropriate for deals that require solidarity, which contrasts with the classical power indices such as the Shapley and Shubik index or the Banzhaf index. Moreover, we provide a new representation for two power indices—the Public Help Index ξ (proposed by Bertini and Stach in 2015) and the particularization of the solidarity value proposed by Nowak and Radzik in 1994—the ψ index—in a simple game using null player free winning coalitions. As it is known, a set of null player free winning coalitions unequivocally determines a simple game. Finally, we compare considered power indices considering some properties in simple games.

Keywords: Cooperative games · Simple games · Null player free winning coalitions · Power indices · Public power indices

1 Introduction

The main issue in the cooperative game theory is, assuming that the grand coalition eventually forms, how to fairly share the joint gain of cooperation (i.e., the grand coalition's worth). Many concepts were proposed in the literature on this topic. This paper focuses on a particular group of one-point solutions concepts from cooperative games—specifically from simple games—power indices that do not satisfy the null player property. The null player property indicates the absence of solidarity among the players. Some scholars have undertaken this topic and introduced—often by modification of the exiting classical solutions—the measures that have such elements of solidarity with those who have a weak quota of participation in the process, see Nowak and Radzik [33], van den Brink [43], van den Brink et al. [44], Casajus and Huettner [15], Chameni-Nembua [16], Malawski [30], Béal et al. [14], Rodríguez-Segura and Sánchez-Pérez [36], Xun-Feng and Deng-Feng [45], Gutiérrez-López [25], for example. In particular, if we deal with sharing public good or a budget among members with different participation quotas in a binary decision-making process, these measures seem appropriate as this kind of situation often requires solidarity with weaker players.

© Springer-Verlag GmbH Germany, part of Springer Nature 2022
N. T. Nguyen et al. (Eds.): Transactions on Computational Collective Intelligence XXXVII,
LNCS 13750, pp. 89–105, 2022.
https://doi.org/10.1007/978-3-662-66597-8_5

The classical power indices such as the Shapley and Shubik index [38] or the Banzhaf index [4, 18, 34] assign zero value to null players. Casajus and Huettner [15] wrote "when the whole society is productive, $v(N) \geq 0$; then it is not *necessary* that any player ends up with a negative payoff. In particular, null players need not receive a negative payoff. Since they do not do any harm to society, they actually should not obtain negative payoffs."

In the paper by Arnsperger and Varoufakis, (2003) [3]—dealing with the concept of solidarity and attempting to estimate the minimal and maximal generosity with weak players—we read something that we can also interpret as a justification of solidarity measures contradicting with classical power indices based on the rationality of the choices: "the essence of solidarity lies in the hypothesis that people are capable of responding sympathetically to (or empathising with) a condition afflicting 'others,' irrespectively of who those others are or whether one cares for them personally. Moreover, when that condition is a social artefact, we argue, solidarity turns radical." Further, they argue "that something else is also born, in addition to justice, at the limits of altruism: Solidarity! It pertains to instances of sacrifice and generosity motivated by 'worthy causes,' rather than by an altruistic urge to contribute to specific individuals."

In particular, in this paper, we focus on the power indices proposed by Rae [35], Nevison [31], König and Bräuninger [27, 32], Bertini, Gambarelli and Stach [7], and Bertini and Stach [6], and the restriction of the solidarity value proposed by Nowak and Radzik [33] in simple games. Some of these indices has been studied as the measures of decisiveness, satisfaction, or success, see Laruelle et al. [29], whereas Bertini and Stach [6] and Stach [40] analyzed some of these indices as being well-defined in the social context.

One of the main proposals of this paper is a new representation of the Public Help index ξ introduced by Bertini and Stach [6] and the solidarity power index ψ (defined in Sect. 3 as a restriction of the solidarity value introduced by Nowak and Radzik [33]) in a simple game using null player free winning coalitions. This idea of a new representation of power indices based on winning coalitions by null player free winning coalitions started in papers by Stach and Bertini [42] and Stach [41]. The winning coalitions without null players were called by Álvarez-Mozos et al. [2]: null player free winning coalitions, and we follow this nomenclature. By the way, the set of all null player free winning coalitions is a very important set of coalitions as it unequivocally determines a simple game. So, this set of coalitions is as important as the set of all winning coalitions or minimal winning coalitions, see Álvarez-Mozos et al. [2], Stach [41], Bertini and Stach (2021) [42].

Consequently, we propose a comparison of the six power indices in terms of some known and desirable properties in simple games. This work is a continuation of the research on power measures in the context of public goods by Bertini ad Stach [6], and Stach [40], where some "solidarity measures" were compared. In this paper, we add to this group the solidarity index ψ, see Sects. 3 and 4.

The rest of this article is structured as follows: in Sect. 2, we introduce the preliminary definitions, concept, and notations of cooperative games, simple games, and power indices. Section 3 provides new formulas for two power indices (the Public Help Index ξ [6] and the restriction of the solidarity value [33] in simple games—the solidarity index ψ) based on null player free winning coalitions. In Sect. 4, we compare all six considered indices taking into account some desirable properties in simple games. For the ψ index, we proved which of the considered properties are satisfied by this index in simple games. For the rest of the indices, we recall results collected and obtained in the previous papers by Bertini et al. [13]; Bertini and Stach [6], Stach [40]. Finally, Sect. 5 concludes the paper.

2 Preliminaries on Cooperative Games and Power Indices

Let $N = \{1, 2, ..., n\}$ be a finite set of *players*, where $n = |N|$ *denotes* the cardinality of N. Let 2^N denote the set of all subsets of N. Any element of 2^N is called a *coalition*, and N is said to be the *grand coalition*.

A cooperative game is a pair (N, v) where v is a mapping from the set of all coalitions to the set of real numbers: $v : 2^N \rightarrow R$ called the characteristic function such that $v(\emptyset) = 0$.

A *value* is a real-valued function that assigns a unique vector $\psi(v) = (\psi_1(v), \psi_2(v), \ldots, \psi_n(v))$ to each cooperative game (N, v). The component $\psi_i(v)$ is said to be an individual value of a player $i \in N$ in (N, v). Different values have been proposed in the topic literature, the best known being the Shapley value [37].

The Shapley value (σ) for each cooperative game (N, v) and each player $i \in N$ is defined as follows:

$$\sigma_i(v) = \sum_{S \subseteq N, i \in S} \frac{(n - |S|)!(|S| - 1)!}{n!} (v(S) - v(S \setminus \{i\})).$$

2.1 Simple Games – Notation and Definitions

A *simple n-person game* is a pair (N, v) where $v : 2^N \rightarrow \{0, 1\}$ satisfies the following conditions: $v(\emptyset) = 0$, $v(N) = 1$, and $v(S) \leq v(T)$ for all coalitions $S \subseteq T \subseteq N$.

A coalition $S \in 2^N$ is a *winning* one if $v(S) = 1$; otherwise, $(v(S) = 0)$ it is said to be a *losing coalition*. A simple game is said to be *proper* if $\forall S \subseteq N$ if $v(S) = 1$, then $v(N \setminus S) = 0$. In this paper, we analyze only proper simple games (for more of a proper simple game, see [40], for example). A player i is said to be *critical* in coalition S if $v(S) = 1$ and $v(S \setminus \{i\}) = 0$. Let $Cr(S)$ denote the number of critical players in S, it means the number of players whose deletion from S is critical. A winning coalition S is said to be a *minimal winning coalition* if $Cr(S) = |S|$. A player $i \in N$ is said to be a *null player* if the following equation holds for each coalition $S \in 2^N$ containing player i: $v(S) = v(S \setminus \{i\})$. A winning coalition S is said to be a *null player free winning coalition* if all of its members are non-null players. Following the notation used in [42], W^{n-} stands for the set of all null player free winning coalitions.

Let W and W^{n-} be the sets of winning coalitions and null player free winning coalitions, respectively, in a simple game (N, v). Then, by W_i and W_i^{n-} we denote the corresponding subsets of W, W^{n-} formed by coalitions that contain player i, Any simple game may be unequivocally determined by W and W^{n-}, (see [2, 41], and [42] for example). Thus, in any simple game (N, v), the set of winning coalitions W can always be described by the set of null player free winning coalitions W^{n-} as follows $W = \{S \in 2^N : \exists T \in W^{n-} | T \subseteq S\}$, for example.

A proper simple game (N, v) is said to be a *weighted game*—denoted by $[q; w_1, \ldots, w_n]$ where $\forall i \in N \ w_i \geq 0$ stands for its *weight* and a non-negative *quota* q satisfies the following double inequality $\frac{\sum_{i \in N} w_i}{2} < q \leq \sum_{i \in N} w_i$—if $v(S) = 1 \Leftrightarrow \sum_{i \in S} w_i \geq q$.

2.2 Power Indices

A *power index* f is a function that assigns a unique real-valued vector $f(v) = (f_1(v), f_2(v), \ldots, f_n(v))$ to every simple game (N, v). Many power indices have been proposed after the most widely applied one proposed by Shapley and Shubik (1954) [38]. Some power indices were proposed as restrictions of the cooperative game solutions—values—for simple games and others autonomously defined in simple games. Power indices are used to measure the power of players in collective decision-making bodies. Interpretations of this power vary depending also on the power index itself and the situation in which it is applied, see [5, 6, 8–13, 20, 24, 29, 40].

The Shapley and Shubik power index (σ) for each simple game (N, v) and each player $i \in N$ is defined as follows:

$$\sigma_i(v) = \sum_{S \in W_i} \frac{(n - |S|)!(|S| - 1)!}{n!} (v(S) - v(S \setminus \{i\})).$$

In the following, we define four power indices that fall in the group of solidarity indices. The rest two are defined in Sect. 3, which also offers a new reformulation of these two indices. The definitions of the power indices below are given for each simple game (N, v) and each player $i \in N$.

The Rae index (R) [35] is defined as follows:

$$R_i(v) = \frac{|\{S : i \in S \in W\}|}{2^n} + \frac{|\{S : i \notin S \notin W\}|}{2^n}.$$

The König and Bräuninger Index (KB) [27, 32], is defined as follows:

$$KB_i(v) = \frac{|W_i|}{|W|}.$$

The Nevison index Z [31] is given by

$$Z_i(W) = \frac{|W_i|}{2^{n-1}}.$$

$$Z_i(W) = \frac{|W_i|}{2^{n-1}}.$$

The Public Help Index Θ (PHI Θ) [7]) is given by:

$$\theta_i(W) = \frac{|W_i|}{\sum_{j \in N} |W_j|}.$$

3   A New Reformulations of Indices ξ and ψ

Stach and Bertini (2021) [42] introduced a representation of the Coleman [17], Rae [35], Nevison [31], and König and Bräuninger [27, 32] indices using null player free winning coalitions. While Stach (2021) [41] proposed a new representation of the PHI θ index [7] also using null player free winning coalitions. This section continues this idea and provides new formulas for the index introduced by Bertini and Stach (2015) [6] and the solidarity value restricted to simple games. Then, in Subsects. 3.1 and 3.2, we define these indices and introduce our propositions for a new representation.

Let N^{n-} be a set of all non-null players in N. Thus, $N = N^{n-} \cup N^{null}$, where N^{null} denotes the set of all null players in (N, v). It is not difficult to show that the following equation holds for each simple game (N, v), see [41], for example.

$$|W| = 2^{|N^{null}|}|W^{n-}|, \tag{1}$$

$$|W_i| = 2^{|N^{null}|}|W_i^{n-}| \text{ for each, } i \in N^{n-} \tag{2}$$

and

$$|W_i| = 2^{|N^{null}|-1}|W^{n-}| \text{ for each } i \in N^{null}. \tag{3}$$

Equations (1)–(3) are used in the demonstrations of Propositions 1 and 2, i.e., to express the solidarity indices by the null player free winning coalitions.

3.1   Public Help Index ξ

The Public Help Index ξ index [6] for each simple game (N, v) and a player $i \in N$ is defined as follows:

$$\xi_i(v) = \frac{1}{\sum_{T \in W} \frac{1}{|T|}} \sum_{S \in W_i} \frac{1}{|S|^2}. \tag{4}$$

Proposition 1.

$$\xi_i(v) = \begin{cases} \dfrac{\displaystyle\sum_{S \in W_i^{n-}} \sum_{j=0}^{|N^{null}|} \dfrac{\binom{|N^{null}|}{j}}{(|S|+j)^2}}{\displaystyle\sum_{T \in W^{n-}} \sum_{l=0}^{|N^{null}|} \dfrac{\binom{|N^{null}|}{l}}{|T|+l}} & \text{if } i \in N^{n-} \\[3em] \dfrac{\displaystyle\sum_{S \in W^{n-}} \sum_{j=0}^{|N^{null}|-1} \dfrac{\binom{|N^{null}|-1}{j}}{(|S|+j+1)^2}}{\displaystyle\sum_{T \in W^{n-}} \sum_{l=0}^{|N^{null}|} \dfrac{\binom{|N^{null}|}{l}}{|T|+l}} & \text{if } i \notin N^{n-} \end{cases} \tag{5}$$

Proof. Consider a simple game (N, v). Looking at Formula (1), we see that from each null player free winning coalition $T \in W^{n-}$ we can obtain all winning coalitions in (N, v). Specifically, from each null player free winning coalition $T \in W^{n-}$ we can obtain $\binom{|N^{null}|}{l}$ different winning coalitions of the cardinalities equal to $(|T|+l)$, where l varies from 0 to $|N^{null}|$. Thus, the denominator in (4) can be expressed as follows:

$$\sum_{T \in W} \frac{1}{|T|} = \sum_{T \in W^{n-}} \sum_{l=0}^{|N^{null}|} \frac{\binom{|N^{null}|}{l}}{|T|+l}. \tag{6}$$

Let i be a null player (i.e., $i \in N^{null}$). Then, from Formula (3), we see that i belongs, in total, to $|W_i| = 2^{|N^{null}|-1}|W^{n-}|$ winning coalitions. In particular, from each null player free winning coalition $S \in W^{n-}$ we can obtain $\binom{|N^{null}|-1}{j}$ different winning coalitions of the cardinalities equal to $(|S|+j+1)$, containing player i, where j varies from 0 to $(|N^{null}|-1)$. So, the nominator in (4) can be expressed as follows:

$$\sum_{S \in W_i} \frac{1}{|S|^2} = \sum_{S \in W^{n-}} \sum_{j=0}^{|N^{null}|-1} \frac{\binom{|N^{null}|-1}{j}}{(|S|+j+1)^2} \text{ for } i \notin N^{n-}. \tag{7}$$

For non-null players, the nominator in (4) is a bit different as a non-null player belongs to null player free winning coalitions and winning coalitions with null players. Let i be a non-null player (i.e., $i \in N^{n-}$). Then, from formula (2), we have that i belongs, in total, to $|W_i| = 2^{|N^{null}|}|W^{n-}|$ winning coalitions. Particularly, from each null player free winning coalition containing player i—$S \in W_i^{n-}$ —we can obtain $\binom{|N^{null}|}{j}$ winning coalitions containing player i of the size $(|S|+j)$ where j vary from 0 to $|N^{null}|$. So, the nominator in (4) can be expressed as follows:

$$\sum_{S \in W_i} \frac{1}{|S|^2} = \sum_{S \in W_i^{n-}} \sum_{j=0}^{|N^{null}|} \frac{\binom{|N^{null}|}{j}}{(|S|+j)^2} \text{ for } i \in N^{n-}. \tag{8}$$

Thus, from (6), (7), and (8), we immediately obtain (5), which is what is needed to be proven.

3.2　Solidarity Index Ψ

The solidarity value, introduced and characterized axiomatically by Nowak and Radzik (1994) [33] is defined by the following for each cooperative game (N, v) and player $i \in N$:

$$\psi_i(v) = \sum_{T \subseteq N, i \in T} \frac{(n-|T|)!(|T|-1)!}{n!} A^v(T),$$

where $A^v(T)$ is the average marginal contribution of a member of coalition T defined for each coalition $T \in 2^N$ as follows: $A^v(T) = \frac{1}{|T|} \sum_{i \in T} (v(T) - v(T \setminus \{i\}))$.

The solidarity value is very close to the Shapley value [37]. Let us cite some words of Nowak and Radzik (1994) [33] about their solidarity value: "Its interpretation can be obtained by replacing the marginal contributions $(v(T) - v(T \setminus \{i\}))$ of player i in the well-known interpretation of the Shapley value by $A^v(T) = \frac{1}{|T|} \sum_{i \in T} (v(T) - v(T \setminus \{i\}))$.

To be more specified, if a player i becomes a member of some coalition T, then he/she obtains (as a payoff) the average marginal contribution $A^v(T)$ of a member of T."

In simple games $A^v(T) = \frac{Cr(S)}{|T|}$, what is not difficult to show. Thus, the restriction of the Nowak and Radzik (1994) [33] solidarity value in a simple game (N, v) can be expressed in the following way:

$$\psi_i(v) = \sum_{T \subseteq N, i \in T} \frac{1}{\binom{n}{|T|}} \frac{Cr(T)}{|T|^2}. \tag{9}$$

Following the queue bargaining model of Shapley and Shubik (1954) [38] we can calculate the solidarity power index as follows:

$$\psi_i(v) = \sum_{T \in W_i} \frac{1}{n!} \frac{|Q \in Q(N) : hpiv(Q) = T|}{|T|} \tag{10}$$

where, $Q(N)$ is a set of all permutations of n players; $Q \in Q(N)$ is a singular permutation (also called a queue or sequential coalition that contain all the players (n) in which the order players are listed reflect the order they joined the coalition; $hpiv(Q)$ stands for a winning coalition consisting of pivot player and all those placed ahead of the pivot player in Q. A player is called a *pivotal player* in a permutation (queue) Q if he/she changes from a losing coalition to a winning one. So, $v(hpiv(Q)) = 1$ and coalition $hpiv(Q)$ is the head of the pivot player in queue Q. In other words, coalition $hpiv(Q)$ consists of the first players from Q, and the last player who joined $hpiv(Q)$ is a pivotal player. $\frac{|Q \in Q(N):hpiv(Q)=T|}{n!}$ is the probability that a given coalition T will form. i.e., the probability that T is the head of the pivot in a queue, see also Felsenthal and Machover (1998) [19]. Note that, in the Shapley and Shubik index, the full value of $v(hpiv(Q)) = 1$ is assigned to a pivotal player, whereas in the solidarity index, this value is divided equally among all members of $hpiv(Q)$. So each member of $hpiv(Q)$ obtains $\frac{1}{|T|}$ in Q, and the rest of the players in Q obtains zero.

Proposition 2. For each simple game (N, v) and player $i \in N$.

$$
\psi_i(v) = \begin{cases}
\displaystyle\sum_{T \in W_i^{n-}} \sum_{j=0}^{|N^{null}|} \frac{\dbinom{|N^{null}|}{j} Cr(T)}{\dbinom{n}{|T|+j}(|T|+j)^2} & \text{if } i \in N^{n-} \\[3em]
\displaystyle\sum_{T \in W^{n-}} \sum_{j=0}^{|N^{null}|-1} \frac{\dbinom{|N^{null}|-1}{j} Cr(T)}{\dbinom{n}{|T|+j+1}(|T|+j+1)^2} & \text{if } i \notin N^{n-}
\end{cases}
\tag{11}
$$

Proof. Consider a simple game (N, v). From Formula (1), we have that from each coalition $T \in W^{n-}$ we can obtain $\dbinom{|N^{null}|}{j}$ different winning coalitions of the cardinalities equal to $(|T|+j)$, where j varies from 0 to $|N^{null}|$. Thus, for each $i \in N^{n-}$ we have

$$
\psi_i(v) = \sum_{T \in W_i^{n-}} \sum_{j=0}^{|N^{null}|} \frac{\dbinom{|N^{null}|}{j} Cr(T)}{\dbinom{n}{|T|+j}(|T|+j)^2} \quad \text{after applying (1) in (9)}.
$$

Let $i \in N^{null}$. Then from Formula (3), we have that from each $T \in W^{n-}$ we can obtain $\dbinom{|N^{null}|-1}{j}$ different winning coalitions of the cardinalities equal to $(|T|+j+1)$, containing player i, where j varies from 0 to $(|N^{null}|-1)$. So, for each $i \in N^{null}$, we have $\psi_i(v) = \displaystyle\sum_{T \in W^{n-}} \sum_{j=0}^{|N^{null}|-1} \frac{\dbinom{|N^{null}|-1}{j} Cr(T)}{\dbinom{n}{|T|+j+1}(|T|+j+1)^2}$ after applying (3) in (9); this completes the proof.

4 Comparison of Power Indices

In the papers by Bertini and Stach (2015) [6] and Stach (2016) [40], some power indices that are well-defined in the social context where goods are public were analyzed. These categories of indices we called here the solidarity power indices. Namely, the following indices were considered: the Public Help Index θ [7], the Public Help index ξ [6], the König and Bräuninger index [27, 32], the Nevison index [31], and the Rae index [35]. In the paper by Stach and Bertini (2021) [42] these indices were reformulated using only the concept of null player free winning coalitions. In the mentioned two papers [6] and [40], these indices were compared considering the various properties, rankings amongst players, and ranges of the power indices. This paper continues the earlier works on these indices (see [6, 40–42]), adding in the group the solidarity index ψ defined and reformulated in Sect. 3.2.

Next, we recall the definitions of some desirable conditions of power indices in simple games, mostly following the notations of an article by Stach (2016) [40] and Bertini et al. (2013) [13]. In particular, we regard the following properties in the alphabetic order: bicameral meet, bloc, dominance, donation, efficiency, non-negativity, null player, null player removable, redistribution, symmetry, and transfer.

Bicameral Meet Property. Let us consider three simple games $v_1 = (N_1, v_1)$, $v_2 = (N_2, v_2)$, (N, v), where $N = N_1 \cup N_2$, $N_1 \cap N_2 = \emptyset$, where the set of winning coalitions in (N, v) is defined as follows: $W(v) = \{S \subseteq N : S \cap N_1 \in W(v_{N_1}) \wedge S \cap N_2 \in W(v_{N_2})\}$. A power index f satisfies the *bicameral meet property* if for any two non-null players $i, j \in N_1$ $f_i(v_1)/f_j(v_1) = f_i(v)/f_j(v)$. Generally, this property states that the ratio of player' powers should be independent of whether the assembly is viewed as a separate legislature or as one chamber of a bicameral system.

The *KB* and Θ indices satisfy the bicameral meet property, see Bertini et al. (2013) [13]. Next, Stach (2016) [40] provided proof that also the Z index satisfies this property. Next, an example of a failure of the bicameral meet property for the R index was given in Bertini et al. (2013) [13]. Then, the same example was used to show a fail of the ξ index in Stach (2016) [40]. Following this example, we can show that the solidarity index ψ, like R and ξ, does not satisfy this property either, see Table 1.

Table 1. An example of a failure of the bicameral meet property of the ψ, R, and ξ indices.

	$v_1 = [3; 2, 1, 1]$	$v_2 = [2; 2], v = [5; 2, 1, 1, 2]$
Power index	$f_1(v_1) / f_2(v_1)$	$f_1(v) / f_2(v)$
ψ	1.60	1.40
R	1.40	1.22
ξ	1.69	1.64

The Bloc Property. Let us consider an n-players simple game and distinguish in this game two players $i, j \in N$ such that $i \neq j$ and j is non-null player. W stands for the set of all winning coalition in (N, v). Let us assume players i and j form a bloc—a single entity—$i\&j$. In this way, we can define a new simple game $v[i\&j]$ determined by the set of all winning coalitions in the following way $W[i\&j] = \{ S \subseteq (N \setminus \{i, j\}) \cup \{i\&j\}$ such that: $S \subseteq N \setminus \{i, j\}$ and $S \in W$ or $S = T \cup \{i\&j\}$ where $T \subseteq N \setminus \{i, j\}$ and $T \cup \{i, j\} \in W \}$. A power index f satisfies the *bloc property* if $f_{i\&j}(v[i\&j]) \geq f_i(v)$. Overall, this property postulates that players should benefit from a merger and playing together, i.e., a bloc between two players should result in greater power value than the power of the single player.

The *KB* and R indices satisfy the bloc property (see Bertini et al. (2013) [13]. Furthermore, Stach (2016) [40] proved that the Z index also satisfies this property. Regarding the θ, ξ, and ψ indices and the bloc property, this is still an open problem, although the authors suspect that these indices satisfy this property.

The Dominance Property. Let $v : [q; w_1, \ldots, w_n]$ be a weighted game. Power index f satisfies the *dominance property* if $w_i \geq w_j$ implies $f_i(v) \geq f_j(v)$ for any players $i, j \in N$ where $i \neq j$. In other words, this property states that: a player with greater weight should not have a lower power value.

The KB and R indices satisfy the dominance property, see [13], for example. Bertini and Stach (2015) [6] proved that the θ, and ξ power indices fulfil this property. Stach (2016) [40] demonstrated that the Z index satisfies this property as well.

Theorem 1. *The solidarity index (ψ) satisfies the dominance property for any weighted game.*

Proof. Let $v : [q; w_1, \ldots, w_n]$ be an arbitrary weighted game, and let $a, b \in N$ be two distinct players such that $w_a \geq w_b$. If a and b are null players, then Formula (10) implies $\psi_a(v) = \psi_b(v)$. Let both players a, $b \in N$ be non-null players or at most one is null player. Then, note that W_a (and also W_b) includes a non-empty subset, $W_{a \cup b}$, of all winning coalitions that contain players a and b. Namely, $W_{a \cup b} = \{S \in W : a \in S \wedge b \in S\}$, $W_{a \cup b} \subset W_a$, and $W_{a \cup b} \subset W_b$. If $w_a \geq w_b$, then for any non-empty coalition $S \in W_b \backslash W_{a \cup b}$ (i.e., $a \notin S$), we have $(S \backslash \{b\} \cup \{a\} \in W_a$ and $|S| = |(S \backslash \{b\}) \cup \{a\}|$; thus, $|W_a| \geq |W_b|$ and $|Q \in Q(N) : hpiv(Q) = T, T \in W_a| \geq |Q \in Q(N) : hpiv(Q) = T, T \in W_b|$. Also, note that the coalitions in W_a—which do not belong to W_b—are not more numerous than the coalitions in W_b. So, using Formula (10), we immediately obtain.

$$\psi_a(v) = \sum_{T \in W_a} \frac{1}{n!} \frac{|Q \in Q(N):hpiv(Q)=T|}{|T|} \geq \sum_{T \in W_b} \frac{1}{n!} \frac{|Q \in Q(N):hpiv(Q)=T|}{|T|} = \psi_b(v),$$

which ends the proof.

The Donation Property. Let $v : [q; w_1, \ldots, w_n]$ and $v' \equiv [q; w'_1, \ldots, w'_n]$ be the two weighted games such that" arising from v by the following redistribution of weights: $\sum_{i=1}^n w_i = \sum_{i=1}^n w'_i$, for only one player i, called donor, $w_i > w'_i$ and only for one recipient j $w_j < w'_j$ and all other players, the weights remain unchanged. A power index f satisfies the *donation property* $f_i(v) \geq f_i(v')$. Generally, this property claims that a player who transmits a part (or total) her or his/her weights to another player should not increase his/her power value.

The KB and R indices satisfy the donation property, see Bertini et al. (2013) [13]. Stach (2016) [40] proved that the Nevison power index Z satisfies this property, Felsenthal and Machover (1998, p. 257) [19] provided an example to show that the normalized Banzahf index [4] and the Johnston index [26] fail the donation property. The same example was used by Bertini et al. (2013) [13] to show a failure of this property for the Public Help index θ. Table 2 calculates the solidarity index ψ for the same example and shows that ψ violates the donation property. In particular, we can observe that player 1—sole donor with the weight 9—gains power, calculated by the ψ and θ indices, "donating" the only recipient (player 4). The PHI ξ index does not present a fail of the donation property in this example. Stach (2016) [40] gave an example where a failure of the donation postulate occurs for PHI ξ.

Table 2. An example of a failure of the donation property of the ψ and θ indices.

Power index	$v = [23; 9, 8, 7, 0, 1, 1, 1, 1, 1, 1]$	$v' = [23; 8, 8, 7, 1, 1, 1, 1, 1, 1, 1]$
	$f_1(v)$	$f_1(v')$
ψ	$108971/907200 \approx 0.1201$	$39217/302400 \approx 0.1297$
θ	$130/849 \approx 0.1531$	$129/841 \approx 0.1534$

The Efficiency Property. A power index f satisfies the *efficiency property* if $\sum_{i \in N} f_i(v) = 1$ for all simple games (N, v). Generally, this property states that the power index is a relative measure of player' power values which add up to 1 for all simple games. For a particular player, it shows her/his percentage share of the grand coalition's total power is held compared to all the other players.

The indices θ, ξ, ψ satisfy the efficiency property by definition, while KB, R, and Z do not, see [6, 7, 13, 33, 40].

The Non-negativity Property. If for any simple game (N, v) and each player $i \in N$ the following inequality holds $f_i(v) \geq 0$, then we said that power index f satisfies the *non-negativity property*. In other words, this property states that the player' power value should not be negative.

All considered indices (θ, ξ, ψ, KB, R, Z) satisfy this property. Moreover, these all indices satisfy the more restrictive property—positivity, i.e., $f_i(v) > 0$ as all these indices violate the null player property. Furthermore, $R_i(v) \geq \frac{1}{2}$, $KB_i(v) \geq \frac{1}{2}$, $Z_i(v) \geq \frac{1}{2^{n-1}}$, and $\theta_i(v) \geq \frac{1}{2^{n-2}}$, see Bertini et al. (2013) [13], Stach (2016) [40], Bertini and Stach (2015) [6].

The Null Player Property. If, for all simple games (N, v), the power value $f_i(v) = 0$ for each null player $i \in N$, then it is said that a power index f satisfies the *null player property*. In other words, this property states that the power value of a player is null if he/she cannot transform any losing coalition into a winning one by joining it.

As a choice of the power indices refers to the solidarity with weak players, it is not strange that all the power indices considered here violate the null player property. Some indices, like KB and R assigned fixed values to null players. Namely, $KB_i(v) = R_i(v) = \frac{1}{2}$ for each null player, see [13, 42], for example. Moreover, in a n-person simple game (N, v), the Z index assigns the same power—$Z_i(v) = \frac{|W|}{2^n}$—to each null player, where $|W|$ denotes the number of all winning coalitions in (N, v) (see [31]). Furthermore, $\theta_i(v) \geq \frac{1}{2^{n-|N^{null}|}}$ for each null player $i \in N$, where $|N^{null}| > 0$ denotes the number of null players in (N, v), see [41].

The Null Player Removable Property. Let us consider a simple game (N, v) with the set of all null players $N^{null} \subset N$. If for all $(N \backslash N^{null}, v')$ arising from v by deleting the null players, the equation $f_i(v) = f_i(v')$ holds for all $i \in N \backslash N^{null}$, then it is said that a power index f fulfils *the null player removable property*. In other words, this postulate states that removing the null players from a game does not change the power value of non-null players.

It is not difficult to show that the θ, ξ, and ψ indices do not satisfy the null player removable property. Namely, these indices satisfy the efficiency property and assign a positive value for each null player, i.e., these indices violate the null player property. So, removing nulls from a game must change the values of the non-null players. Stach (2016) [40] provided an example of a failure of the null player removable property for the PHI θ and ξ indices. In the same example, we can observe a failure of the null player removable property for the ψ index. In particular, let be given a simple game determined by the set of winning coalitions: $W = \{\{1, 2\}, \{1, 3\}, \{1, 2, 3\}, \{1, 2, 4\}, \{1, 3, 4\}, \{1, 2, 3, 4\}\}$. In this game, player 4 is a null player and the distribution of power given by the ψ index is as follows $\left(\frac{53}{144}, \frac{11}{48}, \frac{11}{48}, \frac{25}{144}\right)$. By removing player 4, the game reduces to one with only three winning coalitions:$\{1, 2\}, \{1, 3\}, \{1, 2, 3\}$, and the powers assigned to players 1, 2, and 3 by the ψ index changed to $\left(\frac{4}{9}, \frac{5}{18}, \frac{5}{18}\right)$. Stach (2016) [40] proved that Nevison power index Z satisfies the null player removable property.

The Redistribution Property. This property is a generalization of the donation property, as in the redistribution property, it could be more than one donor and more than one recipient. Namely, it is said that a power index f satisfies the *redistribution property* if in configuration $v = [q; w_1, \ldots, w_n]$, $v' = [q; w'_1, \ldots, w'_n]$, where v' arising from v by the redistribution of weights such that: $\sum_{i=1}^{n} w_i = \sum_{i=1}^{n} w'_i$, the following holds: if player i is a donor ($w_i > w'_i$) then $f_i(v) \geq f_i(v')$; or if some j is a recipient ($w_j < w'_j$) then $f_j(v) \leq f_j(v')$.

Stach (2016) [40] provided an example of a failure of the redistribution property for the θ, ξ, R, and Z indices, see Table 3. In the same example, we can observe a violation of the redistribution property of the solidarity index ψ. In this example player 1 and player 2 are two donors and player 3 is a sole recipient. Considering the solidarity power index ψ, we can see that player 1, by giving one unit of his/her weight to player 3, increases his/her power from 1/3 to 7/18 = 0.389. The power value of player 1, calculated by the *KB* index in both weighted games ($v = [8; 3, 3, 3]$ and $v' = [8; 2, 1, 6]$) is the same and equal to 1. As was mentioned in Stach (2016) [40], we suspect that *KB* satisfies the redistribution property, but this is still not demonstrated.

Table 3. An example of a failure of the redistribution property of the θ, ξ, ψ, R, and Z indices

Power index	$v = [8; 3, 3, 3]$	$v' = [8; 2, 1, 6]$
	$f_1(v)$	$f_1(v')$
PHI θ	≈ 0.333	≈ 0.400
PHI ξ	≈ 0.333	≈ 0.433
ψ	≈ 0.333	≈ 0.389
R	$= 0.625$	≈ 0.750
Z	$= 0.250$	$= 0.500$

The Symmetry (Anonymity) Property. If for all simple games (N, v), each player $i \in N$, and each permutation $\pi : N \to N$ the following equation holds $f_i(v) = f_{\pi(i)}(\pi(v))$, where $(\pi(v))(S) = v(\pi^{-1}(S))$, then it is said that a power index f satisfies the *symmetry property*. In simple words, this property states that the "symmetric" players should have the same power value.

All the considered indices satisfy the symmetry property, and this property often enters in the group of axioms in the axiomatic characterization of the indices, see [1, 6, 7, 13, 31, 33].

The Transfer Property. If for all pairs of simple games (N, v) and (N, v'), it holds $f(v) + f(v') = f(v \cup v') + f(v \cap v')$ where $v \cup v'$ and $v \cap v'$ are counterparts of v and v' with the sets of all winning coalitions defined as follows $W \cap W' = \{S \subseteq N : S \in W \wedge S \in W'\}$, $W \cup W' = \{S \subseteq N : S \in W \vee S \in W'\}$, it is said that power index f satisfies the *transfer property*. In simple words, the transfer postulate states that the power index is a valuation on the lattice of all simple games—defined on N—that redistributes power in the lattice as indicated by the above equation.

The R index satisfies the transfer property, see [13] for example. Stach (2016) [40] proved that the Z index fulfils this property. The ψ index also satisfies the transfer property as the solidarity value satisfies it in cooperative games, see Nowak and Radzik (1994) [33]. By the way, this property is one of the four axioms in the axiomatic characterization of the solidarity value. A failure of this property for the KB and Θ indices was proven by Bertini et al. (2013) [13]. A failure of the transfer property for the ξ index can be observed in the example given in Table 4. Namely, $f_1(v) + f_1(v') = 58/84 + 13/84 = 71/84$ is different than $f_1(v \cup v') + f_1(v \cap v') = 290/690 + 299/690 = 589/690$.

Table 4. An example of a failure of the transfer property for the ξ index.

	$v = [5; 5, 1, 1]$	$v' = [5; 1, 5, 1]$	$v \cup v'$	$v \cap v'$
Power index	$f_1(v)$	$f_1(v')$	$f_1(v \cup v')$	$f_1(v \cap v')$
ξ	58/84	13/84	290/690	299/690

In Table 5 we put all the results of the considered power indices and properties to have full pictures of the relationships between the solidarity power indices considered in this paper.

Table 5. Power indices R, KB, Z, θ, ξ, and ψ in comparison.

Property	Power index					
	R	KB	Z	θ	ξ	ψ
Bicameral Meet	No	Yes	Yes	Yes	No	No
Bloc	Yes	Yes	Yes	?	?	?
Dominance	Yes	Yes	Yes	Yes	Yes	Yes
Donation	Yes	Yes	Yes	No	No	No
Efficiency	No	No	No	Yes	Yes	Yes
Non-negativity	Yes	Yes	Yes	Yes	Yes	Yes
Null player	No	No	No	No	No	No
Null player removable	Yes	Yes	Yes	No	No	No
Redistribution	No	?	No	No	No	No
Symmetry	Yes	Yes	Yes	Yes	Yes	Yes
Transfer	Yes	No	Yes	No	No	Yes

There are some known strict relationships between the Banzhaf index [4, 34] and some of the solidarity power indices, see Dubey and Shapley (1979) [17], Lane and Maeland (2000) [28], Stach (2016) [40], and Stach and Bertini (2021) [42], for example. These relationships were expressed by Stach and Bertini (2021) [42] using the null player free winning coalitions, as well.

5 Conclusion

The novel contributions of this paper is the proposal of a reformulation of two power indices: the Public Help Index ξ [6] and the solidarity index ψ—the restriction of the solidarity value proposed by Nowak and Radzik (1994) [33] in simple games—see Sect. 3.1 and 3.2.

We also offer a new formula for the solidarity index following the queue bargaining model proposed by Shapley and Shubik (1994) [38], see Sect. 3.2 and formula (10).

Another novel contribution is the comparison of solidarity indices in Sect. 4, which considers some desirable properties in simple games. Above all, there are also some demonstrations for the solidarity index.

One further development can be comparing power indices taking into account the ranges of the values assigned to the null players. I.e., minimum and maximum values assigned to nulls in the function of the total number of players in a simple game. Some works in this direction were done by Stach (2021) [41].

As mentioned in Stach and Bertini [42], extending these indices and the notion of a null player free winning coalition to games modelling voting rules with abstention could be a good idea. Some of the indices discussed in this paper are already defined for games with abstention but not all; see Freixas (2012) [21], Freixas (2020) [22], Freixas and Pons (2021) [23], for example.

References

1. Albizuri, M., Laruelle, A.: An axiomatization of success. Soc. Choice Welfare **41**(1), 145–155 (2013). https://doi.org/10.1007/s00355-012-0671-5
2. Álvarez-Mozos, M., Ferreira, F., Alonso-Meijide, J.M., Pinto, A.A.: Characterizations of power indices based on null player free winning coalitions. Optimization: J. Math. Program. Oper. Res. **64**(3), 675–686 (2015). https://doi.org/10.1080/02331934.2012.756878
3. Arnsperger, C., Varoufakis, Y.: Toward a theory of solidarity. Erkenntnis **59**, 157–188 (2003)
4. Banzhaf, J.F.: Weighted voting doesn't work: a mathematical analysis. Rutgers Law Review **19**(2), 317–343 (1965)
5. Bertini, C., Stach, I.: Voting power. In: Dowding, K. (ed.) Encyclopedia of Power, pp. 699–700. SAGE Publications, Los Angeles (2011)
6. Bertini, C., Stach, I.: On public values and power indices. Decis. Mak. Manuf. Serv. **9**(1), 9–25 (2015). https://doi.org/10.7494/dmms.2015.9.1.9
7. Bertini, C., Gambarelli, G., Stach, I.: A public help index. In: Braham, M., Steffen, F. (eds.) Power, Freedom, and Voting, pp. 83–98. Springer Verlag, Heidelberg (2008)
8. Bertini, C., Gambarelli, G., Stach, I.: Some open problems in the application of power indices to politics and finance. In: Holler, M., Nurmi, H. (eds.) Future of power indices, Special Issue of Homo Oeconomicus, vol. 32, no. 1, pp. 147–156. Accedo Verlagsgesellschaft, München (2015)
9. Bertini, C., Gambarelli, G., Stach, I.: Indici di potere in politica e in finanza, Bollettino dei docenti di matematica, No. 72, pp. 9–34. Repubblica e Cantone Ticino Ed., Bellinzona - Svizzera. Power indices in politics and finance, (in Italian) (2016)
10. Bertini, C., Gambarelli, G., Stach, I., Zola, M.: Some results and open problems in applications of cooperative games. Int. J. Econ. Manag. Syst. IARAS **2**, 271–276 (2017)
11. Bertini, C., Gambarelli, G., Stach, I., Zola, M.: Power indices for finance. In: Collan, M., Kacprzyk, J. (eds.) Soft Computing Applications for Group Decision-making and Consensus Modeling. SFSC, vol. 357, pp. 45–69. Springer, Cham (2018). https://doi.org/10.1007/978-3-319-60207-3_4
12. Bertini, C., Gambarelli, G., Stach, I., Zola, M.: The Shapley-shubik index for finance and politics. In: Algaba, E., Fragnelli, V., Sánchez-Soriano, J. (eds.) Handbook of the Shapley Value, pp. 393--417. CRC Press, Taylor & Francis Group, USA (2020). https://doi.org/10.1201/9781351241410
13. Bertini, C., Freixas, J., Gambarelli, G., Stach, I.: Comparing power indices. Int. Game Theory Rev. **15**(2), 1340004-1–1340004-19 (2013)
14. Béal, S., Rémila, E., Solal, P.: Axiomatization and implementation of a class of solidarity values for TU-games. Theor. Decis. **83**(1), 61–94 (2017). https://doi.org/10.1007/s11238-017-9586-z
15. Casajus, A., Huettner, F.: Null players, solidarity, and the egalitarian Shapley values. J. Math. Econ. **49**(1), 58–61 (2013). https://doi.org/10.1016/j.jmateco.2012.09.008
16. Chameni-Nembua, C.: Linear efficient and symmetric values for TU-games: sharing the joint gain of cooperation. Games Econom. Behav. **74**, 431–433 (2012)

17. Coleman, J.S.: Control of collectivities and the power of collectivity to act. In: Liberman, B. (ed.) Social choice, pp. 269–300. Gordon and Breach, New York (1971)

18. Dubey, P., Shapley, L.: Mathematical properties of the Banzhaf power index. Math. Oper. Res. **4**(2), 99–131 (1979). https://doi.org/10.1287/moor.4.2.99

19. Felsenthal, D.S., Machover, M.L: The Measurement of Voting Power: Theory and Practice, Problems and Paradoxes. Edward Elgar, Cheltenham (1998)

20. Felsenthal, D., Machover, M.: Voting power measurement: a story of misreinvention. Social Choice Welfare **25**, 485–506 (2005). https://doi.org/10.1007/s00355-005-0015-9

21. Freixas, J.: Probabilistic power indices for voting rules with abstention. Math. Soc. Sci. **64**(1), 89–99 (2012). https://doi.org/10.1016/j.mathsocsci.2012.01.005

22. Freixas, J.: The Banzhaf value for cooperative and simple multichoice games. Group Decis. Negot. **29**(1), 61–74 (2019). https://doi.org/10.1007/s10726-019-09651-4

23. Freixas, J., Pons, M.: An appropriate way to extend the Banzhaf index for multiple levels of approval. Group Decis. Negot. **30**(2), 447–462 (2021). https://doi.org/10.1007/s10726-020-09718-7

24. Gambarelli, G., Stach, I.: Power indices in politics: some results and open problems. In Holler, M.J., Widgrén, M. (eds.) Essays in Honor of Hannu Nurmi, Homo Oeconomicus, vol. 26(3/4), pp. 417–441 (2009)

25. Gutiérrez-López, E.: Axiomatic characterizations of the egalitarian solidarity values. Math. Social Sci. **108**, 109–115 (2020). https://doi.org/10.1016/j.mathsocsci.2020.04.005

26. Johnston, R.J.: On the measurement of power: some reactions to Laver. Environ. Plan. A **10**, 907–914 (1978)

27. König, T., Bräuninger, T.: The inclusiveness of European decision rules. J. Theor. Polit. **10**, 125–142 (1998). https://doi.org/10.1177/0951692898010001006

28. Lane, J.E., Maeland, R.: Constitutional analysis: the power index approach. Eur. J. Polit. Res. **37**, 31–56 (2000). https://doi.org/10.1111/1475-6765.00503

29. Laruelle, A., Martınez, R., Valenciano, F.: Success versus decisiveness conceptual discussion and case study. J. Theor. Polit. **18**(2), 185–205 (2006). https://doi.org/10.1177/0951629806061866

30. Malawski, M.: "Procedural" values for cooperative games. Int. J. Game Theory **42**, 305–324 (2013). https://doi.org/10.1007/s00182-012-0361-7

31. Nevison, C.H.: Structural power and satisfaction in simple games. Appl. Game Theory, 39–57 (1979). https://doi.org/10.1007/978-3-662-41501-6_3

32. Nevison, C.H., Zicht, B., Schoepke, S.: A naive approach to the Banzhaf index of power. Behav. Sci. **23**(2), 130–131 (1978). https://doi.org/10.1002/bs.3830230209

33. Nowak, A.S., Radzik, T.: A solidarity value for n-person transferable utility games. Int. J. Game Theory **23**, 43–48 (1994). https://doi.org/10.1007/BF01242845

34. Penrose, L.S.: The elementary statistics of majority voting. J. Roy. Stat. Soc. **109**(1), 53–57 (1946). https://doi.org/10.2307/2981392

35. Rae, D.: Decision rules and individual values in constitutional choice. Am. Polit. Sci. Rev. **63**, 40–56 (1969). https://doi.org/10.2307/1954283

36. Rodríguez-Segura, J., Sánchez-Pérez, J.: An extension of the solidarity value for environments with externalities. Int. Game Theory Rev. **19**(2), 1750007 (2017). https://doi.org/10.1142/S0219198917500074

37. Shapley, L.S.: A value for n-person games. In: Tucker, A.W., Kuhn, H.W. (eds.) Contributions to the Theory of Games II, pp. 307–317. Princeton University Press, Princeton (1953)

38. Shapley, L.S., Shubik, M.: A method for evaluating the distribution of power in a committee system. Am. Polit. Sci. Rev. **48**(3), 787–792 (1954)

39. Stach, I.: Proper simple game. In: Dowding, K. (ed.) Encyclopedia of Power, pp 537–539. SAGE Publications, Los Angeles (2011). https://doi.org/10.4135/9781412994088.n295

40. Stach, I.: Power measures and public goods. In: Nguyen, N.T., Kowalczyk, R., Mercik, J. (eds.) Transactions on Computational Collective Intelligence XXIII. LNCS, vol. 9760, pp. 99–110. Springer, Heidelberg (2016). https://doi.org/10.1007/978-3-662-52886-0_6

41. Stach, I.: Reformulation of Public Help Index θ using null player free winning coalitions. Group Decis. Negot. **31**(2), 317–334 (2021). https://doi.org/10.1007/s10726-021-09769-4

42. Stach, I., Bertini, C.: Reformulation of some indices using null player free winning coalitions. In: Nguyen, N.T., Kowalczyk, R., Motylska-Kuźma, A., Mercik, J. (eds.) Transactions on Computational Collective Intelligence XXXVI. LNCS, vol. 13010, pp. 108–115. Springer, Heidelberg (2021). https://doi.org/10.1007/978-3-662-64563-5_6

43. van den Brink, R.: Null or nullifying players: the difference between the Shapley value and equal division solutions. J. Econ. Theory **136**, 767–775 (2007)

44. van den Brink, R., Funaki, Y., Ju, Y.: Reconciling marginalism with egalitarianism: consistency, monotonicity, and implementation of egalitarian Shapley values. Soc. Choice Welfare **40**, 693–714 (2013). https://doi.org/10.1007/s00355-011-0634-2

45. Hu, X.F., Li, D.F.: A new axiomatization of the Shapley-solidarity value for games with a coalition structure. Oper. Res. Lett. **46**(2), 163–167 (2018). https://doi.org/10.1016/j.orl.2017.12.006

Transportation Problem with Fuzzy Unit Costs. Z-fuzzy Numbers Approach

Barbara Gładysz[✉] [ID]

Faculty of Management, Wroclaw University of Science and Technology, Wybrzeże
Wyspiańskiego 27, 50-370 Wrocław, Poland
barbara.gladysz@pwr.edu.pl

Abstract. In the classical version of the transportation problem it is assumed that all the parameters (the unit transport costs, capacities and amounts demanded) are deterministic. In real life problems, these parameters are not deterministic. One way of modeling such problems is by using the concept of fuzzy numbers. An approach using classical fuzzy numbers has been used in a numerous of articles. In proposed in this work transportation models, we assume that demand and supply are deterministic numbers and the uncertainty associated with the transport costs is modeled using Z-fuzzy numbers. A Z-fuzzy number is an ordered pair of fuzzy numbers $Z = (A, B)$. A Z-fuzzy number is associated with a real-valued uncertain variable, X, with the first component, A, playing the role of a fuzzy restriction, $R(X)$, on the values which X can take, written as X is A, where A is a fuzzy set. B is a measure of reliability (certainty) of the A. This allows to include in the model, next to the estimated value of the parameter (here: unit transport cost value), the expert's opinion as to the expert's certainty regarding this estimation. An illustrative example is presented.

Keywords: Transportation problem · Z-fuzzy number · Generative probability distribution

1 Introduction

In 1965 Zadeh proposed his concept of possibility theory, (Zadeh 1965). We will present the basic notions of this theory. First, we will present the concept of a fuzzy variable. Let $\tilde{X}$ be a single valued variable whose value is not precisely known. The possibility distribution for X is a normal, quasi concave and upper semi continuous function $\mu_X : \mathcal{R} \rightarrow [0, 1]$, see (Dubois and Prade 1988), (Zadeh 1978). The value $\mu_X(x)$ for $x \in \mathcal{R}$ denotes the possibility of the event that the fuzzy variable $\tilde{X}$ takes the value of x. We denote this as follows:

$$\mu(x) = Pos\left(\tilde{X} = x\right). \tag{1}$$

For a given fuzzy variable X and a given λ, the λ-level is defined to be the closed interval $\left[\tilde{X}\right]_\lambda = \{x : \mu(x) \geq \lambda\} = \left[\underline{x}(\lambda), \overline{x}(\lambda)\right]$.

© Springer-Verlag GmbH Germany, part of Springer Nature 2022
N. T. Nguyen et al. (Eds.): Transactions on Computational Collective Intelligence XXXVII,
LNCS 13750, pp. 106–116, 2022.
https://doi.org/10.1007/978-3-662-66597-8_6

Dubois and Prade (1978) introduced the following useful definition of the L-R class of fuzzy variables. The fuzzy variable $\tilde{X}$ is called an L-R type fuzzy variable when its membership function takes the following form:

$$
\mu_X(x) = \begin{cases} L\left(\frac{\underline{m}-x}{\alpha}\right) & \text{for } \underline{m} - \alpha < x < \underline{m} \\ 1 & \text{for } \underline{m} \leq x \leq \overline{m} \\ R\left(\frac{x-\overline{m}}{\beta}\right) & \text{for } x > \overline{m} + \beta \\ 0 & \text{otherwise} \end{cases} \tag{2}
$$

where: $L(x)$, $R(x)$ are continuous non-increasing functions x; $\alpha, \beta > 0$, where $\left[\underline{m}, \overline{m}\right]$ are the most possible values, $\alpha = \underline{m} - x(0)$ - left spread, $\beta = \overline{x}(0) - \overline{m}$ - right spread of fuzzy number.

The functions $L(x)$, $R(x)$ are called the left and the right spread functions, respectively. The most commonly used spread functions are: $\max\{0, 1 - x^p\}$ and $\exp(-x^p)$, $x \in [0, +\infty)$, $p \geq 1$. An interval fuzzy variable for which $L(x), R(x) = \max\{0, 1 - x^p\}$ and $\underline{m} = \overline{m} = m$ is called a triangular fuzzy variable $\tilde{X}$ and will be denoted by (m_X, α_X, β_X).

Consider two fuzzy variables X, Y with possibility distributions $\mu_X(x)$, $\mu_Y(y)$, respectively. The possibility distributions of the fuzzy variables $Z = X + Y$ and $V = XY$ are defined by means of Zadeh's extension principle (Zadeh 1975) as follows:

$$
\mu_Z(z) = \sup_{z=x+y}(\min(\mu_X(x), \mu_Y(y))), \tag{3}
$$

$$
\mu_V(v) = \sup_{v=xy}(\min(\mu_X(x), \mu_Y(y))). \tag{4}
$$

Chanas and Nowakowski (1988) proposed the following generative probability distribution for generating values of the fuzzy variable $\tilde{X}$:

$$
U(T, S) = \underline{x}(T) + S\left(\overline{x}(T) - \underline{x}(T)\right), \tag{5}
$$

where T and S are independent random variables with uniform distributions on the intervals $(0, 1]$ and $[0, 1]$, respectively.

The generative distribution given in Eq. (5) defines a two-stage method of generating values of the fuzzy variable $\tilde{X}$. First we generate the λ-level of the fuzzy variable $\tilde{X}$ according to the uniform distribution on $(0, 1]$. Then given this λ-level we generate the value of the fuzzy variable $\tilde{X}$ according to the uniform distribution on the interval $\left[\tilde{X}\right]_\lambda = [\underline{x}(\lambda), \overline{x}(\lambda)]$. The generative expected value and generative variance of such a fuzzy variable are given by:

$$
E\left(\tilde{X}\right) = \frac{1}{2} \int_0^1 \left(\underline{x}(\lambda) + \overline{x}(\lambda)\right)d\lambda, \tag{6}
$$

$$Var\left(\tilde{X}\right) = \frac{1}{3}\int_0^1 \left(\underline{x}^2(\lambda) + \underline{x}(\lambda)\overline{x}(\lambda) + \overline{x}^2(\lambda)\right)d\lambda + \frac{1}{4}\left(\int_0^1 \left(\underline{x}(\lambda) + \overline{x}(\lambda)\right)d\lambda\right)^2 \quad (7)$$

respectively.

Carlsson and Füllér (2001) proposed a different form of generative distribution for a fuzzy variable. Their definition is also based on the concept of the distribution of a random variable, but assumes that T and S are independent random variables with a Beta $(2, 1)$ and a two point distribution, respectively. In this case, their definition corresponds to firstly generating the λ-level of the fuzzy variable $\tilde{X}$ according to the Beta $(2, 1)$ distribution, and then choosing either $\underline{x}(\lambda)$ or $\overline{x}(\lambda)$ according to the two-point distribution $P\left(\underline{x}(\lambda)\right) = P(\overline{x}(\lambda)) = 1/2$. In this case, the generative expected value and the generative variance of the fuzzy variable $\tilde{X}$ are given by:

$$E\left(\tilde{X}\right) = \frac{\int_0^1 \lambda \frac{(\underline{x}(\lambda) + \overline{x}(\lambda))}{2}d\lambda}{\int_0^1 \lambda d\lambda}; \quad (8)$$

$$Var\left(\tilde{X}\right) = \frac{1}{2}\int_0^1 \lambda\left(\overline{x}(\lambda) - \underline{x}(\lambda)\right)^2 d\lambda \quad (9)$$

respectively.

If $\tilde{X}$ is a triangular fuzzy variable $\tilde{X} = (x, l_X, r_X)$, then its expected value based on the generative distribution proposed by Carlsson and Füllér, as well as the one proposed by Chanas and Nowakowski, is equal to.

$$E\left(\tilde{X}\right) = x + \frac{r_X - l_X}{4}. \quad (10)$$

The variances are equal to

$$Var_{CF}\left(\tilde{X}\right) = \frac{(r_X + l_X)^2}{24} \quad (11)$$

and

$$Var_{ChN}\left(\tilde{X}\right) = \frac{7l_X^2 + 7r_X^2 + 2l_X r_X}{144}. \quad (12)$$

respectively.

The generative expected value of a fuzzy variable has the same linearity properties as the expected value of a random variable, i.e.

$$E\left(a\tilde{X}\right) = aE\left(\tilde{X}\right), \quad (13)$$

$$E\left(\tilde{X} + \tilde{Y}\right) = E\left(\tilde{X}\right) + E\left(\tilde{Y}\right). \quad (14)$$

The variance of the generative distribution proposed by Carlsson and Füller (11) is greater than the variance of the generative distribution proposed by Chanas and

Nowakowski (12). Hence, in situations where transport costs are more variable, in order to model them we may use the generative distribution proposed by Chanas and Nowakowski. In cases where the transport costs show less variability, we may use the generative distribution proposed by Carlsson and Füller.

In 2011 Zadeh introduce the concept of Z- fuzzy number (Zadeh 2011). A Z-fuzzy number is an ordered pair of fuzzy numbers $Z = (A, B)$. A Z-fuzzy number is associated with a real-valued uncertain variable, X, with the first component, A, playing the role of a fuzzy restriction, $R(X)$, on the values which X can take, written as X is A, where A is a fuzzy set. B is a measure of reliability (certainty) of the A. In the literature one can find list of triangular fuzzy numbers, each of which corresponds to a linguistic expression, like (reliability) sure, usually, likely, etc. An example of the "dictionary" for the values of B can be found in Table 1.

Table 1. An example of the dictionary for the values of the second component B of Z-fuzzy number.

B	Fuzzy reliability
Sure	(1, 0, 0.2)
Usually	(0.75, 0.1, 0.1)
Likely	(0.6, 0.1, 0.1)

Source: Azadeh and Kokabi (2016)

The crisp equivalent of the second part B (reliability) of Z-number is obtained as a center of gravity method:

$$\theta = \frac{\int_R x\mu_B(x)dx}{\int_R \mu_B(x)dx}. \tag{15}$$

If B is triangular fuzzy number $B = (m_B, \alpha_B, \beta_B)$ then its center of gravity is equal to.

$$\theta = m_B + \frac{\beta_B - \alpha_B}{3}. \tag{16}$$

Z-fuzzy number can be converted into the following classical fuzzy number (Kang et al. 2012; Gündoğdu et al. 2019):

$$Z' = \sqrt{\theta}Z^\theta = \left(\sqrt{\theta}m_A, \sqrt{\theta}\alpha_A, \sqrt{\theta}\beta_A\right). \tag{17}$$

Hence it follows that expected value and variances of converted Z-fuzzy number are equal to.

$$E(Z') = \sqrt{\theta}E(A), \tag{18}$$

$$Var(Z') = \theta Var_{CF}(A), \tag{19}$$

$$Var(Z') = \theta Var_{CnN}(A). \tag{20}$$

The structure of the article is as follows: in the second paragraph, we present the literature review and our new method of fuzzy transportation problem in which the uncertainty associated with the transport cost is modeled using Z-fuzzy numbers. According to the author's knowledge, in literature there are not models of transport problems, in which the uncertainty is modeled with the use of Z-fuzzy numbers. The method presented in this article tries to fill in this research gap. The estimation of model parameters in the form of Z-fuzzy numbers allows to include in the model, next to the estimated value of the parameter (here: unit transport cost), the expert's opinion as to the expert's certainty regarding this estimation. In Paragraph 3 there is present an illustrative example. Finally, we present some conclusions and remarks about future works.

2 Fuzzy Transportation Problems

The classical transportation problem involves the transportation of a homogeneous product from m suppliers to n recipients. The suppliers have capacities of $a_1 \ldots a_m$, and the amounts demanded by the recipients are given by $b_1 \ldots b_n$. The costs of transporting a unit of the good from the i-th supplier to the j-th recipient (the route from i to j) are c_{ij}. The goal is to find a supply plan which satisfies the demands of all the recipients at the lowest possible cost, i.e.

$$\min \sum_{i=1}^{m} \sum_{j=1}^{n} c_{ij} x_{ij} \tag{21}$$

subject to the constraints:

$$\sum_{j=1}^{n} x_{ij} = a_i \; for \; i = 1, \ldots, m,$$
$$\sum_{i=1}^{m} x_{ij} = b_j \; for \; j = 1, \ldots, n,$$
$$x_{ij} \geq 0 \quad for \; i = 1, \ldots, m, j = 1, \ldots, n, \tag{22}$$
$$\sum_{i=1}^{m} a_i = \sum_{j=1}^{n} b_j.$$

In the classical version of the transportation problem it is assumed that all the parameters (the unit transport costs, capacities and amounts demanded) are deterministic. This is an example of a linear programming problem. As well as using standard linear programming algorithms, the algorithm proposed by Dantzig (1951) can be used. When the capacities and amounts demanded take integer values, this algorithm derives a solution according to which the amounts transported along the route from i to j are also integer values.

In real life problems, these parameters are not deterministic. One way of modeling such problems is by using the concept of fuzzy numbers. An approach using interval fuzzy numbers has been used in a number of articles, e.g. (Chanas and Kuchta 1966), (Chanas et al. 1984), (Dinigar and Palanivel 2009), (Hussain and Jayaraman 2014),

(Mohideen and Kumar 2010), (Kaur and Kumar 2011), (Liu and Kao 2006), (Gani and Razak 2006), (Narayanamoorthy et al. 2013), (Pandian and Natarajan 2010), (Solaiappan and Jeyaraman 2010). The review of the methods for fuzzy transportation problems may be found in the work by Chhiber et al. (2021).

This article proposes a model of the transportation problem in which the uncertainty associated with the transport costs is modeled using Z-fuzzy numbers.

Let's assume that the costs of transporting one unit of the good from the i-th supplier to the j-th recipient are given by a triangular Z-fuzzy numbers $Z_{ij} = (A_{ij}, B_{ij})$. Let's assume father that experts estimate the most possible c_{ij}, optimistic $\overline{c}_{ij}$ and pessimistic $\underline{c}_{ij}$ costs of transporting a unit of the good for each route (i, j) from the i-th supplier to the j-th recipient; $i = 1, .., m, j = 1, .., n$. They also gives information about reliability of such costs B_{ij} (for example: sure, usually, likely). As a result we get the parameter of Z - fuzzy number: $Z_{ij} = (A_{ij}, B_{ij})$, where $A_{ij} = (c_{ij}, \alpha_{ij}, \beta_{ij}) = ((c_{ij}, c_{ij} - \underline{c}_{ij}, c_{ij} + \overline{c}_{ij}), sure)$ - classical fuzzy number.

For example, an expert estimates the unit cost of transport on the route (i, j) as "certainly about 10 (he/she estimate that the optimistic, most likely and pessimistic unit cost are equal respectively: 5, 10, 12), which we model as Z-fuzzy number of the form $Z_{ij} = (A_{ij}, B_{ij}) = ((c_{ij}, \alpha_{ij}, \beta_{ij}), sure) = ((c_{ij}, c_{ij} - \underline{c}_{ij}, c_{ij} + \overline{c}_{ij}), sure) = ((10, 5, 2), sure)$. In the next step, we will transform the linguistic description of uncertainty B_{ij} into a classical fuzzy number, see Table 1. Obviously, other transformations could be used. As a result, we get a cost estimate in the form of the Z-fuzzy number: $Z_{ij}=((10, 5, 2) (1, 0, 0.2))$. Next on the base of Eqs. (15)–(17), we transform Z-fuzzy number $Z_{ij}=((10, 5, 2), (1, 0, 0.2))$ into classical fuzzy number $\tilde{Z}_{ij}' = (c_{ij}', \alpha_{ij}', \beta_{ij}') = (0.66, 4.83, 1.03)$.

The total transport costs are given by a fuzzy number of the form:

$$\tilde{C}' = \sum_{i=1}^{m} \sum_{j=1}^{n} \tilde{C}'_{ij} x_{ij} = \left(\sum_{i=1}^{m} \sum_{j=1}^{n} c'_{ij} x_{ij}, \sum_{i=1}^{m} \sum_{j=1}^{n} \alpha'_{ij} x_{ij}, \sum_{i=1}^{m} \sum_{j=1}^{n} \beta'_{ij} x_{ij} \right)$$

where: $\tilde{C}_{ij}' = (c_{ij}', \alpha_{ij}', \beta_{ij}')$ – Z-fuzzy number that represents unit transport cost on the route (i, j) after transformation into classical fuzzy number.

We consider the transportation problems corresponding to the following optimization criteria:

- minimization of the expected transport costs $F_1 : minE(\tilde{C}')$, and
- minimization of the variance of the transport costs $F_2 : min\ Var(\tilde{C}')$.

Using the linearity properties of the expected value (13–14), the F_1 optimality criterion can be written in the following form:

$$F_1 : minE(\tilde{C}') = \min \sum_{i=1}^{m} \sum_{j=1}^{n} E(\tilde{C}'_{ij}) x_{ij} = \min \sum_{i=1}^{m} \sum_{j=1}^{n} \left(c'_{ij} + \frac{\beta'_{ij} - \alpha'_{ij}}{4} \right) x_{ij}.$$

Hence, the transportation problem with the F_1 optimality criterion and constraints given by (22) is also a linear programming problem. Thus it may be solved using either the simplex algorithm or Dantzig's algorithm.

Now consider the problem associated with the optimality condition of minimizing the variation of total transport costs. Applying Eqs. (11) and (12) to the optimality criterion F_2, we obtain:

- for the generative distribution proposed by Carlsson and Füller

$$F_2 : \min Var_{CF}\left(\widetilde{C}'\right) = \min \frac{\left(\sum_{i=1}^{m}\sum_{j=1}^{n}\alpha'_{ij}x_{ij} + \sum_{i=1}^{m}\sum_{j=1}^{n}\beta'_{ij}x_{ij}\right)^2}{24},$$

- for the generative distribution proposed by Chanas and Nowakowski

$$F_2 : \min Var_{ChN}\left(\widetilde{C}'\right) =$$

$$\min \frac{7\left(\sum_{i=1}^{m}\sum_{j=1}^{n}\alpha'_{ij}x_{ij}\right)^2 + 7\left(\sum_{i=1}^{m}\sum_{j=1}^{n}\beta'_{ij}x_{ij}\right)^2 + 2\sum_{i=1}^{m}\sum_{j=1}^{n}\alpha'_{ij}x_{ij}\sum_{i=1}^{m}\sum_{j=1}^{n}\beta'_{ij}x_{ij}}{144}.$$

In both cases, the objective function is quadratic. Hence, in order to solve such problems we should use an algorithm for solving quadratic programming problems. In particular, we may use the algorithm proposed by Adlakha and Kowalski (2013) for solving transportation problems with a quadratic objective function.

3   Example

We consider the transportation problem with two suppliers and three recipients. The transportation costs on these routes are affected by a number of factors, which implies a significant diversity in the total costs depending on the present situation. Let's assume that the unit transport costs are given by experts in a form of Z-fuzzy numbers $Z_{ij} = \left(A_{ij}, B_{ij}\right)$, see Table 2.

Table 2. Unit transport costs, capacities and amounts demanded.

Supplier	Recipient			Supply
	R1	R2	R3	
S1	((10, 5, 2), likely)	((20, 3, 5), sure)	((30, 4, 2), sure)	10
S2	((60, 5, 3), usually)	((20, 3, 1), usually)	((50, 5, 7), likely)	10
Demand	10	9	1	

The expected values and variances of these unit transport costs are given in Table 3 (calculated using Eqs. (18) and (20)).

It should be emphasized that the generative expected value as well as the generative variance of Z'_{ij} are smaller than the expected value (variance) of A_{ij}. Thus, in practical situations, if there is such a possibility, transport costs can be estimated by several experts. Then the estimated cost on the route (i, j) takes the form (Azadeh and Kokabi 2016):

$$Z_{ij} = \left(\left(\frac{1}{K}\sum_k A_{ij}^k, \frac{1}{K}\sum_k B_{ij}^k\right)\right)$$

where: K- number of experts, $Z_{ij}^k = \left(A_{ij}^k, B_{ij}^k\right)$ – cost estimated by k-th expert in the form of Z- fuzzy number (B_{ij}^k- a linguistic evaluation of an expert certainty (e.g.: sure, usually, likely) transformed into a classical fuzzy number.

In the case when only one expert estimates the unit costs of transport, he/she should provide estimates for particularly unfavorable conditions.

In the literature (Kang et al. 2012; Azadeh and Kokabi 2016; Gündoğdu and Kahraman 2019) there is a few proposal of transformation Z-fuzzy number in simplified form (classical fuzzy number or crisp number). In specific practical situations, we may apply a different procedure of transformation.

Table 3. Expected values and variances of the unit transport costs.

Supplier	Recipient					
	R1		R2		R3	
	$E\left(\widetilde{C}'\right)$	$\text{Var}\left(\widetilde{C}'\right)$	$E\left(\widetilde{C}'\right)$	$\text{Var}\left(\widetilde{C}'\right)$	$E\left(\widetilde{C}'\right)$	$\text{Var}\left(\widetilde{C}'\right)$
S1	7.17	0.93	19.80	1.74	28.5	1.01
S2	51.53	1.04	16.89	0.40	39.12	2.45

The optimal supply plans P1, P2 according to the two optimality criteria used: minimizing the expected costs (F_1), as well as minimizing the variance of the costs (F_2) are presented in Table 4.

Table 4. Optimal solutions corresponding to the F_1 and F_2 criteria.

Criterion	F1: minimize expected costs				F2: minimize variance			
Supplier	Recipient			Demand	Recipient			Demand
	R1	R2	R3		R1	R2	R3	
S1	10	0	0	10	9	0	1	10
S2	0	9	1	10	1	9	0	10
Supply	10	9	1		10	9	1	

When the expected transport costs are minimized, the total transport costs C' are a triangular fuzzy number of the form (272.07, 65.99, 28.71) with an generative expected value of 262.75 and variance of 278.03. Using the criterion of minimizing the variance of these costs, the total transport costs C' are a triangular fuzzy number of the form (306.54, 66.43, 26.27) with an expected value of 296.5 and variance of 272.32. The total transport costs C' corresponding to criteria F1 and F2 are presented in Fig. 1.

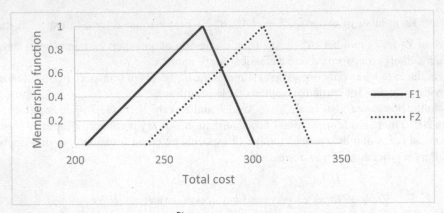

Fig. 1. The total transport costs $\tilde{C}'$ corresponding to the optimality criteria F_1 and F_2.

In a given real life situation, a decision maker should choose the appropriate strategy. For example, using strategy P1, the expected costs incurred by the decision maker are 278.03, but these costs may vary over the interval (206.1, 300.8). Applying strategy P2, the expected costs incurred by the decision maker are 296.5 (greater by 18.47 units). On the other hand, the variance of the costs of strategy P2 is lower by 5.71 and the costs vary over the interval (240.1, 332.8) with smaller wide.

The P1 and P2 strategies are different. In particular, in the P1 strategy, goods are transported via three routes: (1, 2), (2, 1) and (2, 3). In the case of the P2 commodity strategy, there are 4 routes (1.1), (1.3), (3.1) and (3.2). The advantage of the P1 strategy is that the expected transport total cost is lower and the fact that we use fewer routes to transport goods. What can be a significant advantage of this strategy in practice from the point of view of the organization of transport services. On the other hand, the P2 strategy has the advantage that overall transport costs are less heterogeneous.

According to the author's knowledge, in the literature there are not transportation models in which the uncertainty is modeled with the use of Z-fuzzy numbers. Therefore, wanting to compare the obtained solutions with the results obtained by other methods of solving transportation problems for fuzzy data, we would have to do this comparison by omitting the information provided by the second component B of Z-fuzzy number. Thus, we lose a significant component of the information contained in the data. Using, for example, the Chanas-Kuchta model (1996), we get the same solution, exactly P2 strategy. However, we get a different value of the total transport cost (360, 81, 32), with a smaller expectation - 347.75 and variance - 404.72. This is due to the properties of the generative expected value and the variance of Z-fuzzy number (see: formulas 18–20).

4   Conclusions

This article has considered the modeling of uncertain transport costs using Z-fuzzy numbers. The concept of a Z-fuzzy number has a potential for many applications, especially in the realms of characterization of imprecise functions and relations. The novelty in the proposed model of the transportation problem is the use of Z-fuzzy numbers to evaluate the unknown parameters of the model. This allows to include in the model, next to the estimated value of the parameter (here: unit transport cost value), the expert's opinion as to the expert's certainty regarding this estimation. Two optimality criteria have been used: minimization of the expected total costs and minimization of the variance of total transport costs. Based on the two criteria proposed, it is also possible to construct an analogous model of a multi-criterion decision problem.

In further works, the author intends to model supply and demand in the form of Z-fuzzy numbers in addition to the unit cost of transport. Both of these limitations of the transport model are non-deterministic in many practical situations.

Acknowledgments. The paper was funded under subvention funds for the WSB University in Wroclaw (Seminar: Quantitative Methods of Group Decision Making) and Wrocław University of Sciences and Technology.

Conflicts of Interest. The author declares no conflict of interest.

References

1. Adlakha, V., Kowalski, K.: On the quadratic transportation problem. Open J. Optim. **2**, 89–94 (2013)
2. Azadeh, A., Kokabi, R.: Z-number DEA: a new possibilistic DEA in the context of Z-numbers. Adv. Eng. Inform. **30**, 604–617 (2016)
3. Carlsson, C., Fullér, R.: On possibilistic mean value and variance of fuzzy variable. Fuzzy Sets Syst. **122**, 315–326 (2001)
4. Chanas, S., Kuchta, D.: A concept of the optimal solution of the transportation problem with fuzzy cost coefficients. Fuzzy Sets Syst. **82**, 299–305 (1996)
5. Chanas, S., Kołodziejczyk, W., Machaj, A.: A fuzzy approach to the transportation problem. Fuzzy Sets Syst. **13**, 211–221 (1984)
6. Chanas, S., Nowakowsk,i M.: Single value simulation of fuzzy variable. Fuzzy Sets Syst. **25**, 43-57 (1988)
7. Chhibber, D., Srivastava, P.K., Bisht, D.C.S: From fuzzy transportation problem to non-linear intuitionistic fuzzy multi-objective transportation problem: a literature review. Int. J. Model. Simul. **41**(5), 335–350 (2021)
8. Dantzig, G.B.: Application of the simplex method to a transportation problem. In: Koopmans, T.C. (ed.) Activity Analysis of Production and Allocation, John Wiley and Sons, New York (1951)
9. Dinagar, S., Palanivel, K.: The transportation problem in fuzzy environment. Int. J. Algorithms Comput. Math. **2**(3), 65–71 (2009)
10. Dubois, D., Prade, H.: Algorithmes de plus courts Chemins pour traiter des donnees floues. RAIRO Recherche operationelle/Oper. Res. **12**, 213–227 (1978)

11. Dubois, D., Prade, H.: Possibility Theory: An Approach to Computerized Processing of Uncertainty. Plenum Press, New York (1988)
12. Gündoğdu, F.K., Kahraman, C.: Spherical fuzzy sets and spherical fuzzy TOPSIS method. J. Intell. Fuzzy Syst. **36**, 337–352 (2019)
13. Hussain, R.-J., Jayaraman, P.: A fuzzy transportation problem using improved fuzzy Russells method. Int. J. Math. Trends Technol. **5**, 50–59 (2014)
14. Ismail Mohideen, S., Senthil Kumar, S.: Comparative study on transportation problem in fuzzy environment. Int. J. Math. Res. **2**(1), 151–158 (2010)
15. Kang, B., Wei, D., Li, Y., Deng, Y.: A method of converting Z-number to classical fuzzy number. J. Inf. Comput. Sci. **9**, 703–709 (2012)
16. Kaur, A., Kumar, A.: A new method for solving fuzzy transportation problem using ranking function. Appl. Math. Model. **35**, 5652–5661 (2011)
17. Liu, S.-T.: Kao, C: Solving fuzzy transportation problem based on extension principle. J. Phys. Sci. **10**, 63–69 (2006)
18. Nagoor Gani, A., Abdul Razak, K.: Two stage fuzzy transportation problem. J. Phys. Sci. **10**, 63–69 (2006)
19. Narayanamoorthy, S., Saranya, S., Maheswari, S.: A method for solving fuzzy transportation problem (FTP) using fuzzy Russell's method. Int. J. Intell. Syst. Appl. **2**, 71–75 (2013)
20. Pandian, P., Natarajan, G.: A new algorithm for finding a fuzzy optimal solution for fuzzy transportation problems. Appl. Math. Sci. **4**, 79–90 (2010)
21. Solaiappan, S., Jeyaraman, K.: A new optimal solution method for trapezoidal fuzzy transportation problem. Int. J. Adv. Res. **2**(1), 933–942 (2014)
22. Zadeh, L.A.: A note on Z-numbers. Inf. Sci. **181**, 2923–2932 (2011)
23. Zadeh, L.A.: The concept of a linguistic variable and its application to approximate reasoning. Inf. Sci. **8**(3), 199–249 (1975)
24. Zadeh, L.A.: Fuzzy sets. Inf. Control **8**, 338–353 (1965)
25. Zadeh, L.A.: Fuzzy sets as a basis of theory of possibility. Fuzzy Sets Syst. **1**, 3–28 (1978)

The New Ecological Paradigm, Functional Stupidity and University Sustainability – A Polish Case Study

Johannes (Joost) Platje[1]([✉]) [iD], Anna Motylska-Kuzma[1] [iD], Marjolein Caniels[2] [iD], and Markus Will[3,4] [iD]

[1] WSB University in Wroclaw, Fabryczna 29-31, 53-609 Wrocław, Poland
{johannes.platje,anna.motylska-kuzma}@wsb.wroclaw.pl
[2] Faculty of Management, Open Universiteit (The Netherlands), P.O. Box 2960, 6401 DL Heerlen, The Netherlands
marjolein.caniels@ou.nl
[3] Faculty of Natural and Environmental Sciences, University of Applied Sciences Zittau/Görlitz, Theodor-Körner-Allee 16, 02763 Zittau, Germany
m.will@hszg.de
[4] European School of Sustainability Science and Research, Faculty of Life Sciences, Hamburg University of Applied Sciences, Ulmenliet 20, 21033 Hamburg, Germany

Abstract. The New Ecological Paradigm (NEP) reflects fragility in nature, limits to growth and the perceived ability of mankind to deal with all kinds of challenges to sustainable development. Functional Stupidity (FS) concerns the willingness to use and apply knowledge, while being able to go beyond short-term, myopic goals. Both concepts bear on the capacity to create a policy for and redefine goals for sustainable development. This study aims to provide a picture of the adherence to the New Ecological Paradigm and the level of Functional Stupidity of a group of business and economics students. By means of a survey and a teaching intervention, data was gathered among Polish business and economics students (N = 428) in April-May 2019. Fuzzy logic was found suitable to analyse the data, as worldviews tend to be general and imprecise. The results show that worldviews of the students are very similar and do not depend on specific characteristic like gender, employment, etc. The only one exception is the direction of the study, which show little influence on the specific view. Interestingly, the teaching intervention does not change specific views. The lack of reflection and justification, as well as the belief in unlimited growth, may lead students to believe that human intervention, when using a system approach, can prevent different types of adverse side effects. Adherence to the New Ecological Paradigm is neutral or positive.

Keywords: New ecological paradigm · Functional stupidity · Fuzzy logic · Economics of information · Education for sustainable development

© Springer-Verlag GmbH Germany, part of Springer Nature 2022
N. T. Nguyen et al. (Eds.): Transactions on Computational Collective Intelligence XXXVII, LNCS 13750, pp. 117–135, 2022.
https://doi.org/10.1007/978-3-662-66597-8_7

1 Introduction

The engagement of universities in the sustainability discourse can be approached in different ways [29], as the role model of universities [60] and activities in the field of sustainability should fit in the university profile as well as strategical and operational planning. Following Lozano et al. [33, 34], Lambrechts, Platje and Van Dam [28] identify campus operations, institutional framework, assessment and reporting, on-campus experiences, education, research, outreach and collaboration. Universities have an important role in supporting intra- and inter-general equity, i.e., a good life now without compromising future generations to realize their developmental aims [30, 61]. However, disagreement tends to appear when discussing particular elements of sustainable development, as well as the way a sustainable world should be created. This disagreement, among other reasons, is determined by worldviews.

Sustainability is about prevention of non-linear, irreversible damage of ecosystems [9] and social, economic and political systems (see [44]). For this reason, understanding of low probability, high impact events becomes important [56]. In this context, worldviews are important, being a determinant of human and organizational goals [37], and an element of the willingness to ignore or deal with signals of potential threats [43] and information on long term costs and system risks. The diversity in worldviews [59] means that a diversity of views should be considered in collaborative research and as a consequence in education as well as cost-benefit analyses for policy for sustainable development.

In this paper, two indicators of the capacity for a university to develop sustainability related policies are presented: the New Ecological Paradigm (NEP) and Functional Stupidity (FS). NEP can be treated as a measure of ecological beliefs, attitudes or worldviews, being a predictor of environmental attitudes and behaviours (e.g. [20, 48, 53–55]). The NEP scale has been used by economists as a predictor of willingness to pay in contingent valuation studies (e.g. [8, 27]) and in studies about risk perception (e.g. [21, 51]). An interesting approach is the effort to make the NEP scale suitable for investigating ecological worldviews among children (e.g. [17, 36]).

FS shows the unwillingness to use and apply knowledge, and develop goals beyond myopic, short term profit, company value, efficiency improvements, etc. [1]. These elements of FS reduce the capacity to create an Early Warning System for non-linear, irreversible, extreme events [43–45], and as such for preventing system and organizational collapse scenarios.

NEP and FS can be useful measures for an organization's capacity to identify and deal with threats to sustainability. A description of the profile of students can help to develop policy for sustainable development, identify challenges in policy implementation, as well as development of education for sustainable development. The adherence to NEP and the level of FS is assessed among students of business (logistics, management) from a private university and economics students from a state university in Poland (N = 428). A picture of the students' worldview and their opinions on FS is created, using fuzzy logic for analysing questionnaire results. Fuzzy logic is applied as peoples' worldviews often embrace conflicting and unclear ideas [2, 22, 25], where a more traditional statistical analysis may provide an illusion of preciseness.

The results are analysed for age, gender, employment, private vs. state university and direction of studies. Furthermore, the impact of a teaching experiment on the level of NEP and FS is assessed, based on the results of a pre-test ($N = 134$) and post-test ($N = 128$). The general working hypothesis for the research is that a low level of FS is a descriptor for adherence to NEP. In other words, the willingness to use and apply knowledge translates into the acknowledgement of limits to growth, limitations to human ingenuity finding solutions for all types of problems, the vulnerability of ecosystems and the possibility of an ecocrisis.

In the remainder of this paper we first present the theoretical framework of NEP and FS in the context of university sustainability. Then, we explained why fuzzy logic is suitable to analyse our data. After an elaboration of research methodology, data are presented and discussed. Finally, conclusions of the research and implications for future research are presented.

2 Theoretical Framework

While sustainable development is often approached from the point of view of social, economic and environmental aims, and assumes a good life should be achieved for current and future generations [52, 61], trade-offs exist between these goals. Sustainable development can be interpreted as management of scarce resources [46], where ecological collapse scenarios [9] should be prevented, while also economic, social and political resilience is elementary. The world has become interconnected at an increasing rate, creating serious system threats to, e.g., the global financial system [57]. Ecosystems are interconnected through increased global travel and trade [22], while integrated IT networks create small probability, high impact threats in case of, e.g., an energy blackout or a super-virus [7]. Against this background, the notion of Functional Stupidity (FS, [1]) may be a useful concept to identify the level of reflection, justification of choices and a broader view on organizational goals. The concept of Functional Stupidity reflects support for (re-)defining goals, change of system structures and the rules of the game (formal institutions [39]) in an organization. In addition, given the current challenges in sustainable development, such as climate change or the process of globalization accompanied by economic and social inequalities as well as increasing populism and nationalism (see [16]), the power to change a worldview [37] may be elementary.

A lack of adherence to NEP and a high level of FS may hamper universities' and other organizations' engagement in sustainability issues. An example is business incubators, which are aimed at promoting "the creation of successful entrepreneurial companies", "to develop small companies in a protected environment" that due to their innovativeness can "have a significant impact on the local economy" ([32]). The mindset of students may have an important impact on the goals of the ventures, and their focus on sustainability. With a techno-optimistic, anti-NEP mindset and a high level of FS, students starting up business may approach sustainability from the point of view that innovation will not have side effects that threaten different elements of sustainability.

The New Ecological Paradigm (NEP) is widely used as a measure of worldviews [23]. It contains an extensively applied, coherent set of questions [13]. NEP, first published in the *Journal of Environmental Education* in 1978 by Dunlap and Van Liere [12], has become a well-known measure of pro-environmental orientation and an instrument used to research environmental attitude. This conceptualization focuses on beliefs about humanity's ability to upset the balance of nature, the existence of limits to growth in the human societies, and humanity's right to rule over the rest of nature. The authors found that a set of 12 Likert items measuring these three facets of new social paradigm or world-view exhibited a high level of internal consistency and strongly discriminated between known environmentalists and the general public. Despite the wide discussion about the contrast between the environmental paradigm and the dominant social paradigm (Brown, 1981), surveyed by many authors (e.g. [10, 38, 41]), the NEP scale has become a far more widely used measure of an environmental worldview, or what is a much more appropriate label, "ecological" worldview [14]. Because of global environmental changes, issues such as balance of nature, existence of limits of growth or the humanity's influence on nature, have become more relevant now than in the 1970s. Thus, the NEP Scale has also become a popular measure of environmental concern, with endorsement of NEP treated as reflecting pro-environmental orientation.

More than two decades after the first publication of the NEP items, Dunlap et al. [14] added three items. The 15 items included 8 pro-NEP and 7 anti-NEP items to ensure that no single facet was measured with items worded only in one direction. These items are presented in Table 1.

Table 1. The NEP scale's items

NEP item	Question
The fragility of nature's balance	3. When humans interfere with nature it often produces disastrous consequences (+) 8. The balance of nature is strong enough to cope with the impacts of modern industrial nations (−) 13. The balance of nature is very delicate and easily upset (+)
Possibility of an ecocrisis	5. Human are severely abusing the environment (+) 10. The so-called "ecological crisis" facing humankind has been greatly exaggerated (−) 15. If things continue on their present course we will soon experience a major ecological catastrophe (+)
Rejection of exemptionalism	4. Human ingenuity will ensure that we do not make the earth unliveable (+) 9. Despite their special abilities humans are still subject to the laws of nature (−) 14. Humans will eventually learn enough about how nature works to be able to control it (+)

(*continued*)

Table 1. (*continued*)

NEP item	Question
Limits to growth (Ecological worldview)	1. We are approaching the limit of the number of people the earth can support (+) 6. The earth has plenty of natural resources if we just learn how to develop them (−) 11. The earth is like a spaceship with very limited room and resources(+)
Antianthropocentrism	2. Humans have the right to modify the natural environment to suits their needs (+) 7. Plants and animals have as much right as human to exist (−) 12. Humans are meant to rule over the rest of nature (+)

(+) agreement means a pro-NEP attitude ("rejection of exemptionalism has an inverted Likert item scale, (−) means a pro-NEP attitude), (−) agreement means an anti-NEP attitude (for "rejection of exemptionalism (+) means a pro-NEP attitude). Questions are numbered according to the original scale.
Source: [13, 14].

FS concerns the lack of capacity or willingness to use and apply knowledge [1] and to deal with uncertainty, as well as low probability and high-impact events, in decision-making. Regarding FS, two types of categories were distinguished (see Table 2): FS1 (questions regarding reflexivity) and FS2 (questions regarding substantive reasoning). This distinction was made as FS1 concerns information flows and willingness to discuss and communicate, while FS2 concerns the inclusion of small probability, difficult to measure, high impact events in an organization's strategical management.

Following Platje et al. [44], (based on [1, 14, 19, 35, 57]) it can be argued that FS tends to be a rational strategy in times of prosperity, when considerations about problems, vulnerabilities and long-term threats to sustainability are rather a cost, reducing, e.g., short-term profits or revenues. A short-term focus reduces the capacity to prepare for future challenges, while it may lead to ignorance of signals of potential threats to organizational sustainability. FS may lead to lack of learning from mistakes (related to a lack of awareness of vulnerabilities and the related non-linear threats to sustainability), and have a negative impact on inclusion of weaker stakeholders in policy for sustainable development. Low FS is a determinant of the capacity to create an Early Warning System for catching weak signals of potential threats to university sustainability, as well as potential negative impacts of university outreach on the sustainability of development. It is related to the question whether universities produce students with a "fragilizing mindset", potentially creating vulnerabilities as these are ignored on assessment of innovations (see [3, 44, 63]), ignoring, e.g., rebound effects in innovative activities. NEP, generally speaking, shows a rather techno-pessimistic worldview, contradicting weak sustainability, while appreciating vulnerabilities of ecosystems. This might create challenges for

Table 2. Question set for functional stupidity

FS item	Question
FS1 (reflexivity, justification)	1. Mistakes are not discussed 2. It is impossible to doubt or criticize management decisions 3. Changes in the rules are not openly discussed 4. Management does not provide reasons and explanations for their decisions 5. People do not provide feedback to other people
FS2 (substantive reasoning)	1. Threats to the companies' existence which are difficult to quantify are ignored 2. Low probability threats are ignored 3. Low probability threats are ignored 4. An organization should take unlikely disasters into consideration in crisis management 5. Organizations can neglect low probability threats in their risk management

Source: authors' own elaboration

business-oriented innovations and university sustainability incubators, as solutions need to be assessed from a broader point of view than profit, labour market, etc.

3   Fuzzy Logic

In this study we use fuzzy logic to analyse the importance of the New Ecological Paradigm and Functional Stupidity. Fuzzy logic is particularly suitable to analysing opinions and beliefs, where no clear zero-one picture tends to exist. A worldview is messy, often full of internal contradictions (e.g., [22]). The fuzzy approach allows for providing probably a kind of sketch in a situation where opinions are not always very clear.

In the context of statistical theory, data sets are generally considered as representative cross-sections of theoretical populations [5]. It means, that most of the used tools consists of estimating the parameters of the hypothetical underlying distribution of the sample. However, data usually contain intrinsic uncertainty or imprecision induced by the acquisition, the nature of the data, etc. Thus, it is impossible to make the assumptions on the data distributions needed by classical statistical and probability tools [6, 18]. The theory of fuzzy sets and the probabilistic approach, are common ways to deal with imprecision, noisy information and uncertainty [5].

The main idea of fuzzy logic is that the world is not black-white, with binary yes-no, 0–1 or true-false decisions [26]. Decisions often involve „notions that cannot be defined precisely, but which depend on their context" ([4], p. 6). The real world is characterized by high dynamics and/or dependencies that are difficult to describe properly. People tend to describe reality in a verbal way is a reason for the internal fuzzyness. When asking for opinions, there is always uncertainty about the accuracy of answers. Respondents can have a limited perception of reality, due to the existence of lack of information [50] as well as limits to the human brain in explaining reality [2]. Human preferences may change based on situations [24, 49], while a ranking of these preferences as well as different goals to be achieved is troublesome [42]. In short, there is not only informational fuzziness, but also "internal fuzziness" regarding, for example, world views and paradigms. As "[p]opulations vary in terms of how well their belief systems are organized in coherent frameworks ([14], p. 431)", fuzzy logic may be a useful instrument to provide a general picture.

Following the [62] and [11] a triangular fuzzy number is $A = (\alpha, m, \beta)$, where m is the most probable/expected value and the α and β – left and right spread, respectively. The sum of two fuzzy numbers $X = (\alpha_x, m_x, \beta_x)$ and $Y = (\alpha_y, m_y, \beta_y)$ is a triangular fuzzy number $X + Y = (\alpha_x + \alpha_y, m_x + m_y, \beta_x + \beta_y)$. The multiplication of fuzzy numbers X and Y is a triangular fuzzy number $X \otimes Y = (\alpha_x \bullet \alpha_y, m_x \bullet m_y, \beta_x \bullet \beta_y)$ if the $\alpha_x, \alpha_y, m_x, m_y, \beta_x, \beta_y$ are positive numbers. In the case of assessment the complex phenomenon it is crucial to know the ratings of the detailed elements as well the weights/importance of this elements. Thus, let Rj and Wj, where $j = 1, 2,..., n$, be the fuzzy rating and fuzzy weighting given to factor j, respectively. To know the general assessment, it can follow the procedure of [31] to consolidate of the fuzzy numbers and calculate the fuzzy attractiveness ratio (FAR):

$$FAR = \frac{\sum_{j=1}^{n}(W_j \otimes R_j)}{\sum_{j=1}^{n} W_j} \qquad (1)$$

The fuzzy attractiveness ratio FAR, consolidates fuzzy ratings and fuzzy weights of all the factors that will influence on some decision or general assessment. FAR is the mean assessment for a particular group of respondents, which consolidates the ratings and the importance of the element. It is not the simple mean of all answers, but the mean including the preferences of the respondents. In our case, the weights are equal for every question, thus the FAR will be calculated not as a weighted average but the simple average of all membership of the fuzzy numbers. FAR represents the overall merit of the whole category of NEP or FS by the selected group of respondents, e.g. men/women, employed/unemployed, showing whether FS and anti-NEP go in pair.

Once the FAR has been calculated, this value can be approximated by a similar close linguistic term (LT) from the fuzzy values predefined scale. Several methods for approximating the FAR with an appropriate corresponding linguistic term have been proposed (e.g. [15, 47]). The Euclidean distance will be used since it is the most intuitive from the human perception of approximation and the most commonly used method [31]. If the natural – language expression set LT is {very low, low, fair, high, very high}, then the distance between FAR and each fuzzy number member of LT can be calculated as follows:

$$D(FAR, LTi) = \left\{ \sum_{x=1}^{t} (fFAR(x) - fLTi(x))^2 \right\}^{1/2} \qquad (2)$$

4 Research Methodology

The research was conducted in April and May 2019 at two universities in Poland – WSB University in Wroclaw and the University in Opole (N-428 – sample characteristics presented in Table 3). The first one is the largest private university in the south – west of Poland. The second one is a state university, situated in the same region. The respondents were the students from three faculties: Logistics, Management (WSB) and Economics (Opole). Logistics students have a strong business profile with a focus on quantitative matters, e.g. efficiency improvements in logistic chains. Management students have a qualitative focus. Economics students tend to adopt a balanced approach, combining qualitative and quantitative aspects. While the logistics and management students were first-year BA students, the sample of the economics students embraced BA and MA students from all years of studies. Thus, every group of students has a different background which could influence their worldviews. Students were involved in a questionnaire as well as a teaching experiment.

The results were analysed using Excel. The sampling was purposive, i.e., non-random. One of the authors provided classes in transport economics, where the questionnaire was used as a teaching instrument. This group was used for the teaching intervention, where at the beginning of the course (pre-test, $N = 134$) and at the end (post-test, $N = 128$) the questionnaire was filled out by the students. The teaching intervention consisted of the inclusion of different elements of the New Ecological Paradigm in lectures and exercises.

Table 3. Sample characteristics (N = 428)

Factor	Percentage of respondents
State university	N = 177 (41.36%)
Private university	N = 251 (58.64%)
Economics	N = 92 (21.49%)
Management	N = 147 (34.35%)
Logistics	N = 164 (38.32%)
Male	N = 173 (46.26%)
Female	N = 230 (53.74%)
Employed	N = 258 (64.18%)
Unemployed	N = 144 (35.82%)
≤25 years	N = 370 (91.36%)
>25 years	N = 35 (8.64%)
Teaching intervention, pre-test	N = 134 (51.15%)
Teaching intervention - post-test	N = 128 (48.85%)

Source: Authors' calculations

As shown earlier in Table 2, regarding FS, two types of categories were distinguished: FS1 (questions regarding reflexivity) and FS2 (questions regarding substantive reasoning). In order to assess the level of FS1, on a Likert item scale respondents were asked to indicate to what extent they consider five issues as very unproblematic (1) to very problematic (5). Answering (very) problematic would mean low level of FS1. This same scale was used to first two questions in FS2. Two other questions were formulated as statements which could be assessed from 1 (strongly disagree) to 5 (strongly agree), with 3 being neither agree nor disagree. As the agreement with the second statement would mean high FS2, for the statistical analysis, the scale was inverted.

Taking into account the aggregation of the items proposed by Dunlap et al. [12] and Dunlap [13] (see Table 1), it was assumed that in each of the five categories the questions presented similar issues which were formulated in a different way. The Likert item of part of the questions was recalculated so that the results could be ordered from anti-NEP (1 and 2), to pro-NEP (4 and 5). The same approach was used for Functional Stupidity. The authors gathered the questions into two groups (FS1 and FS2), recalculated the answers so that the results could be ordered in the same directions and build on that basis the fuzzy number for each respondent (see Table 4).

Table 4. Fuzzy values for linguistic terms and their values for NEP and FS.

Linguistic terms (LT)		Generalized fuzzy numbers
NEP	FS	
(1) Strong anti-NEP	(1) Very high FS	(1, 1, 2)
(2) Anti-NEP	(2) High FS	(1, 2, 3)
(3) Neither anti- nor pro-NEP (neutral)	(3) Neither high nor low FS (neutral)	(2, 3, 4)
(4) Pro-NEP	(4) Low FS	(3, 4, 5)
(5) Strong pro-NEP	(5) Very low FS	(4, 5, 5)

Source: Authors' calculations

The teaching experiment focused on NEP. The fragility of nature's balance and the possibility of an ecocrisis were discussed during a lecture on sustainable transport, energy dependency and non-linear threats of climate change. Ecosystem vulnerability was discussed on the example of the impact of disappearing of bees on food production. Rejection of exemptionalism was dealt with during a lecture and an in-depth exercise on the system approach, showing that road construction does not solve the problem of traffic jams, but magnifies the problem after some years. This was discussed in the context of transport policy that could prevent side effects such as decline of public transport. Limits to growth (Ecological worldview) was shortly dealt with in the introduction lecture of the relation between scarcity and transport economics. Hypothetical cases were presented, such as "what would happen when every citizen goes four times per year on a flight holiday to Spain" or "what would happen when every inhabitant of the planet possesses and drives a car". Anti-Anthropocentrism was not specifically dealt with in class.

Due to the subjective nature of the evaluation criteria as well the vague and imprecise nature of available information, it is easier to express the values in the natural language terms (LT) rather than using crisp values, what is possible through the use of fuzzy logic. Thus, comparing the Likert scale used in the research and the fuzzy logic, we set the linguistic terms and their corresponding values (generalized fuzzy numbers) as presented in Table 4. While the NEP shows the eco-centeredness of the respondents [40], here the terms anti-NEP and pro-NEP were used. This same approach was used to the set the linguistic terms and their corresponding values in the case of functional stupidity (Table 6). The level of FS was assessed from very high (1) to very low (5).

Note that the left spread for linguistic term (1) and right spread for linguistic term (5) is not symmetrical, because the ratings relate to 5-point Likert scale and thus must be cut accordingly. In other cases we assume that respondents are symmetrical in their assessments, i.e. they have no tendency to underestimated or overestimated scores.

For each student the fuzzy number was created as follows: the left spread is the minimum rate gave by individual students to the item within the selected category. The right spread is the maximum rate given by individual students to the item within the selected category. m is the mean of all answers in selected category. In the next step, we divided the students into groups and calculated for every group the fuzzy attractiveness ratio (FAR) and the Euclidean distance to each fuzzy number member of LT (dFAR). The closest linguistic expression is the one with minimum distance value (dFAR). The Euclidean distance is described in formula 2 and the preceding paragraph. If FAR is the measure of mean attitude to, e.g., NEP, dFAR is the measure how far is the mean attitude from the linguistic expression. The nearest expression (the minimum distance value) provides information which expression on the linguistic scale is proper for this mean value.

5   Results and Discussion

The results of the data analysis for NEP are presented in Tables 5 and 6. The numbers underlined in bold show the lowest distance to the selected fuzzy number member. These numbers shows the assessment of respondents the particular category on a linguistic scale. The grey coloured categories indicate the group of respondents showing a different opinion.

In general, the worldviews do not seem to differ radically. For general NEP, the outcome is neutral for all groups. Balance of nature/ecocrisis are rather pro-NEP, while anti-exceptionalism and limits to growth, neither anti- nor pro-NEP (3 on the 1–5 scale). Analysing for private vs. public university, they assess the balance of nature, ecocrisis and limits to growth similarly. Some difference was observed regarding anti-anthropocentrism. In both cases, students from the private university seem to be pro-NEP when considering anti-exemptionalism, while students from the state university tend to be somewhat neutral.

Table 5. Comparison of the groups of students – NEP (part 1)

Group of students		Aggregate NEP category	dFAR				
			Strong anti-NEP	Anti-NEP	Neutral	Pro-NEP	Strong pro-NEP
Ownership of the university	State university	Balance of Nature	4.1962	3.0809	1.4269	**0.7617**	1.6487
		Ecocrisis	4.3293	3.2054	1.5359	**0.6655**	1.5215
		Anti – Exceptionalism	3.5577	2.3819	**0.7122**	1.1582	2.3228
		Limits to Growth	2.4134	1.1201	**0.6120**	2.3440	3.5914
		Anti - Anthropocentrism	3.7634	2.5619	**0.8458**	0.9314	2.1701
		NEP	3.6742	2.2860	**0.9664**	1.6254	2.9651
	Private university	Balance of Nature	4.4320	3.3083	1.6350	**0.6336**	1.4196
		Ecocrisis	4.4177	3.2800	1.5970	**0.5852**	1.4381
		Anti – Exceptionalism	3.1758	2.5418	**0.8584**	1.0064	2.1668
		Limits to Growth	2.6818	1.3521	**0.4316**	2.1317	3.4188
		Anti - Anthropocentrism	3.8918	2.6989	0.9890	**0.8199**	2.0199
		NEP	3.7934	2.4025	**1.0592**	1.5723	2.8948
Gender	Female	Balance of Nature	4.3864	3.2684	1.6020	**0.6712**	1.4623
		Ecocrisis	4.5846	3.4590	1.7789	**0.6039**	1.2707
		Anti – Exceptionalism	3.7116	2.5608	**0.9065**	1.0420	2.1745
		Limits to Growth	2.4763	1.1824	**0.5497**	2.2817	3.5347
		Anti - Anthropocentrism	3.9808	2.7847	1.0680	**0.7257**	1.9464
		NEP	3.7909	2.4032	**1.0340**	1.5373	2.8627
	Male	Balance of Nature	4.1560	3.0349	1.3779	**0.7660**	1.6896
		Ecocrisis	4.0579	2.9108	1.2356	**0.7621**	1.7996
		Anti – Exceptionalism	3.5504	2.3395	**0.6287**	1.1478	2.3777
		Limits to Growth	2.6726	1.3553	**0.4013**	2.1177	3.3939
		Anti - Anthropocentrism	3.6350	2.4362	**0.7314**	1.0653	2.2792
		NEP	3.6835	2.2904	**1.0178**	1.6810	3.0169
Age	≤25	Balance of Nature	4.2614	3.1416	1.4798	**0.7140**	1.5855
		Ecocrisis	4.3221	3.1863	1.5081	**0.6297**	1.5318
		Anti – Exceptionalism	3.6423	2.4723	**0.8001**	1.0808	2.2343
		Limits to Growth	2.5329	1.2320	**0.5019**	2.2329	3.4916
		Anti - Anthropocentrism	3.8065	2.6076	**0.8942**	**0.8942**	2.1165
		NEP	3.7249	2.3349	**1.0076**	1.6058	2.9377
	>25	Balance of Nature	4.4272	3.3115	1.6425	**0.6558**	1.4283
		Ecocrisis	4.0013	2.9500	1.3633	**1.0073**	2.0240
		Anti – Exceptionalism	3.6891	2.4657	**0.7412**	1.0097	2.2666
		Limits to Growth	3.0174	1.6772	**0.3273**	1.8442	3.1602
		Anti - Anthropocentrism	4.1864	3.1056	1.3114	**0.5880**	1.7070
		NEP	3.9250	2.5337	**1.1609**	1.5086	2.8139

Analysing for gender, women tend to be pro-NEP regarding to Anti-Anthropocentrism, while men tend to be neutral. For age, no differences have been observed. This is in accordance with observations made by Hawcroft and Milfront [23] who, using traditional statistics, did not observe significant correlations with gender and age. Also, employed students tend to be more anti-anthropocentric than the non-employed students. Being employed and studying at a private university is strongly

Table 6. Comparison of the groups of students – NEP (part 2)

Group of students		Aggregate NEP category	dFAR				
			Strong anti-NEP	Anti-NEP	Neutral	Pro-NEP	Strong pro-NEP
employment	Employed	Balance of Nature	4.3824	3.2716	1.6105	**0.6955**	1.4676
		Ecocrisis	4.3688	3.2383	1.5630	**0.6318**	1.4822
		Anti – Exceptionalism	3.7449	2.5605	**0.8649**	0.9696	2.1499
		Limits to Growth	2.5903	1.2727	**0.4753**	2.9181	3.4689
		Anti - Anthropocentrism	3.9151	2.7273	1.0190	**0.7990**	1.9936
		NEP	3.7848	2.3904	**1.0796**	1.6177	2.9367
	unemployed	Balance of Nature	4.1721	3.0529	1.3966	**0.7620**	1.6735
		Ecocrisis	4.2966	3.1565	1.4749	**0.6224**	1.5612
		Anti – Exceptionalism	3.4673	2.3000	**0.6573**	1.2546	2.4025
		Limits to Growth	2.5199	1.2368	**0.4958**	2.2275	3.4779
		Anti - Anthropocentrism	3.7042	2.4902	**0.7688**	0.9905	2.2426
		NEP	3.6816	2.2999	**0.9298**	1.5618	2.9077
Direction of study	Logistics	Balance of Nature	4.5198	3.4169	1.7582	**0.7122**	1.3301
		Ecocrisis	4.3702	3.2313	1.5490	**0.5978**	1.4857
		Anti – Exceptionalism	3.8152	2.6511	0.9727	**0.9296**	2.0562
		Limits to Growth	2.5371	1.2136	**0.5413**	2.2612	3.5379
		Anti - Anthropocentrism	3.8072	2.5955	**0.8768**	0.8948	2.1286
		NEP	3.7815	2.3920	**1.0401**	1.5626	2.8879
	Economy	Balance of Nature	4.1474	3.0198	1.3569	**0.7504**	1.7009
		Ecocrisis	4.3608	3.2352	1.5617	**0.6411**	1.4936
		Anti – Exceptionalism	3.5571	2.3819	**0.7122**	1.1581	2.3228
		Limits to Growth	2.3303	1.0336	**0.6988**	2.4307	3.6775
		Anti - Anthropocentrism	3.7634	2.5619	**0.8458**	0.9314	2.1701
		NEP	3.6742	2.2860	**0.9664**	1.6254	2.9651
	Management	Balance of Nature	4.2659	3.1209	1.4360	0.6198	1.5963
		Ecocrisis	4.3938	3.2609	1.5835	0.6176	1.4572
		Anti – Exceptionalism	3.6008	2.4149	0.7250	1.1043	2.2964
		Limits to Growth	2.3105	1.1182	0.8697	2.5024	3.6280
		Anti - Anthropocentrism	3.9921	2.8205	1.1221	0.7503	1.8971
		NEP	3.8066	2.4142	**1.0799**	1.5825	2.9018
Interference	Pre-test	Balance of Nature	4.5198	3.4169	1.7582	**0.7122**	1.3301
		Ecocrisis	4.3702	3.2313	1.5490	**0.5978**	1.4857
		Anti – Exceptionalism	3.8152	2.6511	0.9727	**0.9296**	2.0562
		Limits to Growth	2.5371	1.2136	**0.5413**	2.2612	3.5379
		Anti - Anthropocentrism	3.8068	2.5949	**0.8761**	0.8953	2.1292
		NEP	3.7815	2.3920	**1.0400**	1.5626	2.8879
	Post-test	Balance of Nature	4.1425	3.0296	1.3888	**0.8238**	1.6937
		Ecocrisis	4.1816	3.0361	1.3564	**0.6797**	1.6757
		Anti – Exceptionalism	3.7434	2.5925	**0.9344**	1.0125	2.1164
		Limits to Growth	2.5949	1.3334	**0.4098**	2.1349	3.3713
		Anti - Anthropocentrism	3.8713	2.7034	1.0132	**0.8629**	2.0126
		NEP	3.6983	2.3254	**0.8760**	1.4585	2.8002

related as more than 75% of this university's students are part-time, going to class during the weekend and working during weekdays. These students pay for their studies, opposed to the full-time students from the public university.

When analysing the subject of studies, logistics students tend to be pro-NEP regarding anti-exemptionalism, and regarding the other two groups rather neutral. Management students have a rather pro-NEP attitude regarding anti-anthropocentrism, while the other two are rather assessed neutral. A reason may be that logistics students are often focusing on innovation as a solution for problems, without considering rebound effects, while repeating "continuous improvement" like embedded in Kaizen and Lean Management as a kind of mantra.

The teaching intervention seems to have had little impact. When comparing the pre- and post-test of the logistics students, Anti-Exemptionalism changed from pro-NEP to rather neutral, and anti-anthropocentrism from rather neutral to pro-NEP. Explanations may be:

- Worldviews do not change fast. The change seems to be minor.
- A system approach with deep exercises may change specific views (e.g., on the impact of road construction on traffic jams, increasing the problem in time through positive feedback loops), but a radical shift is unlikely to happen in a short time (see [44]).
- The system approach may have convinced students that human intervention when using a system approach, can prevent different types of adverse side effects.

The results of the levels of FS are presented in Table 7. The level of FS1, embracing the reflection on mistakes and justification of managerial decisions, is low in all groups. Also, as a whole, the level of FS (embracing FS1 and FS2) is low. However, the picture becomes different for FS2, the importance of small probability events, which are difficult to quantify, potentially having non-linear irreversible impact on organizational sustainability. All groups are characterized by a neutral position, except for women and logistics students, who are characterized by a low level of FS2. The teaching intervention did neither have an impact on FS, nor FS1. FS2 declined from pro-NEP to neutral for logistics intervention. A reason may be that the difference observed in the pre-test was a statistical coincidence.

In order to assess the relation between FS and NEP, the adherence to NEP was calculated for respondents characterized by low FS and high FS (Table 8). When comparing high FS and low FS, only a difference was observed for the category "limits to growth" – a neutral position for low FS and an anti-NEP position for high FS.

Regarding FS1, low FS is related to a higher perceived fragility of the balance of nature, and a higher level of anti-anthropocentrism, and this a more pro-NEP attitude. Low FS 2 is related to a pro-NEP attitude regarding anti-anthropocentrism, compared to a neutral position for high levels of FS2.

Table 7. Comparison of the groups of students – Functional stupidity (FS)

Group of students		Aggregate FS category	dFAR				
			Strong anti-NEP	Anti-NEP	Neutral	Pro-NEP	Strong pro-NEP
Ownership of the University	State University	FS1	4.4129	3.2422	1.5335	**0.4377**	1.4851
		FS2	3.7339	2.5515	**0.8581**	0.9810	2.1588
		FS	4.0718	2.8021	1.0778	**0.6868**	2.0327
	Private University	FS1	4.5257	3.3485	1.6329	**0.3468**	1.3951
		FS2	3.7138	2.5021	**0.7856**	0.9901	2.2150
		FS	4.1412	2.8485	1.1419	**0.7028**	2.0654
Gender	Female	FS1	4.5921	3.4275	1.7181	**0.3946**	1.3099
		FS2	3.8127	2.6215	0.9178	**0.9013**	2.0905
		FS	4.1836	2.9063	1.1868	**0.6087**	1.9613
	Male	FS1	4.3371	3.1477	1.4291	**0.4199**	1.5926
		FS2	3.5932	2.3798	**0.6674**	1.1079	2.3361
		FS	4.0070	2.7126	1.0092	**0.8237**	2.1892
Age	≤25	FS1	4.5006	3.3265	1.6136	**0.3764**	1.4099
		FS2	3.7305	2.5319	**0.8262**	0.9770	2.1800
		FS	4.1184	2.8347	1.1196	**0.6867**	2.0429
	>25	FS1	4.3506	3.1629	1.4422	**0.3949**	1.5950
		FS2	3.5510	2.3340	**0.6176**	1.1469	2.3878
		FS	4.0191	2.7250	1.0254	**0.8231**	2.2026
Employment	employed	FS1	4.4957	3.3165	1.6010	**0.3566**	1.4231
		FS2	3.6970	2.4823	**0.7666**	1.0068	2.2355
		FS	4.1109	2.8252	1.1116	**0.7386**	2.0985
	unemployed	FS1	4.4630	3.2952	1.5857	**0.4128**	1.4403
		FS2	3.5517	2.2681	**0.5765**	1.2330	2.4872
		FS	4.1171	2.8542	1.1270	**0.6278**	1.9774
Direction of study	Logistics	FS1	4.6114	3.4187	1.6951	**0.2435**	1.3481
		FS2	3.9160	2.7113	0.9946	**0.7920**	2.0113
		FS	4.2693	2.9797	1.2700	**0.5890**	1.9496
	Economy	FS1	4.4129	3.2422	1.5335	**0.4377**	1.4851
		FS2	3.7339	2.5515	**0.8581**	0.9810	2.1588
		FS	4.0718	2.8021	1.0778	**0.6868**	2.0327
	Management	FS1	4.4302	3.2721	1.5698	**0.4715**	1.4568
		FS2	3.4915	2.2721	**0.5621**	1.2127	2.4398
		FS	3.9975	2.7008	0.9992	**0.8380**	2.1982
Interference	Pre-test	FS1	4.6114	3.4187	1.6951	**0.2435**	1.3488
		FS2	3.9168	2.7113	0.9946	**0.7920**	2.0113
		FS	4.2693	2.9797	1.2700	**0.5890**	1.9496
	Post-test	FS1	4.2794	3.1031	1.3948	**0.5113**	1.6185
		FS2	3.6794	2.4839	**0.7847**	1.0304	2.2239
		FS	4.0392	2.7548	1.0406	**0.7595**	2.1201

Table 8. Level of functional stupidity vs aggregate NEP category

Group of students		Aggregate NEP category	dFAR				
			Strong anti-NEP	Anti-NEP	Neutral	Pro-NEP	Strong pro-NEP
Functional stupidity	High level	Balance of Nature	4.0537	2.8105	1.0793	**0.6564**	1.9740
		Ecocrisis	4.1508	2.9939	1.3028	**0.6573**	1.7220
		Anti – Exceptionalism	3.0777	1.7142	**0.4522**	1.8629	3.1838
		Limits to Growth	1.9740	**0.6564**	1.0793	2.8105	4.0537
		Anti - Anthropocentrism	3.5837	2.2309	**0.7248**	1.4300	2.7891
		NEP	3.5999	2.2148	**1.0254**	1.7882	3.1533
	Low level	Balance of Nature	4.4746	3.3588	1.6911	**0.6616**	1.3747
		Ecocrisis	4.5410	3.4153	1.7367	**0.6069**	1.3131
		Anti – Exceptionalism	3.7583	2.5832	**0.8973**	0.9681	2.1239
		Limits to Growth	2.5419	1.2235	**0.5206**	2.2461	3.5127
		Anti - Anthropocentrism	4.0467	2.8597	1.1471	**0.6737**	1.8687
		NEP	3.8289	2.4378	**1.0876**	1.5566	2.8752
Functional stupidity 1	High level	Balance of Nature	3.6160	2.4096	**0.6989**	1.0822	2.3086
		Ecocrisis	4.1484	2.9926	1.3045	**0.6691**	1.7192
		Anti – Exceptionalism	3.7192	2.4561	**0.7293**	1.0161	2.3092
		Limits to Growth	2.3310	1.0564	**0.6820**	2.4113	3.6478
		Anti - Anthropocentrism	3.7853	2.5219	**0.7936**	0.9485	2.2632
		NEP	3.6078	2.2126	**1.0066**	1.7694	3.1103
	Low level	Balance of Nature	4.4517	3.3433	1.6833	**0.6992**	1.3955
		Ecocrisis	4.4720	3.3419	1.6626	**0.5999**	1.3818
		Anti – Exceptionalism	3.7539	2.5875	**0.9105**	0.9813	2.1199
		Limits to Growth	2.5951	1.2843	**0.4583**	2.1842	3.4527
		Anti - Anthropocentrism	3.9534	2.2789	1.0613	**0.7652**	1.9535
		NEP	3.8090	2.4226	**1.0396**	1.5141	2.8396
Functional stupidity 2	High level	Balance of Nature	3.8555	2.6829	0.9929	**0.8796**	2.0266
		Ecocrisis	4.1523	2.9948	1.3024	**0.6508**	1.7231
		Anti – Exceptionalism	3.4540	2.2452	**0.5432**	1.2446	2.4675
		Limits to Growth	2.3071	1.0097	**0.7312**	2.4596	3.7199
		Anti - Anthropocentrism	3.4839	2.2397	**0.5084**	1.2251	2.5077
		NEP	3.5395	2.1489	**0.9428**	1.7776	3.1297
	Low level	Balance of Nature	4.4302	3.3098	1.6401	**0.6523**	1.4187
		Ecocrisis	4.5481	3.4079	1.7186	**0.5412**	1.3132
		Anti – Exceptionalism	3.7429	2.5710	**0.8896**	0.9861	2.1356
		Limits to Growth	2.5414	1.2103	**0.5526**	2.2684	3.5470
		Anti - Anthropocentrism	3.9792	2.7813	1.0633	**0.7250**	1.9518
		NEP	3.8021	2.4073	**1.0962**	1.6151	2.9322

6 Conclusions

As sustainable development concerns management of scarce resources [46], and critical challenges for sustainable development are featured by non-linear, irreversible threats to system or organizational sustainability, the New Ecological Paradigm (NEP) and Functional Stupidity (FS) can be useful measures for the university's capacity to identify and deal with threats to sustainability. Worldviews create order in an uncertain and complex world [22], and are a basis for co-operation or conflict in setting the goals of an organization.

Low FS (the willingness to use and apply knowledge and setting broad, strategic goals) and the adherence to NEP (recognition of limits to growth, limits to human ingenuity, acknowledgement of rights of nature, vulnerability of nature's and possible ecocrises) are instrumental in assessing whether universities "produce" students with a so-called "fragilizing mindset", not considering vulnerabilities and non-linear consequences of policy measures, as well as different types of innovations for sustainable development [44].

In the case study resented, students reported to have a rather neutral attitude towards NEP, with a pro-NEP attitude towards a balance of nature and the possibility of an ecocrisis. Management students and employed students tend to have a rather Anti-Anthropocentric attitude. The relation between type of study, working experience and NEP requires more profound research.

All groups showed a low level of FS. However, regarding difficult-to-measure, low probability and high impact events, the attitude was neutral. This confirms the idea that people tend to have difficulties in understanding non-linear, random events in complex systems due to cognitive limitations and dissonances [25, 58]. An implication may be that in education more attention needs to be drawn to such issues. The lack of change in FS and NEP after the teaching intervention confirms the observation that teaching and intensive system-oriented classes tend to have impact on specific issues, but do not lead quickly to a radical change in mindsets [44].

As a relation between low FS and adherence to NEP, as well as high FS and the belief in unlimited growth was observed, a hypothesis for further research is that reducing FS, i.e. supporting reflective thinking, justification and substantive reasoning, leads to an increasing support of the NEP. This change in mental models may lead to a change in the goals of the system, governance structures and rules of the game. As a consequence, including issues regarding worldviews in the university curriculum may be an important contribution to university sustainability.

As the research presented in this paper is an explorative case study, the results have to be interpreted with care. The relation between FS and NEP requires deeper elaboration, and may be related to the issue whether lack of reflection, justification and substantive reasoning is related to optimism regarding opportunities for growth. A theoretical explanation may be that functional stupidity included the focus on myopic, short-term goals, where reflection on long-term sustainability would contradict short-term goals.

References

1. Alvesson, M., Spicer, A.: A stupidity-based theory or organizations. J. Manage. Stud. **49**(7), 1186–1220 (2012). https://doi.org/10.1111/j.467-6486.2012.01072.x
2. Beck, H.: Mózg się myli (original: Irren ist nützlich). Wydawnictwo JK, Łódź (2018)
3. Bertoncel, T., Erenda, I., Pejić Bach, M., Roblek, V., Meško, M.: A managerial early warning system at a smart factory: an intuitive decision-making perspective. Syst. Res. Behav. Sci. **35**, 406–416 (2018). https://doi.org/10.1002/sres.2542
4. Bih, J.: Paradigm shift - an introduction to fuzzy logic. Potent. IEEE **25**, 6–21 (2006). https://doi.org/10.1109/MP.2006.1635021

5. Blanchard, F., Vautrot, P., Akdag, H., Herbin, M.: Data representativeness based on fuzzy set theory. J. Uncert. Syst. **4**(3), 216–228 (2010)
6. Bonett, D.G.: Approximate confidence interval for standard deviation of nonnormal distributions. Comput. Stat. Data Anal. **50**, 775–782 (2006). https://doi.org/10.1016/j.csda.2004. 10.003
7. Casti, J.L.: X-Events – Complexity Overload and the Collapse of Everything. Harper Collins Publishers, New York (2013)
8. Cooper, P., Poe, G.L., Bateman, I.J.: The structure of motivation for contingent values: a case study of lake water quality improvement. Ecol. Econ. **50**, 69–82 (2004). https://doi.org/10. 1016/j.ecolecon.2004.02.009
9. Costanza, R., Daly, H.E., Bartholomew, J.A.: Goals, agendas and policy recommendations for ecological economics. In: Costanza, R. (ed.) Ecological Economics – the Science and Management of Sustainability, pp. 1–20. Columbia University Press, New York (1991)
10. Cotgrove, S.: Catastrophe or Cornucopia. Wiley, New York (1982)
11. Dubois, D., Prade, H.: Possibility theory, probability theory and multiple-valued logics: a clarification. Ann. Math. Artif. Intell. **32**, 35–66 (2001). https://doi.org/10.1023/A:101674 0830286
12. Dunlap, R.E., Van Liere, K.D.: The "new environmental paradigm": a proposed measuring instrument and preliminary results. J. Environ.Educ. **9**, 10–19 (1978). https://doi.org/10.1080/ 00958964.1978.10801875
13. Dunlap, R.E.: The New Environmental Paradigm Scale: From marginality to worldwide use. J. Environ. Educ. **40**, 3–18 (2008). https://doi.org/10.3200/JOEE.40.1.3-18
14. Dunlap, R.E., Van Liere, K.D., Mertig, A.G., Jones, R.E.: Measuring endorsement of the new ecological paradigm: a revised NEP scale. J. Soc. Issues **56**(3), 425–442 (2000). https://doi. org/10.1111/0022-4537.00176
15. Eshragh, F., Mandani, E.H.: A general approach to linguistic approximation. Int. J. Man-Mach. Stud. **11**, 501–519 (1979). https://doi.org/10.1016/S0020-7373(79)80040-1
16. Etzioni, A.: Law and Society in a Populist Age: Balancing Individual Rights and the Common Good. Bristol University Press, Bristol (2018). https://doi.org/10.2307/j.ctv56fgtg
17. Evans, G.W., Brauchle, G., Haq, A., Stecker, R., Wong, K., Shapiro, E.: Young children's environmental attitudes and behaviors. Environ. Behav. **39**, 645–659 (2007). https://doi.org/ 10.1177/0013916506294252
18. Friedman, M.: The use of ranks to avoid the assumption of normality implicit in the analysis of variance. J. Am. Stat. Assoc. **32**(200), 675–701 (1937). https://doi.org/10.1080/01621459. 1937.10503522
19. Gladwin, T.N., Kennelly, J.J., Krause, T.-S.: Shifting paradigms for sustainable development: implementations for management theory and research. Acad. Manag. Rev. **20**(4), 874–907 (1995). https://doi.org/10.2307/258959
20. Groot, J.I.M., Steg, L.: Value orientations to explain beliefs related to environmental significant behavior. Environ. Behav. **40**, 330–354 (2008). https://doi.org/10.1177/001391650629 7831
21. Hall, C., Moran, D.: Investigating GM risk perceptions: a survey of anti-GM and environmental campaign group members. J. Rural. Stud. **22**, 29–37 (2006). https://doi.org/10.1016/ j.jrurstud.2005.05.010
22. Harari, Y.N.: Sapiens – A Brief History of Humankind. Vintage, London (2018)
23. Hawcroft, L.J., Milfont, T.L.: The use (and abuse) of the new environmental paradigm scale over the past 30 years: a meta-analysis. J. Environ. Psychol. **30**, 143–158 (2010). https://doi. org/10.1016/j.jenvp.2009.10.003
24. Kacelnik A., Meaning of rationality. In: Hurley, S., Nudds, M. (eds.) Rational Animals?, pp. 87–106. Oxford University Press, Oxford (2005). https://doi.org/10.1093/acprof:oso/978 0198528272.001.0001

25. Kahneman, D.: Thinking, Fast and Slow. Penguin Books, London (2011)
26. Kosko, B.: Fuzzy Thinking: the New Science of Fuzzy Logic. Hyperion, New York (1993)
27. Kotchen, M.J., Reiling, S.D.: Environmental attitudes, motivations, and contingent valuation of nonuse values. Ecol. Econ. **32**, 93–107 (2000). https://doi.org/10.1016/S0921-8009(99)000 69-5
28. Lambrechts, W., Platje, J., Van Dam, Y.: Guest Editorial - the university as an arena forsustainability transition. Int. J. Sustain. High. Educ. **30**(7), 1101–1108 (2019). https://doi.org/ 10.1108/IJSHE-11-2019-240
29. Leal Filho, W.: Sustainability and University Life. Int. J. Sustain. High. Educ. **1**(1) (2000). https://doi.org/10.1108/ijshe.2000.24901aae.005
30. Levin, K., Cashore, B., Bernstein, S., Auld, G.: Overcoming the tragedy of super wicked problems: constraining our future selves to ameliorate global climate change. Policy Sci. **45**(2), 123–152 (2012). https://doi.org/10.1007/s11077-012-9151-0
31. Lin, C., Chen, Y.: Bid/no-bid decision-making—a fuzzy linguistic approach. Int. J. Proj. Manage. **22**, 585–593 (2004). https://doi.org/10.1016/j.ijproman.2004.01.005
32. Lose, T., Tengeh, R.K.: The sustainability and challenges of business incubators in the Western Cape Province, South Africa. Sustainability **7**, 14344–14357 (2015). https://doi.org/10.3390/ su71014334
33. Lozano, R., et al.: A review of commitment and implementation of sustainable development in higher education: results from a worldwide survey. J. Clean. Prod. **108**, 1–18 (2015). https:// doi.org/10.1016/j.jclepro.2014.09.048
34. Lozano, R., Lukman, R., Lozano, F.J., Huisingh, D., Lambrechts, W.: Declarations for sustainability in higher education: becoming better leaders, through addressing the university system. J. Clean. Prod. **48**, 10–19 (2013). https://doi.org/10.1016/j.jclepro.2011.10.006
35. Mandelbrot, M., Hudson, R.L.: The (Mis)behaviour of Markets. Profile Books, London (2008)
36. Manoli, C.C., Johnson, B., Dunlap, R.E.: Assessing children's environmental worldviews: modifying and validating the new ecological paradigm scale for use with children. J. Environ. Educ. **38**(4), 3–13 (2007). https://doi.org/10.3200/JOEE.38.4.3-13
37. Meadows, D.: Leverage Points – places to intervene in a system. The Sustainability Institute, Hartland (1999)
38. Milbrath, L.W.: Environmentalists: Vanguard for a New Society. State University of New York Press, Albany (1984)
39. North, D.C.: Institutions, Institutional Change, and Economic Performance. Cambridge University Press, Cambridge (1990). https://doi.org/10.1017/CBO9780511808678
40. Ntanos, S., Kyriakopoulos, G., Skordoulis, M., Chaliklas, M. Arabatzis, G.: An application of the new ecological paradigm (NEP) scale in a Greek context. Energies **12**(239) (2019). https://doi.org/10.3390/en12020239
41. Olsen, M.E., Lodwick, D.G., Dunlap, R.E.: Viewing the world ecologically. Westview, Boulder (1992). https://doi.org/10.4324/9780429267048
42. Over, D.: Rationality and the normative/descriptive distinction. In: Koehler, D.J., Harvey, N. (eds.) Blackwell Handbook of Judgment and Decision Making, pp. 3–18. Blackwell Publishing, Malden (2004). https://doi.org/10.1002/9780470752937.ch1
43. Platje, J.(: The capacity of companies to create an early warning system for unexpected events – an explorative study. In: Nguyen, N.T., Kowalczyk, R., Mercik, J., Motylska-Kuźma, A. (eds.) Transactions on Computational Collective Intelligence XXXIV. LNCS, vol. 11890, pp. 47–62. Springer, Heidelberg (2019). https://doi.org/10.1007/978-3-662-60555-4_4
44. Platje, J., Will, M., Van Dam, Y.: A fragility approach to sustainability – researching effects of education. Int. J. Sustain. High. Educ. **20**(7), 1220–1239 (2019). https://doi.org/10.1108/ IJSHE-11-2018-0212

45. Platje, J., Quintana, D.S.Z.: Business unsustainability and early warning systems. In: Filho, W.L. (ed.) Encyclopedia of Sustainability in Higher Education, pp. 1–8. Springer, Cham (2019). https://doi.org/10.1007/978-3-319-63951-2_263-1

46. Ryden, L.: Tools for Integrated Sustainability Management in Cities and Towns. Baltic University Press, Uppsala (2008)

47. Schmucker, K.J.: Fuzzy Sets, Natural Language Computations, and Risk Analysis. Computer Science Press, USA (1985)

48. Schultz, P.W., Zelezny, L.C.: Values and proenvironmental behavior: a five-country survey. J. Cross Cult. Psychol. **29**, 540–558 (1998). https://doi.org/10.1177/0022022198294003

49. Sen, A.: Internal consistency of choice. Econometrica **61**, 495–521 (1993). https://doi.org/10.2307/2951715

50. Simon, H.A.: Models of Man; Social and Rational. Wiley, New York (1957)

51. Slimak, M.W., Dietz, T.: Personal values, beliefs, and ecological risk perception. Risk Anal. **26**(6), 1689–1705 (2006). https://doi.org/10.1111/j.1539-6924.2006.00832.x

52. Sterman, J.D.: Business Dynamics: System Thinking and Modelling for a Complex World. Irwin/McGraw Hill, Boston (2000)

53. Stern, P.C., Dietz, T., Guagnano, G.A.: The new ecological paradigm in social-psychological context. Environ. Behav. **27**, 723–743 (1995). https://doi.org/10.1177/0013916595276001

54. Stern, P.C., Dietz, T., Kalof, L., Guagnano, G.A.: Values, beliefs, and proenvironmental attitude formation toward emergent attitude objects. J. Appl. Soc. Psychol. **25**, 1611–1636 (1995). https://doi.org/10.1111/j.1559-1816.1995.tb02636.x

55. Stern, P.C., Dietz, T., Abel, T., Guagnano, G.A., Kalof, L.: A value-belief-norm theory of support for social movements: the case of environmentalism. Hum. Ecol. Rev. **6**, 81–97 (1998)

56. Taleb, N.N.: The Black Swan - The Impact of the Highly Improbable. Penguin Books, London (2007)

57. Taleb, N.N.: Antifragile - Things that Gain from Disorder. Penguin Books, London (2012)

58. Taleb, N.N., Read, R., Douady, R., Norman, J., Bar-Yam, Y.: The precautionary principle: fragility and black swans from policy actions. Extreme Risk Initiative – NYU School of Engineering Working Paper Series (2014). https://arxiv.org/pdf/1410.5787.pdf

59. Van Opstal, M., Huge, J.: Knowledge for sustainable development: a worldviews perspective. Environ. Dev. Sustain. **15**, 687–709 (2013). https://doi.org/10.1007/s10668-012-9401-5

60. Verhulst, E., Lambrechts, W.: Fostering the incorporation of sustainable development in higher education. Lessons learned from a change management perspective. J. Clean. Prod. **106**, 189–204 (2015). https://doi.org/10.1016/j.jclepro.2014.09.049

61. WCED: Our Common Future. Oxford University Press, Oxford (1987)

62. Zadeh, L.A.: Fuzzy sets. Inf. Control **8**, 338–353 (1965). https://doi.org/10.1016/S0019-9958(65)90241-X

63. Zepeda Quintana, D.S., Esquer, J., Anaya, C.: Teaching and mindsets regarding sustainable development – a Mexican case study. Cent. Eur. Rev. Econ. Manag. **3**(4), 91–102 (2019). https://doi.org/10.29015/cerem.860

The Polish Market of Equity Crowdfunding - Pre and During Pandemic COVID-19 Situation

Przemyslaw Klocek[1](✉) ⓘ and Anna Motylska-Kuzma[2] ⓘ

[1] WSB University in Wrocław, Fabryczna 28-31, 53-609 Wrocław, Poland
przemyslaw.klocek@wsb.wroclaw.pl
[2] University of Lower Silesia, Strzegomska 55, 53-611 Wrocław, Poland
anna.motylska-kuzma@dsw.edu.pl

Abstract. The main aim of this paper is to identify the changes on the Polish market of equity crowdfunding on the cusp of disturbing external factors, such as the pandemic COVID-19. The authors analyzed data from the four leading equity crowdfunding platforms: beesfund, crowdway, findfunds and crowdconnect through the prism of the basic efficiency factors. Comparing the reached results within the time before pandemic to the period of years 2020 and 2021 shows that Polish equity crowdfunding market is very resistant to such unpredictable conditions as pandemic COVID-19 and develops in a very stable way, in meantime experiencing a challenging process of professionalization and matching the rules of law to the requirements of the EU.

Keywords: Equity crowdfunding · COVID-19 · Social financing

1 Introduction

Since 2015, online alternative finance actors have provided financing to individuals and businesses across the globe in a myriad of ways. The idea to draw funds from the anonymous crowd via the internet originated with small loans in developing countries [1, 11]. Thus, the crowdfunding is considered as the demand-oriented way of financing. The success of the campaign is the result of the sufficient demand, but the raised funds are not only one advantage of this model of financing. The authors of the project get feedback that could be used to further improve the ideas. Moreover, crowdfunding enables supporting an atypical project, which could not be financed by the traditional financial institutions, or to meet the expectations and interest of such institution. Due to these reasons today, this approach increases competition with traditional financing agents such as venture capitalists (VCs), business angels (BAs), and banks [12, 18], and provides new opportunities for individuals and entrepreneurs in need of financing [5]. Low entry barriers stimulate the abnormal growth of this market, and the digital channels of crowdfunding platforms are open to almost anyone with the internet connection.

The pandemic COVID-19 changed the situation in many sectors of economy and generated big challenges for companies around the world. The hard lockdowns, limited

© Springer-Verlag GmbH Germany, part of Springer Nature 2022
N. T. Nguyen et al. (Eds.): Transactions on Computational Collective Intelligence XXXVII,
LNCS 13750, pp. 136–156, 2022.
https://doi.org/10.1007/978-3-662-66597-8_8

movements and contacts between people as well the restrictions in traveling resulted in problems with daily economic operations and planning of future investments. On the other hand, people closed in their homes having limited possibilities to spend their money, were generating financial surplus and looking for the new opportunities (also for investments). Crowdfunding could have appeared for them as a good alternative, therefore the main aim of this article is to identify the changes on the Polish market of equity crowdfunding on the cusp of disturbing external factors, such as the pandemic COVID-19.

2 Crowdfunding – Social Financing

Crowdfunding appeared as an alternative solution to the problem of access to capital among young enterprises in the initial phase of their activity, the so-called start-ups, and it was quickly adopted by entities characterized by above-average pace of development [2]. It is connected with the financing process using an online platform through which a sufficiently large number of small investors can support a project by paying small amounts in a predetermined amount of time (usually a few weeks) [12]. However, such ventures, especially the social ones, utilize crowdfunding as a mechanism not only to finance their initiatives and programs, but also to entice the individuals who are interested more in the proposed idea itself, rather than future cash flows or profits [2, 15]. It is worth noting that at the beginning of existing the crowdfunding platform, most crowd investors were not very sophisticated. They were common individual investors who avoided business plans, cash-flow liquidity, collateral, rational economic analysis, etc. Nevertheless, along with the growth of the popularity of crowdfunding, there increases also the selectivity of the crowd funders. As equity crowdfunding platforms have expanded and attracted an increasing number of interesting investment opportunities, professional and institutional investors have begun to look to them for opportunities [6].

Currently, the online platforms provide several different models of crowdfunding that vary according to the incentives they offer to the crowd. The literature distinguishes among donation-based, reward-based, debt-based, and equity-based crowdfunding [3, 14]. Donation-based crowdfunding collects a specific type of backers who do not expect return or benefits from their support to the project. The model offers the donors a contract without any physical or financial rewards. It is commonly used for social campaigns whose main goals are not connected with the business itself, but with charity (e.g., GoFoundMe or Crowdrise.com). In reward-based crowdfunding, investors receive perks such as advanced versions of funded products (e.g., Pebble Smartwatch) rather than receiving a financial return on their contributions [9]. Equity-based crowdfunding is the most sophisticated form of financing the entrepreneurships activity, most often through the purchase of the shares of an unlisted company [16]. The Cambridge Centre of Alternative Finance adopted the taxonomy of 16 models of crowdfunding which can be broadly divided into Debt, Equity, and Non-investment models [7]. Debt models include non-deposit taking platforms that facilitate online credits for individuals, business or other borrower-entities from individual lenders or institutional investors. This debt can be in the form of secured or unsecured loan, a bond or another debtor-note. Equity-based models relate to activities where the individuals or institutions invest in over-the-counter shares or securities issued by an unlisted business, typically a start-up. The best-known equity-based model is the equity-based crowdfunding, where the individuals or institutions purchase equity issued by a company. Other flourishing models, are Real Estate Crowdfunding and Property-based crowdfunding, where the individuals or institutions purchase the equity or subordinated debt financing the real estate. The last one from the equity-based models is the Revenue/Profit sharing, where the individuals or institutions purchase securities from a company, such as shares or bonds, and then share the profits or royalties of business. The Non-investment models include Reward-based and Donation-based crowdfunding. In these models individuals or institutions provide funding to the project, an individual or a business without any obligation from the fundraiser to provide the monetary return for the funds raised.

3   COVID-19 Situation and Its Influence on Market

In the autumn of 2019, the epidemic of SARS-COV-2 (COVID-19) broke out in the People's Republic of China, and subsequently it has spread to all the countries in the world. The economic crisis resulting from the emergence of the new disease has also spread to almost all the countries on the globe. Thus, it will be the most widespread and severe socio-economic scourge since the Great Depression of 1929–1933. After thirty years of uninterrupted economic growth, Poland was also affected by this crisis. Gross Domestic Product fell by 8.3p.p. in the second quarter of 2020, and at the end of that year Poland's GDP declined by 2.7p.p. of the previous year [4]. At the beginning of January 2020 were introduced the first regulations in Poland aimed to limit the spread of the virus, e.g. the obligation of wearing masks. The 'patient zero' appeared at the beginning of March 2020 and in the middle of March further restrictions were introduced. They included limits in movement, contacting others, education and the organisation of mass events. On 20 March 2020 the government imposed the state of epidemic in the whole country and introduced the hard lock down, which covered almost all economic and daily activities, e.g. shopping centres, libraries, museums, art galleries, hotels and medical rehabilitation facilities did not operate, as well as the nurseries, kindergartens, hairdressers and beauty salons. Restaurants, bars, cinemas, theatres, opera houses, swimming pools, fitness clubs, play and amusement parks, saunas and solariums were also closed. These restrictions were in force till the summer of 2020 and were partially reintroduced in November 2020. In January/February 2021, the restrictions were again partially lifted, however the real chance of lifting the restrictions and some normalisation came with the vaccination programme. Unfortunately, the next wave of infections in March 2021 meant that the restrictions were set again, and some of them remained in place until May and June. The introduction and lifting of restrictions took place cyclically together with further waves of new mutations of SARS-CoV-2 (COVID-19), until 28.03.2022.

According to data from the Federation of Polish Entrepreneurs, the Polish economy in 2020 lost PLN 185 billion as a result of the coronavirus pandemic. GDP declined by 2.8 percent and investments by 8.4 percent [8]. However, as the experience of the first lockdown in 2020 showed, many companies learned from the experience of 2020 and adapted their business operations to the new realities and challenges. In 2020 companies in the hospitality industry, the broader HoReCa channel and training and education sector were the most challenged. However, looking at the bigger picture and reviewing the data on how business has fared during the COVID years shows that there are industries that have suffered only marginally. There are also those that have grown in recent months. In 2020 and the early months of 2021, the pandemic also hit extracurricular forms of education very hard. Many sports, dance and hobby classes were cancelled or temporarily suspended. If they did take place, they attracted only a small number of participants. For most of the year, decreases were recorded in the field of learning foreign languages. Construction works businesses experienced a decrease in the revenues, e.g. in June 2020, when they invoiced 27% less than in February. Later in the year, there is a clear rebound in construction works invoicing, with 224% of invoices compared to February [8].

The industries that have benefited from COVID-19 are fairly easy to pinpoint: internet sales, courier activities, data processing or the activity connected somehow with health care and medicine. In general, the industry related to broadly defined IT and "coding" proved to be one of the most resilient to the pandemic crisis.

4 Law Requirements to the Equity Crowdfunding

The main idea of equity crowdfunding is to raise funds from individual retail investors via on-line platforms and invest them into incorporated entities. Although in many countries the equity crowdfunding is a regulated activity and allowed to act the platforms as a funding venue for startups and early stage companies, only one out of four countries state that the operation of a secondary market is a permitted activity in their jurisdiction [19]. In Table 1 the most common permissible activities for regulated equity crowdfunding firms are presented.

Table 1. Permissible activities for regulated equity crowdfunding firms

Activity	Percent of surveyed regulators
Fundraising for incorporated entities	97%
Promotions to individual investors	85%
Holding client assets to facilitate transactions	50%
Access to relevant credit/transaction data on users from the public registry or the mandated open data	35%
Operation of a fund or insurance product for the purpose of compensating investors in the event of losses	35%
Fundraising for individuals or unincorporated entities	35%
Operation of secondary market	26%

Source: [19].

Every jurisdiction which actively regulates equity crowdfunding requires platforms to communications to be accurate and complete. It means that the platforms are obliged to provide the standardized information to the investors and adhere to Anti – Money Laundering regulations including Know Your Customer requirements. Additionally, very common requirement is that the money that investors place on the platform is held separately from the platform to ensure funds are not co-mingled. Furthermore, the platforms are required to ensure that fundraising entities meet an eligibility requirement before they can solicit funds from potential investors via the platform.

The biggest divergence amongst regulators is apparent in the approach to marketing and promotion based on the level of wealth and experience of investors. These requirements are connected with e.g. special treatment of the less knowledgeable investors, limitation of the period of investment's amount for a single fundraiser or the limitation of the amount which the single investor may provide to a single fundraiser, etc. Table 2 sets out the selected regulatory obligations for regulated equity crowdfunding firms.

Table 2. Selected regulatory obligations for regulated equity crowdfunding firms

Activity	Percent of surveyed regulators
Ensure communication with customers is accurate and complete	100%
Provide standardized information to investors (e.g. risk warning, costs, incentive structures, etc.)	91%
Comply with Anti-Money Laundering (e.g.KYC) rules specific to this type of firm	88%
Comply with mandatory governance requirements (e.g. independent risk management, internal audit)	85%
Separate client assets from firm assets	82%
Ensure eligibility criteria are met before fundraising (e.g. minimum company age, profitability)	82%
Comply with complaints handling requirements	76%
Verify the claims made by fundraiser (incl via third party)	74%
Provide fundraisers/investors with cancellation rights	59%
Have a "wind-down" plan to minimize impact of platform failure (e.g. resolution packs or living wills)	53%
Cap the amount invested by an individual at the defined percentage of their wealth or income	53%
Promote to investors differently, based on wealth and/or experience	47%
Maintain the minimum amount of capital	38%
Cap the amount that may be raised over e.g. 12 months	35%
Cap the amount that a single investor may provide a single fundraiser	35%

(*continued*)

Table 2. (*continued*)

Activity	Percent of surveyed regulators
Comply with restrictions of advertising using specific types of media (e.g. social media)	29%
Hold capital proportionate to total amount invested on the platform	21%
Share relevant user data (e.g. with a public or private credit registry)	21%

Source: [19].

Despite all these regulations, most regulators argue that the crucial risks connected with equity crowdfunding are still not very well covered by these law requirements. The most challenging is fraud, capital losses for investors and misuse for criminal purposes (money laundering).

In Poland the equity crowdfunding is supposed to be a typical offer to purchase "shares" in limited companies, targeted at an unrestricted recipient [16]. The only problem is that the notion of "participation" does not fall within the definition of securities (in the light of the share of joint-stock company that is a security). This means that the "shares" in limited companies are not subject to a public offering regime within the meaning of the Act on Public Offering and Conditions Governing the Introduction of Financial Instruments to Organized Trading System and Public Companies ("Act on Public Offering"). This frees the limited company from the necessity to complete a number of formalities related to the public issue of securities, in particular as regards preparation and availability of information memorandum or prospectus. There exist a number of legal barriers to limited companies trading in shares, necessitating many other activities before the notary, such as adopting resolutions on capital increase or submitting notifications of shareholdings or, last but not least, regulating the internal organization of the company.

Partially this problem was resolved by the amendment of the Code of Commercial Companies, which entered into force on April 1, 2016. It allows limited companies created by means of a template, in accordance with the provisions of the Code of Commercial Companies, to perform actions connected with the amendment of the company's contract via the teleinformatic system. These regulations, assessed from the perspective of equity crowdfunding, should have a positive influence on its development in Poland, and thus on the increase in the number of companies that benefit from this method of raising capital. An additional advantage of the amendment, which is the advantage for both sides - the limited company as well as the investor, is a reduction of the notary costs. However, till today many platforms require from the potential fundraisers to reorganize theirs business into the joint stock company before setting the campaign just to be sure that regulator would not have the objections according to legality of the process.

The Polish government also introduced in July, 2021 into the Code of Commercial Companies a new form of business activity – the simple joint-stock company (PSA), which is based on the French experience with Société par Actions Simplifiée – SAS and the Slovakia solution (Jednoduchá Spoločnosť na Akcie). Thanks to uncomplicated registration and low capital requirements, the proposed solutions should make it easier to raise funds for all those who base their idea on knowledge and have the skills to develop it, but might have neither professional economic or legal knowledge nor high financial means. It is dedicated especially for start-ups and crowdfunding.

According to the regulations which are provided by the EU, the Polish government is obliged to match them with solutions used in Poland. The basic changes which are currently being discussed and planned to introduce in November, 2022 are as follows:

- setting the Polish Financial Supervision Authority (KNF) the main regulator for the equity crowdfunding market;
- introducing the concept of crowdfunding service provider, which would be the licenced activity given by KNF;
- forbidding offering the shares in private limited companies;
- increasing the limit of amount to raise per single fundraiser – during the first year (probably till 2023) 2.5mln EUR, then – 5mln EUR.

There is still lack of regulations about possibilities of going out from such investments. It means, in Poland it is almost impossible to plan the completion of the investment and to start to operate on the secondary market, which in many cases is considered as a very big disadvantage. The only one existing alternative is the NewConnect market. However, this solution is time-consuming for the fundraisers and in many cases not very suitable.

5 Polish Equity Crowdfunding Market

The world crowdfunding market is quite young and Poland is present on it almost from its beginning. Of course, the history shows the cases of raising the funds from the society much before the Internet (e.g. the platform under the Statue of Liberty in 1885 or Panorama of the Battle of Racławice in 1894), however the real development of this market was possible thanks to the incredible technological progress and its influence on the communication as well the financial operations.

From the beginning of offering, the crowdfunding financing in the Polish market is one of the fastest-growing in Central and Eastern Europe, and not only there [15]. In 2016, the value of the Polish alternative finance market reached the level of 38.1 million EUR, which was more than 272% higher than in 2015. According to Zieger et al. [20], debt-based crowdfunding increased circa 700% year-to-year, and equity crowdfunding increased 350%. In comparison, in the same time, the biggest alternative market in the world—the Asia and Pacific Region—grew by 136%, Europe grew by 101%, the UK grew by 43%, and the American market grew by 23% (see [20, 21] or [10]).

The oldest Polish platform offering equity crowdfunding is beesfund [22]. It is a definite precursor of crowdfunding in Poland, set up in 2012 and engages more than 75 thousand investors. Beesfund offers a flexible financing model (the fundraiser receives all raised funds, regardless of whether their amount exceeds the assumed goal or not). The limit of a single campaign is set according to the law requirement – 1mln EUR denoted to PLN (by official current exchange rate). The costs of cooperation include two components: commission - percentage of the collected amount and a transaction fee for using the online payment option. Additionally to that, platform charges the entrance fee from potential fundraisers within which it guarantees the law and marketing service as well the advice and IT service before starting the campaign.

Till the end of 2019, 55 campaigns were finished with the total raised funds 8.2 million EUR and the average rate of success was 55%. On average, the number of investor per single campaign was around 1103 funders and the single remittance – 313.84 EUR (see Table 3). At least one per every five campaigns was connected with the mobile apps and e-commerce (12 out of 55), however the highest funds were raised by the craft alcohol campaigns (about 0.5 million EUR on average), despite the highest single remittance was transferred to the finance services.

Table 3. The basic data about the activity of beesfund till 2019

Sector	Percent of finished campaigns	Percent of raised funds	Rate of success	Average raised amount per single campaign [EUR]	Average number of investors per single campaign	Average remittance per single investor [EUR]
Mobile apps and e-commerce	21.8% (12)	12.9%	59.0%	87 565.25	201	435.65
Entertainment	12.7% (7)	16.9%	31.0%	196 350.50	2 618	75.00
Food	12.7% (7)	4.5%	36.0%	52 435.25	179	292.93
Craft alcohol	9.0% (5)	30.1%	66.0%	488 905.50	1 663	293.99
Finance service	7.2% (4)	5.7%	66.0%	116 343.25	154	755.48
Medicine	5.7% (3)	5.4%	20.0%	146 538.50	445	329.30
Moto service	1.8% (1)	0.1%	3.0%	12 060.00	74	162.97
Clothes	1.8% (1)	0.2%	16.0%	16 380.00	N/A	N/A
Gaming	1.8% (1)	0.6%	17.0%	51 807.00	92	563.12
Others	25.5% (14)	23.5%	67.0%	131 867.37	395	333.84
Total[a]	**100% (55)**	**100%**	**55.0%**	**239 748.44**	**1 102.66**	**313.84**

Source: own calculation based on the data from [23].
[a] All the averages are weighed by the share in the raised funds.

In 2020 (see Table 4), when the first pandemic restrictions were introduced, 31 campaigns were finished on beesfund.pl, which is more than 56% of succeed campaigns from all previous years. However, the rate of success decreased about 9p.p. to 43.71%. The average amount per single campaign went up about 16%, which in comparison with lower average number of investors per single campaign (-14%) resulted in higher average amount invested (376.21 EUR versus 313.84 EUR before 2020). According to the above data, it can be noticed that higher expectations or valuations of the company looking for the financing met with higher willingness to invest by the investors. These results are compatible with the previous research about the behavior of the companies in the terms of crisis (e.g. [13, 17]). Due to possible problems with the sales and liquidity, the firms are looking for the new markets and the innovations which could be introduced into the daily activities to maintain the status quo or push the company on the higher level of development. Crowdfunding is a mean to achieve such goals, not only because of the capital itself but also because of the direct proof of concept. From the other side, the investors are looking for the alternatives which in the period of crisis could bring the better efficiency and be used to diversify the investment portfolio, especially if the situation on the market resulted in the significant increase of inflation.

Table 4. The basic data about the activity of beesfund in 2020

Sector	Percent of finished campaigns	Percent of raised funds	Rate of success	Average raised amount per single campaign [EUR]	Average number of investors per single campaign	Average remittance per single investor [EUR]
Entertainment	16.13% (5)	17.3%	29.0%	213 547.55	2 244	95.16
Craft alcohol	16.13% (5)	33.8%	47.0%	416 117.80	1 011	411.59
Food	9.68% (3)	5.5%	39.0%	113 743.00	423	268.90
Clothes	6.45% (2)	10.2%	63.0%	315 166.75	376	838.21
Mobile apps and e-commerce	3.23% (1)	6.0%	55.0%	370 263.00	551	671.98
Finance service	3.23% (1)	0.4%	5.0%	21 600.00	42	514.29
Real estate*	3.23% (1)	5.3%	65.0%	326 988.75	769	425.21
Interior furnishings*	3.23% (1)	1.6%	40.0%	95 972.75	233	411.90
Renewable energy*	3.23% (1)	0.5%	3.0%	30 196.25	N/A	N/A
Medicine	– (0)	–	–	–	–	–
Moto service	– (0)	–	–	–	–	–
Gaming	– (0)	–	–	–	–	–
Others	35.48% (11)	19.4%	35.0%	108 623.36	432	251.73
Total[a]	**100% (31)**	**100%**	**43.71%**	**278 525.20**	**953.79**	**376.21**

*The new sectors.
Source: own calculation based on the data from [23].
[a] All the averages are weighed by the share in the raised funds.

Looking into sectors (Table 4), it can be noticed that before pandemic and in the first year the most popular sectors which used the crowdfunding campaign are the "craft alcohol", and "entertainment". These sectors are not only the most frequent users but raise the highest amount of funds. In 2020 there could be observed a little change in the other sectors. In "Mobile apps and e-commerce" only one campaign was finished, whereas before pandemic it was 12 campaigns. In the "clothes" sector significantly increased the amount of raised funds (from the 0.2% of all raised funds to 10.2%, growth about 3850%). In this year appeared also three new sectors: "Real estate", "Interior furnishing" and "Renewable energy". It is quite similar to the changes on the market. The people, who were closed at homes, started to reorganized their close environment due to matching it with longer stay at home and work from home. They were looking for the private piece of ground with access to greenery and trees, were moving to apartments outside the cities, etc. Therefore, the property market, interior furnishing as well the renewable energy market were blooming. According to demand, the very quick adopting companies saw an opportunity in this situation. Nevertheless, three of the sectors ("Medicine", "Moto service" and "Gaming") didn't finish any campaign, which could be a little surprise, especially that the situation created big demand on medicine service and products, and the gaming sector itself was the best developing line of business in Poland before the pandemic.

In 2021 (see Table 5) were finished 26 equity campaigns, what is further decline about 16% according to the 2020 (about 53% according to the time before the pandemic). This decrease was seen also in the total amount of raised funds (2021 – 4.46mln EUR; 2020 – 6.16mln EUR; before 2020 – 8.13mln EUR). However, the average success rate per single campaign was growing about 25% (reached 54.3%) likewise the average amount of raised funds – about 39.35% (reached 388 117.38 EUR). The average number of investors per single campaign dropped down to 331.06 (about 65%) resulting in rising of average amount invested per one person by about 150% (reached the level 937.53 EUR).

The most of campaigns were set up by the "Mobile apps and e-commerce" sector (5 out of 26), however, one EUR per every five was engaged in the "Hemp company" sector. This sector also involved the highest number of investors. The most successful line of business was the "Food" sector with the success rate 100%.

After the two years of pandemic times, analyzing only the data from the beesfund platform, it could be concluded that the market of equity crowdfunding is in a very good condition. Although the number of finished campaigns is slightly on the decline, the efficiency is still improving. It could be observed in the average of raised funds per one campaign or the average of invested amount by a single investor.

The second biggest equity crowdfunding platform in Poland is crowdway [24]. At the beginning this platform offered besides the equity crowdfunding also other models of crowdfunding. Today, it offers only the equity crowdfunding in the flexible financing model. The basic cost related to cooperation with the platform is the commission on the raised funds, but its amount is determined individually, depending on the idea and fundraiser. Till today, 41 campaigns have been completed on the platform, most of them within the last two years (29 out of 41), which raised almost 21.5mln EUR.

Table 5. The basic data about the activity of beesfund in 2021

Sector	Percent of finished campaigns	Percent of raised funds	Rate of success	Average raised amount per single campaign [EUR]	Average number of investors per single campaign	Average remittance per single investor [EUR]
Mobile apps and e-commerce	19.23% (5)	16.4%	40.0%	146 492.35	142	1 031.64
Real estate	15.38% (4)	4.9%	7.0%	54 128.56	51	1 061.34
Craft alcohol	11.54% (3)	8.8%	13.0%	131 043.67	386	339.49
Entertainment	7.69% (2)	0.7%	3.0%	15 060.00	32	470.63
Cosmetics*	7.69% (2)	11.3%	81.0%	250 949.13	241	1 041.28
Food	3.85% (1)	12.3%	100.0%	549 702.00	690	796.67
Medicine	3.85% (1)	1.1%	10.0%	47 646.00	69	690.52
Moto service	3.85% (1)	2.0%	19.0%	87 045.75	82	1 061.53
Clothes	3.85% (1)	2.4%	21.0%	105 940.00	113	937.52
Marketing*	3.85% (1)	5.1%	23.0%	229 135.00	87	2 633.74
Interior furnishings	3.85% (1)	0.6%	5.0%	26 800.25	15	1 786.68
Hemp company*	3.85% (1)	20.0%	79.0%	889 520.50	735	1 210.23
Renewable energy	3.85% (1)	11.3%	46.0%	504 898.00	N/A	N/A
Finance services	– (0)	–	–	–	–	–
Gaming	– (0)	–	–	–	–	–
Others	7.69% (2)	3.2%	50.0%	70 775.75	76	931.26
Total[a]	**100% (26)**	**100%**	**54.30%**	**388 117.38**	**331.06**	**937.53**

*The new sectors.
Source: own calculation based on the data from [23].
[a] All the averages are weighed by the share in the raised funds.

Before the pandemic time, on the crowdway were completed 13 campaigns, which raised almost 5mln EUR. The average rate of success was 83.96% what is a better result than in comparable time on beesfunds. The average raised amount per single campaign reached the level 599 360.97 EUR – double more than on beesfunds.pl. It was possible due to lower number of engaged investors and higher average remittance per single investor.

Table 6. The basic data about the activity of crowdway till 2019

Sector	Percent of finished campaigns	Percent of raised funds	Rate of success	Average raised amount per single campaign [EUR]	Average number of investors per single campaign	Average remittance per single investor [EUR]
Food	23.08% (3)	9.6%	16.0%	158 736.33	160	992.10
Craft alcohol	15.38% (2)	41.9%	100.0%	1 041 230.75	1 334	780.53
Clothes	7.69% (1)	7.8%	39.0%	385 725.00	460	838.53
Others	53.85% (7)	40.8%	92.0%	289 566.04	116	2 496.26
Total[a]	**100% (13)**	**100%**	**83.96%**	**599 360.97**	**657.12**	**1 504.85**

Source: own calculation based on the data from [23].
[a] All the averages are weighed by the share in the raised funds.

Crowdway.pl focused only on three specific sectors: food, craft alcohol and clothes. The middle one attracts almost 42% of the total raised funds with the 100% success rate (Table 6).

Table 7. The basic data about the activity of crowdway in 2020

Sector	Percent of finished campaigns	Percent of raised funds	Rate of success	Average raised amount per single campaign [EUR]	Average number of investors per single campaign	Average remittance per single investor [EUR]
Craft alcohol	33.33% (4)	49.2%	76.0%	788 603.25	746	1057.11
Entertainment*	16.67% (2)	10.2%	84.0%	325 625.00	168	1938.24
Food	16.67% (2)	11.8%	100.0%	376 986.38	466	808.98
Clothes	8.33% (1)	3.9%	100.0%	249 999.75	554	451.26
Gaming*	8.33% (1)	6.1%	78.0%	390 541.00	216	1808.06
Hemp company*	8.33% (1)	16.4%	100.0%	1 050 000.00	895	1173.18
Others	8.33% (1)	2.5%	64.0%	160 261.25	311	515.31
Total[a]	**100% (12)**	**100%**	**84.32%**	**675 006.46**	**628.10**	**1 145.03**

*The new sectors.
Source: own calculation based on the data from [23].
[a] All the averages are weighed by the share in the raised funds.

In 2020 (see Table 7) the number of completed campaigns slightly declined to 12 (instead of 13 before), however the rate of success remained on a stable high level (84%). The other factors like the average amount of raised funds per single campaign, average number of investors or the average transfer were steady. Comparing these results with the situation in the beesfund in the same time, it could be noticed that crowdway operated much more effectively and the first year of pandemic did not influence their activity.

Table 8. The basic data about the activity of crowdway in 2021

Sector	Percent of finished campaigns	Percent of raised funds	Rate of success	Average raised amount per single campaign [EUR]	Average number of investors per single campaign	Average remittance per single investor [EUR]
Hemp company	25.00% (4)	35.2%	91.0%	889 081.25	618	1 438.64
Craft alcohol	18.73% (3)	23.3%	83.0%	784 417.67	701	1 119.00
Food	12.50% (2)	13.2%	80.0%	664 633.50	595	1 117.03
Medicine*	12.50% (2)	4.9%	33.0%	246 112.13	221	1 113.63
Clothes	12.50% (2)	5.4%	56.0%	274 798.25	386	711.91
Entertainment	6.25% (1)	3.0%	42.0%	301 668.25	228	1 323.11
Gaming	6.25% (1)	3.7%	34.0%	378 060.00	364	1 038.63
Renewable energy*	6.25% (1)	11.3%	41.0%	1 141 855.50	366	3 119.82
Total[a]	**100% (16)**	**100%**	**73.71%**	**762 326.06**	**552.71**	**1 438.10**

*The new sectors.
Source: own calculation based on the data from [23].
[a] All the averages are weighed by the share in the raised funds.

In 2021 the situation was very similar (see Table 8). There could be observed a slight increase in the number of finished campaigns (to 16), which raised above 10mln EUR with an average success rate on the level of 73.71%. This result is a bit worse than in previous years however, still it is much higher than on beesfund. The average amount of raised funds per single campaign (about 13%) was rising significantly, which together with lower average number of investors gave the results in higher average single transfer.

The ¼ of all campaigns were set up by the "hemp company" sector, however the highest transfer was made in "renewable energy" sector. Very popular was also the "craft alcohol" sector with the three finished campaigns and 23.3% of all raised funds.

The data from the crowdway show that although the pandemic stopped the activity of many companies and brought the higher uncertainty about the future, the equity crowdfunding market in Poland was not infected by these disruptors and has been developing in a very stable way. It attracts even more investors and improves the success rates, caring about the quality of the offers and choosing only those projects which guarantee the real sufficient return simultaneously minimalizing the risk of investment.

Another equity platform on Polish market is findfunds [25]. The method of financing it uses is situated somewhere between the rigid and the flexible model. This means that the fundraiser has the possibility to define the financial goal in the form of a range of values. All other platforms assume a specific amount as a financial goal that the fundraiser is applying for. According to this range of values, a range of shares is offered, thus the goal is a bit more flexible. As part of the cooperation, commission costs are incurred, determined as 5% of the raised amount.

Table 9. The basic data about the activity of findfunds till 2019

Sector	Percent of finished campaigns	Percent of raised funds	Rate of success	Average raised amount per single campaign [EUR]	Average number of investors per single campaign	Average remittance per single investor [EUR]
Gaming	70.00% (7)	96.5%	123.0%	303 787.82	75	4050.50
Mobile apps and e-commerce	10.00% (1)	0.2%	19.0%	4 725.00	3	1575.00
Food	10.00% (1)	2.2%	385.0%	48 093.75	22	2186.08
Interior furnishings	10.00% (1)	1.1%	100.0%	24 968.75	12	2080.73
Total[a]	100% (10)	100%	128.23%	220 430.23	72.98	3 982.21

Source: own calculation based on the data from [23].
[a] All the averages are weighed by the share in the raised funds.

Findfunds finished 10 campaigns before the pandemic, which raised together 2.2mln EUR. Most of them were suited in the gaming sector (70%) and reached the abnormal rate of success (average rate – 128.23%) which exceeds the set goal (Table 9). The highest excess could be noticed in the "food" sector, which reached the level 385%. This result was possible due to the accepted financing model – setting the goal as a range of values instead of the single strict value. Thus the success rate was calculated taking into account the lowest value from the range and comparing it with the real raised funds. On other platforms which offer the equity crowdfunding such success rate is impossible due to the rule of finishing the campaign where all the offered shares were sold. Thereby exceeding 100% is not allowed.

The average amount of raised funds per single campaign was 220 430.23 EUR. However, besides the gaming sector, in other sectors this number is much lower. Although the same situation could be observed in the number of investors, the average amount raised per single funder were very comparable between the sectors and were close to the total average amount.

Table 10. The basic data about the activity of findfunds in 2020

Sector	Percent of finished campaigns	Percent of raised funds	Rate of success	Average raised amount per single campaign [EUR]	Average number of investors per single campaign	Average remittance per single investor [EUR]
Gaming	80.00% (4)	82.0%	123.0%	284 403.13	64	4 443.80
Entertainment*	20.00% (1)	18.0%	125.0%	250 000.00	59	4 237.29
Mobile apps and e-commerce	– (0)	–	–	–	–	–
Food	– (0)	–	–	–	–	–
Interior furnishings	– (0)	–	–	–	–	–
Total[a]	**100% (5)**	**100%**	**123.36%**	**278 204.87**	**63.10**	**4 406.59**

*The new sectors.
Source: own calculation based on the data from [23].
[a] All the averages are weighed by the share in the raised funds.

The year 2020 was not very good for the findfunds platform (see Table 10). Only five campaigns were finished, which is 50% less than before pandemic. All the raised funds amounted at 1.4mln EUR and the rate of success was stable, however there could be observed a slight increase in average raised funds per single campaign. Most of the funds were engaged by the gaming sector (82% of all raised funds), but the entertainment sector attracted very similar number of investors (per one campaign), average transfer per single funder and also the average raised amount (per single campaign). Although the results which were stable despite the disruptors, the number of finished campaigns could suggest the problem with efficiency of this platform. Focusing only on the one sector is very dangerous and could limit the investors who looks for the diversification on their investment portfolio.

In 2021 findfunds finished 10 campaigns with the final effect of 3mln EUR. The success rate achieved the level 110.01%, what was a bit lower than in previous years, but the average raised amount per single campaign was increased by 19%, whereas the average amount transfer per single investor grew rapidly by 60.5% comparing to the year 2020. This atypical rise is a result of the very high single transfer made in the mobile apps and e-commerce sector, where the one campaign gathered 17.5% of all raised funds via the platform in 2021, engaging only 31 investors (Table 11).

The findfunds was focusing still on the gaming sector in 2021, however there appeared the campaigns in other sectors, from which the most impressive (taking into account efficiency counted as the average raised amount per campaign or the average single transfer) was the mobile apps and e-commerce as well the hemp company.

Comparing the situation with other platforms, it could be noticed that findfunds is still deviating from the leading platforms, i.e. beesfund or crowdway. Both the number

Table 11. The basic data about the activity of findfunds in 2021

Sector	Percent of finished campaigns	Percent of raised funds	Rate of success	Average raised amount per single campaign [EUR]	Average number of investors per single campaign	Average remittance per single investor [EUR]
Gaming	50.00% (5)	45.2%	115.0%	271 100.00	60	4 518.33
Finance service*	20.00% (2)	16.7%	113.0%	250 000.00	63	3 968.25
Mobile apps and e-commerce	10.00% (1)	17.5%	106.0%	525 000.00	31	16 935.48
Hemp company*	10.00% (1)	14.7%	100.0%	439 375.00	50	8 787.50
Real estate*	10.00% (1)	5.9%	100.0%	176 250.00	94	1 875.00
Total[a]	**100% (10)**	**100%**	**110.01%**	**331 166.26**	**55.95**	**7 072.91**

*The new sectors.
Source: own calculation based on the data from [23].
[a] All the averages are weighed by the share in the raised funds.

of finished campaigns as well the raised funds or diversification of the offer expose findfunds to the turbulence on the market. The results of it could be observed in 2020.

The last equity platform with a significant share in the Polish market is crowdconnect [26]. This platform is the first official partner for Polish Stock Market (GPW) and is the part of the INC Group, which is the certified financial institution with allowance to trade the financial instruments and lead the process of IPO. Thus the platform finally guarantees the launch on the NewConnect market of companies firstly seeking financing through crowdfunding. It is very important information for the potential investors, who always ask about possibilities of going out from such investments and assess this factor as a basic determinant for their decision.

Till the end of 2019, the only one campaign has been completed on the platform, which raised 304 425 EUR and engaged 177 investors. In 2020 crowdconnect signed official documents about the partnership with Polish Stock Market (GPW) and started a quick development.

In 2020 ten campaigns were finished, which gathered together 6.1mln EUR with the average success rate on the level 99.83%. The average raised amount per single campaign was 730 139.08 EUR and this was the best result ongoing from all leading platforms. The average number of investors was quite low, comparing to beesfund or crowdway, however the average single transfer was much higher but not as high as in findfunds (Table 12).

Table 12. The basic data about the activity of crowdconnect in 2020

Sector	Percent of finished campaigns	Percent of raised funds	Rate of success	Average raised amount per single campaign [EUR]	Average number of investors per single campaign	Average remittance per single investor [EUR]
Gaming	30.00% (3)	23.4%	100.0%	472 917.00	217	2 179.34
Craft alcohol	10.00% (1)	18.0%	100.0%	1 093 750.00	324	3 375.77
Renewable energy	10.00% (1)	16.5%	100.0%	1 000 000.00	523	1 912.05
Real estate	10.00% (1)	8.2%	100.0%	500 650.00	194	2 580.67
Entertainment	10.00% (1)	4.5%	100.0%	275 000.00	144	1 909.72
Mobile apps and e-commerce	10.00% (1)	4.1%	96.0%	251 250.00	193	1 301.81
others	20.00% (2)	25.3%	100.00%	767 750.00	183	4 206.85
Total[a]	**100% (10)**	**100%**	**99.83%**	**730 139.08**	**271.72**	**2 847.80**

*The new sectors.
Source: own calculation based on the data from [23].
[a]All the averages are weighed by the share in the raised funds.

The majority of campaigns were realized in the gaming sector (30%) but the highest raised amount per single campaign was obtained in the craft alcohol and the renewable energy sectors. It was above 1mln EUR.

In 2021 fourteen campaigns were finished, with the total effect of 8.67mln EUR. Most of the campaigns were realized in the gaming sector (57.14%) and this is about twice more than in the previous year. On the second place is the sector of mobile apps and e-commerce, which realized 21.43% of all campaigns. However, both of those sectors attract a lower average amount per single campaign. Moreover, he success rates were also lower compared to others lines of business. The best effects calculated as the average raised amount per single campaign was achieved in marketing sector, which together with a low number of engaged investors resulted in a very high average single transfer (12 926.14 EUR). Whereas the average raised amount per single campaign declined slightly about 10%, the average single remittance increased rapidly about 104%, basically due to the results in marketing sector (Table 13).

Table 13. The basic data about the activity of crowdconnect in 2021

Sector	Percent of finished campaigns	Percent of raised funds	Rate of success	Average raised amount per single campaign [EUR]	Average number of investors per single campaign	Average remittance per single investor [EUR]
Gaming	57.14% (8)	53.4%	94.0%	578 694.00	132	4 384.05
Mobile apps and e-commerce	21.43% (3)	17.7%	59.0%	510 765.83	86	5 939.14
Marketing	7.14% (1)	13.1%	101.0%	1 137 500.00	88	12 926.14
Renewable energy	7.14% (1)	8.6%	100.0%	750 007.75	168	4 464.33
Clothes	7.14% (1)	7.2%	200.0%	624 997.75	134	4 664.16
Total[a]	**100% (14)**	**100%**	**96.89%**	**658 121.47**	**121.36**	**5 806.03**

*The new sectors.

Source: own calculation based on the data from [23].

[a] All the averages are weighed by the share in the raised funds.

Table 14 shows basic data from four leading platforms, which are also the biggest influencers on Polish equity crowdfunding market. The summarized raised funds suggest that the pandemic was not a disruptor for this market. On the contrary, it pushed equity crowdfunding on the higher level of development. Only two platforms (beesfund and findfunds) experienced a slight influence observed in the decline of raised funds.

The average rate of success throughout all those years was quite high (about 80%) and remained stable. The increase of this rate in 2020 is worht to be notice, which is the another argument showing the opposite influence of pandemic on the market.

The efficiency of this market is observed also in the increase in average amount of raised funds per single campaign. This effect is mostly connected with changing the limit of amount raised in a single campaign from the 100 000 EUR to 1mln EUR, however the pandemic did not stop also this trend. This same effect could be noticed in the average amount of raised funds per single investor, yet it is not an effect of changing the limits. More probably, it outflows from the rising interest of crowdfunding as well as trust in such a form of investing. It could be also the effect of attracting more wealthy investors or even financial institutions like venture capital or investment funds. A good proof of this thesis could be the average number of investors engaged in a single campaign. This figure decreased in the analyzed period about 50%, which along with observed increase in the total raised amount suggest that the funders have to invest higher amounts.

The attractiveness of equity market could be also observed in the time needed to gather all funds. In 2021 was beaten a new record. The "Kombinat Konopny" raised 1 mln EUR in 7 min. This is another argument which shows that pandemic time did not disturb the impressive development of equity crowdfunding in Poland.

Table 14. The summary data from four above analyzed platform

Sector	Beesfund	Crowdway	Findfunds	Crowdconnect	Total
Amount of raised funds [EUR]					
Before the end of 2019	8 133 514.75	4 971 357.75	2 204 302.25	304 425.00	15 613 599.75
2020	6 159 767.00	6 410 437.75	1 387 612.50	6 074 901.00	20 032 718.25
2021	4 456 364.25	10 102 249.50	2 996 125.00	8 674 355.00	26 229 093.75
Average rate of success [%]					
Before the end of 2019	55.07%	83.96%	128.23%	51.00%	79.57%
2020	43.71%	84.32%	123.36%	99.83%	87.81%
2021	54.30%	73.71%	110.01%	96.89%	83.73%
Average amount of raised funds per single campaign [EUR]					
Before the end of 2019	239 748.44	599 360.97	220 430.23	304 425.00	340 991.16
2020	278 525.20	675 006.46	278 204.87	730 139.08	490 468.90
2021	388 117.38	762 326.06	331 166.26	658 121.47	534 932.79
Average number of investors per single campaign					
Before the end of 2019	1 102.66	657.12	72.98	177.00	502.44
2020	953.79	628.10	63.10	271.72	479.18
2021	331.06	552.71	55.95	121.36	265.27
Average amount of raised funds per single investor [EUR]					
Before the end of 2019	313.84	1 504.85	3 982.21	1 719.92	1 880.20
2020	376.21	1 145.03	4 406.59	2 847.80	2 193.91
2021	937.53	1 438.10	7 072.91	5 806.03	3 813.64

Source: own calculation based on the data from [23].

6 Conclusions and Future Research

The main objective of this paper was to identify the changes on the Polish market of
equity crowdfunding on the cusp of disturbing external factors as the pandemic COVID-
19. Focusing on the four leading equity platforms operated on Polish market: beesfund,
crowdway, findfunds and crowdconnect, the authors analysed the changes in basic data,
e.g. amount of raised funds, average rate of success, average raised amount per single
campaign, average number of investors and the average raised amount per single investor.
All the data show lack of influence of pandemic and even if it appeared in single cases,
it was not significant.

Although as the above analysis indicates, the equity crowdfunding market is undergo-
ing permanent development, there are a lot of problems connected with law requirements
(still not enacted the law which regulates the market and match the requirements and
obligations with the EU directives) and the possibility of getting out from the investments. Additionally, the gaps in information published and given by the fundraisers as
well as the platforms set limits for further growth. Thus the main disruptors are today
related to internal problems on the market and the pandemic is not one of them.

References

1. Agrawal, A., Catalini, C., Goldfarb, A.: Crowdfunding: geography, social networks, and the
   timing of investment decisions. J. Econ. Manag. Strategy **24**, 253–274 (2015)

2. Allison, T.H., Davis, B.C., Short, J.C., Webb, J.W.: Crowdfunding in a prosocial microlending environment: examining the role of intrinsic versus extrinsic cues. Entrepreneurship Theory Pract. **39**(1), 53–73 (2014)
3. Baeck, P., Collins, L.: Not Disrupting, Building—Crowdfunding and P2P Lending Will Be an Integral Part of New Financial Systems in Developing Economies, 15 July 2015. http://www.nesta.org.uk/blog/not-disrupting-building-crowdfunding-and-p2p-len ding-will-be-integral-part-new-financial-systems-developing-economies. Accessed 12 June 2017
4. Biuletyn Statystyczny Nr 8/2021, GUS. https://stat.gov.pl/obszary-tematyczne/inne-opraco wania/informacje-o-sytuacji-spoleczno-gospodarczej/biuletyn-statystyczny-nr-82021,4,115. html. Accessed 28 Mar 2022
5. Bruton, G., Khavul, S., Siegel, D., Wright, M.: New financial alternatives in seeding entrepreneurship: microfinance, crowdfunding, and peer-to-peer innovations. Entrep. Theory Pract. **39**, 9–26 (2015)
6. Burtch, G., Ghose, A., Wattal, S.: An empirical examination of the antecedents and consequences of contribution patterns in crowd-funded markets. Inf. Syst. Res. **24**, 499–519 (2013)
7. CCAF: The 2nd Global Alternative Finance Market Benchmarking Report (2021)
8. www.ceo.com.pl/jak-biznes-zniosl-rok-covidu. Accessed 28 Mar 2022
9. Collins, L., Pierrakis, Y.: The Venture Crowd: Crowdfunding Equity Investment into Business, NESTA, London, 3 July 2012. http://www.nesta.org.uk/publications/venture-crowd. Accessed 1 July 2015
10. Gravery, K.: Cultivating Growth: The 2nd Asia Pacific Region Alternative Finance Industry Report; Cambridge Centre for Alternative Finance: Cambridge, UK (2017). https://www.jbs. cam.ac.uk/fileadmin/user_upload/research/centres/alternative-finance/downloads/2017-09-cultivating-growth.pdf. Accessed 2 Oct 2018
11. Khavul, S.: Microfinance: creating opportunities for the poor? Acad. Manag. Perspect. **24**, 58–72 (2010)
12. Khavul, S., Chavez, H., Bruton, G.D.: When institutional change outruns the change agent: the contested terrain of entrepreneurial microfinance for those in poverty. J. Bus. Ventur. **28**(1), 30–50 (2013)
13. Kotler, P., Caslione, J.: Chaotics: The Business of Managing and Marketing in the Age of Turbulence. Amacom, New York (2009)
14. Kuppuswamy, V., Bayus, B.L.: Crowdfunding creative ideas: the dynamics of project backers in Kickstarter. SSRN Electron. J. (2014). https://doi.org/10.2139/ssrn.2234765
15. Motylska-Kuzma, A.: Crowdfunding and sustainable development. Sustainability **10**(12), 4650 (2018). https://doi.org/10.3390/su10124650
16. Motylska-Kuźma, A.: The problem of alternative financing sources management – the equity crowdfunding case. Financ. Internet Q. "e-Finanse" **15**(4), 12–24 (2019). https://doi.org/10. 2478/fiqf-2019-0024
17. Orłowski, W., Pasternak, R., Flaht, K., Szubert, D.: Procesy inwestycyjne i strategie przedsiębiorstw w czasach kryzysu (eng. Investment processes and strategies of enterprises in times of crisis), PARP, Warszawa (2010)
18. Steinberg, D.: The Kickstarter Handbook: Real-Life Success Stories of Artists, Inventors, and Entrepreneurs. Quirk Books, Philadelphia (2012)
19. World Bank and CCAF: Regulating Alternative Finance: Results from a Global Regulatory Survey (2019)
20. Zieger, T., et al.: Expanding Horizon; The 3rd European Alternative Finance Industry Report; Cambridge Centre for Alternative Finance, Cambridge, UK (2017). https://papers.ssrn.com/ sol3/papers.cfm?abstract_id=3106911. Accessed 21 Feb 2018

21. Zhang, B., Garvey, K., Burton, J., Ziegler, T., Ridler, S., Yerolemou, N.: Entrenching Innovation; The 4th UK Alternative Finance Industry Report; Cambridge Centre for Alternative Finance: Cambridge, UK (2017). https://www.jbs.cam.ac.uk/faculty-research/centres/alternative-finance/publications/entrenching-innovation. Accessed 3 Oct 2018
22. www.beesfund.pl. Accessed 28 Mar 2022
23. https://inqube.pl/platforma-emisji-crowdfundingowych/. Accessed 28 Mar 2022
24. www.crowdway.pl. Accessed 28 Mar 2022
25. www.findfunds.pl. Accessed 28 Mar 2022
26. www.crowdconnect.pl. Accessed 28 Mar 2022

A Model of a Parallel Design Environment for the Development of Decision-Making IoT Systems

Anna Łuczak[(⊠)], Konrad Stróżański, and Cezary Orłowski

Faculty of Computer Science and New Technologies, WSB University in Gdańsk, IBM Centre for Advanced Studies, Aleja Grunwaldzka 238 A, 80-266 Gdansk, Poland
a.luczak.3miasto@gmail.com

Abstract. The aim of the article is to present a model of building a parallel design environment using containerization processes for Internet of Things (IoT) systems supported by local environments and their orchestration. According to the currently dominant approach in IT, which is the maximum automation of the software development process, special emphasis is placed on the processes of Continuous Integration and Continuous Delivery (CI / CD). They are supported by such solutions as Docker Compose, Swarm and Pipeline.

CI / CD is a response to such common problems related to software development as slow product growth, lack of transparency in the cooperation of the development team, lack of predictability and the possibility of estimating project duration, late implementation of changes, repeatable errors caused by the human factor and many others. These challenges translate into the final product and customer satisfaction, and thus the success of the project or even the financial result of the enterprise. Although Continuous Integration and Delivery are not new concepts (the first mention of Continuous Integration dates back to 1991), thanks to the continuous improvement of these methods, many tools and new approaches are created.

Therefore, in this article, the authors consider the research problems of building a decision-making system using Continuous Integration and Continuous Delivery processes. For this purpose, a model of the decision-making process was built using both of the above-mentioned processes and then it was verified in a parallel design environment.

Keywords: IoT design environment · IoT decision systems · Docker processes · Continuous integration · Continuous delivery

1 The Main Processes of Software Development for Decision-Making Processes

In order to start building the model, it is necessary to present the main processes in the development and delivery of software. It is necessary to analyze software development

© Springer-Verlag GmbH Germany, part of Springer Nature 2022
N. T. Nguyen et al. (Eds.): Transactions on Computational Collective Intelligence XXXVII,
LNCS 13750, pp. 157–170, 2022.
https://doi.org/10.1007/978-3-662-66597-8_9

cycles, software development models and methods of IT project management. Their number is significant, but their analysis also indicates the key importance of two of them: CI and CD processes (Fig. 1). Therefore, in the remainder of the work, the authors attention will be focused on these processes.

Continuous Integration (CI) is a method in which code development, compilation, testing and integration of changes with the current repository are fully automated [15, 16]. In practice, this means that after each change is approved, the code is verified for coincidence with the already created main branch. Continuous Delivery (CD) automates the next phase of software development, that is, placing a given artefact in the desired (most often production) environment, where it awaits approval for implementation [21]. The combination of both of these practices (CI / CD) brings numerous benefits related to the process of building software as well as business potential [22]:

- software development time is shortened thanks to the elimination of many manual steps;
- changes to the code are more frequent and more significant;
- all changes are automatically verified and tested, which reduces the chance of errors and allows you to see changes between the stages of the project;
- team efficiency is increased by avoiding sudden, hard-to-find mistakes;
- new software versions are ready for production at any time, so new solutions are created and made available to users more efficiently and at a lower cost;
- project risks related to software development are minimized.

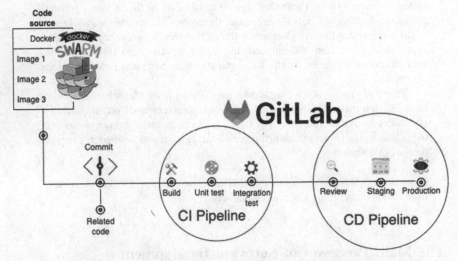

Fig. 1. Decision processes and CI/CD path used in model building

The software development process established in this way allows for the expansion of solutions with new functionalities and the delivery of innovative products much faster, which positively affects the interest of potential customers. Docker [1, 2] is a key element of this process.

Docker is containerization software, that is, creating and running applications distributed using containers. Containerization allows you to collect and isolate the necessary parts of the application, such as system libraries, configuration files, and local databases. Thanks to such a solution, it is possible to freely transfer the containers to other machines with Linux system, with the certainty that the application will work identically [3, 4].

Docker also allows running processes in an isolated environment, where each process becomes a separate container that can be freely managed. Such isolation allows you to create autonomous units with specific functions, and the entire environment can be run on any operating system. The division of the IT system into independent containers lowers both the cost of software development and shortens the development time, thanks to the possibility of starting the environment with one command on any machine, regardless of the base device [5, 6].

1.1 Methods of Implementing Continuous Integration and Continuous Delivery Processes in Docker Compose and Pipelines for Decision-Making Processes

The containers are created using self-created images (the image is a read-mode unified files pattern - the base unit of the container) or available on the official Docker Hub site [7]. For the basic launch of the environment, a Linux system is needed, the libraries of which are used, but with the help of virtualization and ready-made tools, the container can be run on any operating system [17].

Swarm is a set of nodes that runs Docker Engine processes in building the infrastructure. It is a Docker process that allows you to create, run and manage (orchestrate) distributed applications as well as create clusters. The tool that automates the installation on the host system is Docker Machine, which allows you to install Docker Engine on virtual machines or other operating systems and manage them using docker-machine commands [24, 25].

Another important element related to the implementation of CI / CD using Docker is the Pipeline created in a repository such as GitLab [8]. Pipeline is a tool for simultaneous processing by the processor of many instructions and commands in a logical, organized manner using the possibility of building new branches in the repository. The coder writer makes changes to the local repository and then uploads them to the remote repository on the newly created branch. After uploading a new branch to the remote repository, the defined Pipeline starts. This way of processing tasks significantly improves the software development process and increases the team's efficiency and the speed of project implementation [9, 10].

A linked process is version control, which is the systematic tracking of changes made to files. In order to fully automate the processes of continuous integration and delivery, GitLab uses Pipeline, supporting not only the construction and testing of the application but also enabling the review of changes according to the influencing branches. When the build and testing processes are properly completed, Gitlab will automatically deliver the new version to the production environment. Moreover, if there were errors not detected during the tests, it will be possible to return to earlier versions of the software by referring to given branches [11, 12].

Most common IoT architectures include data generators, databases, and a loopback implementation environment. Since the RabbitMQ broker was used to generate the traffic, an explanation of the MQTT (MQ Telemetry Transport) protocol is necessary. It is a code-light data transfer protocol that provides resource-constrained network clients with a simple means of delivering telemetry information. The protocol uses the publish (send data) / subscribe (receive data) pattern and is used for machine-to-machine communication, involving both the information broker and the client. The broker acts as a server to which clients, i.e. connected devices, connect. If the connection between the broker and the client is broken, the broker will buffer (queue) messages and resend them when the client is available again [13, 14].

Another data generator used for the project is Gstreamer - a multimedia structure that allows you to create any type of application for multimedia streaming, editing, audio and video recording and more. It was created for writing applications that handle audio and video, and which can be a kind of data flow at the same time. The wide range of multimedia formats used by this solution and the ability to add plugins allow for any expansion and editing of the environment. The tool is distributed under a free license, so it can be adapted to your needs.

2   Model of a Parallel Design Environment for IoT Systems and Its Implementation

As part of the conducted experiments, a parallel design environment was built, in which the previously discussed technologies for the implementation of the CI / CD model were prepared and tested [18]. In order to demonstrate the purposefulness of the experiments, the term of parallel design environment should be explained. It is an environment in which processes are created concurrently, including both infrastructure construction and software development [19].

For the purposes of this article, a parallel development environment is defined as an environment in which containers based on the Linux operating system are created using the three previously discussed Docker processes. It was assumed that services and a stack will be built on the first cluster, and the stack will be tested on the second cluster. This structure of the environment was created through gaining experience while writing this article and knowledge gained from the descriptions of individual images on Docker Hub (Fig. 2).

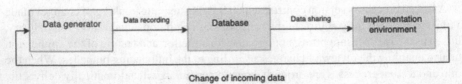

Change of incoming data

Fig. 2. Process implementation of a parallel design environment for IoT systems Source: Own elaboration

Thanks to the use of feedback processes, it is possible to obtain opinions on the data collected in databases and to change them as a result of the client's observations [29, 30].

2.1 Assumptions for Building the Model and Its Implementation

The project involved conducting research in the previously discussed parallel design environment. Various data generators and databases were used in the experiments. They were implemented in three Docker processes: Docker Compose, Docker Swarm and Pipelines. During the preparation of these experiments, an environment was created using the services defined in the process, which were then combined in Docker Compose and subsequently launched in Docker Swarm. Then the environment was shared with the GitLab tool and run on a second machine with Docker Swarm [20].

The purpose of building the environment is to run two environments on separate machines, creating an environment parallel to Docker in the Swarm process. The assumption of the first Docker Compose environment is the creation of services and preparation of Stacks enabling the launch of queuing processes, which results in the generation of data for the database. The task of the second environment is to start the processes of generating video images with the use of GStreamer, which in consequence is to generate bitmaps of these images and save them in the database.

The Python programming language was used for this purpose. At the same time, the assumption is to study the behaviour of these environments when switching between two built Stacks on both clusters in a parallel design environment. Both stacks are to be run in the same environment, thanks to which we can gain experience in transferring them to different clusters, as well as see if there are differences in the consumption of server data components and check the complex processes of moving these services.

2.2 Experience from Model Building and Its Implementation

When creating the environment model, many problems were encountered related to many different aspects, the successive resolution of which contributed to the final success of the experiments and the acquisition of valuable experiences. Generating environments initially caused a lot of errors when running them from the command line, which made the code unreadable. Connecting images so that they could communicate with each other was limited to links using "links", but Docker Compose turned out to be a comprehensive solution. Using this process made it easier to control and test the environments. Another problem encountered was the adjustment of the MySQL database version to run the Joomla CMS system, which was not described by the creators of the image, the problem was solved using the well-known development portal which is stackoverflow.com, the solution to this problem was to use MySQL version 5.7. Another problem that arose when creating Joomla sites with PostgreSQL was the error that the "makedb.php" file was missing, inferring from the errors displayed in the logs, this file was created locally and assigned to Joomla. As a result, it was possible to remember the connection with this database and to start the website correctly. While creating the parallel environment and moving the sites for validation purposes, the actions generated several problems, such as not remembering the changes that took place after the environment was launched.

Another problem was the communication of the virtual machine on which the cluster was placed with the external network, which limited the possibility of creating containers and services. A common problem that arose when using the Swarmpit environment was the stopping of Stacks, the user interface often crashed and blocked the stopping of running services. The final shape of the environment and services was therefore achieved mainly thanks to the use of Docker tools.

3 Verification of the Design Environment Model

The aim of the first research experiment was to start the process of creating services using the described stack. Working together, services are to generate data via applications written with the Python language, which will then be transferred to the database. The consequence of this connection is the display of data via the CMS system.

3.1 Model Verification - Research Experiment No._1

The research experiment begins by creating a new stack. To do this, go to the Swarmpit user interface, and then to the "Stacks" tab. The implementation of the Docker Compose code that was used to create this environment is shown in Fig. 3. Thanks to the implementation of the code presented, the first environment was created and launched: Joomla, MySQL, GStreamer, RabbitMQ and PhpMyAdmin.

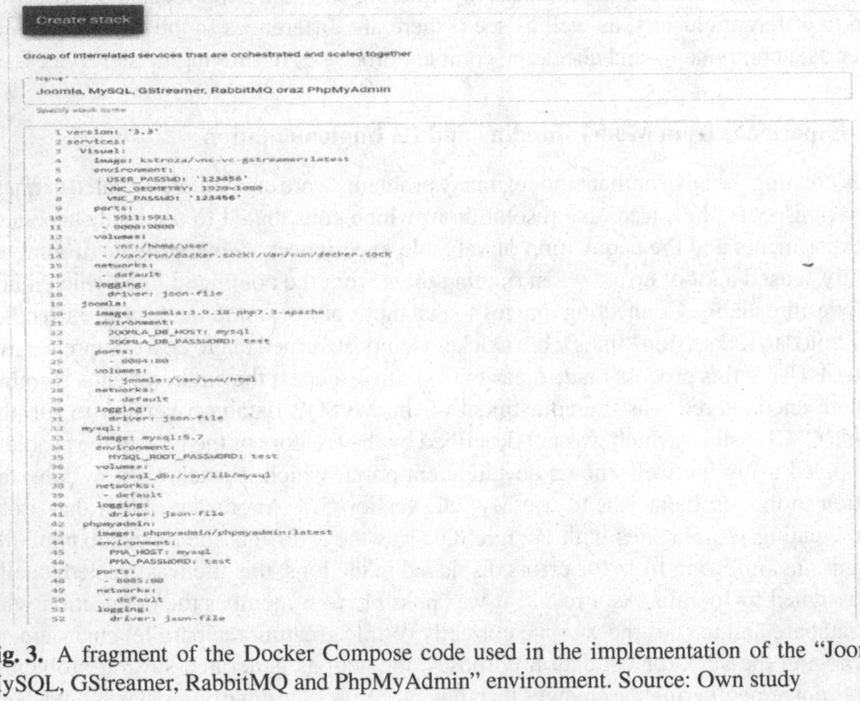

Fig. 3. A fragment of the Docker Compose code used in the implementation of the "Joomla, MySQL, GStreamer, RabbitMQ and PhpMyAdmin" environment. Source: Own study

After launching the environment, the user is transferred to the RabbitMQ website. You need to create an exchange and a queue. After entering the graphic interface available at port "8087", a request to log in is displayed, where the login and password are "guest". Successively, in the "Exchanges" tab, a new exchange is created under the name "data_exchange". "Queues" are started and a new queue is created under the name "data_queue". The next element will be editing the queue by clicking on it and adding Bindings, where "From exchange" should be "data_exchange" and "Routing key" should be "data_queue" (Fig. 4).

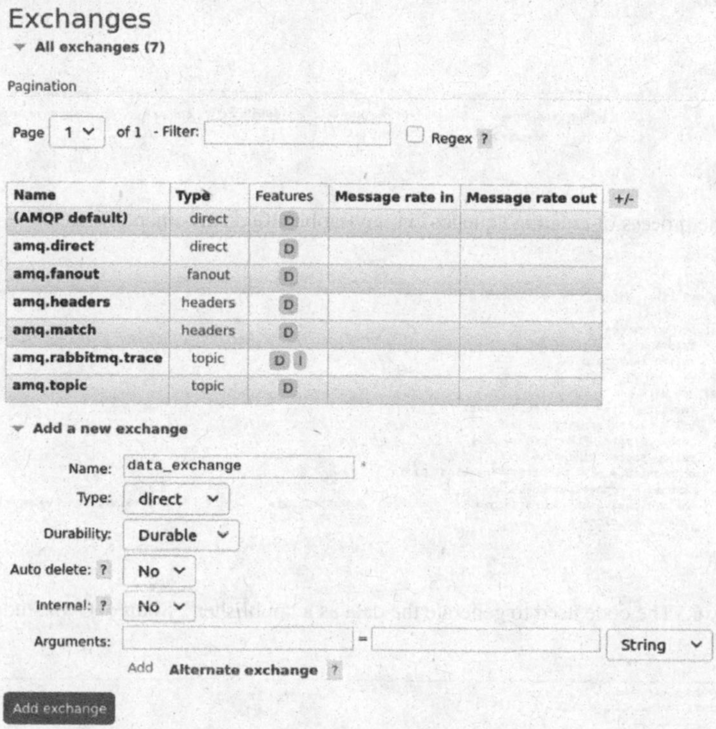

Fig. 4. The process of creating "exchange" in RabbitMQ environment. Source: Own study

After such preparation of the environment, data exchange was connected to the created queue. Now it is possible to go to the GStreamer which is located under the port "9000". The Gstreamer container contains VNC (Virtual Network Computing) technology with Visual Studio Code installed. With this software, applications are written in Python, Publisher (Fig.5) and Subscriber (Fig.6) will be launched. This software was executed via the command line using the command line built into Visual Studio Code. The commands to run the software are "python3 Publisher.py" followed by "python3 Subscriber.py", the code works in a loop to generate and retrieve data (Fig. 7).

The experiment is carried out on two different machines, in which Subscriber is stopped using the "ctrl + c" keys, and after restarting, it is possible to check whether the data that has not been downloaded will be properly handled and displayed in the

Queues

▾ **All queues (0)**

Pagination

Page [∨] of 0 - Filter: [   ] ☐ Regex ?

... no queues ...

▾ **Add a new queue**

Type:	Classic ∨
Name:	data_queue
Durability:	Durable ∨
Auto delete: ?	No ∨
Arguments:	[ ] = [ ] String ∨

Add **Message TTL** ? | **Auto expire** ? | **Max length** ? | **Max length bytes** ? | **Overflow behaviour** ?
Dead letter exchange ? | **Dead letter routing key** ? | **Single active consumer** ? | **Maximum priority** ?
Lazy mode ? **Master locator** ?

Add queue

Fig. 5. The process of creating "queues" in the RabbitMQ environment. Source: Own study

```
1    import pika, os, threading, random
2
3    def get_somenumber():
4        randomnum = round(random.uniform(-30, 30), 1)
5        return randomnum
6
7    def queue():
8        threading.Timer(5.0, queue).start()
9        url = os.environ.get('rabbitmq', 'amqp://guest:guest@rabbitmq/%2f')
10       params = pika.URLParameters(url)
11       params.socket_timeout = 5
12       connection = pika.BlockingConnection(params)
13       channel = connection.channel()
14       channel.basic_publish(exchange='data_exchange', routing_key='data_queue', body=str(get_somenumber()))
15       connection.close()
16
17   queue()
```

Fig. 6. The code used to generate the data as a "publisher". Source: Own study

```
1    import pika, os
2    import mysql.connector
3
4    connectMySQL = mysql.connector.connect(user='root', password='test', host='mysql', database='jooml
5    cursor = connectMySQL.cursor()
6    cursor.execute("CREATE TABLE IF NOT EXISTS weather (temp float(30));")
7
8    url = os.environ.get('rabbitmq', 'amqp://guest:guest@rabbitmq/%2f')
9    params = pika.URLParameters(url)
10   params.socket_timeout = 5
11   connection = pika.BlockingConnection(params)
12   channel = connection.channel()
13   def callback(ch, method, preporties, body):
14       print(" Received %r" % body)
15       cursor.execute("""INSERT INTO weather (temp) VALUES ({%f})""" % (float(body)))
16       connectMySQL.commit()
17
18   channel.basic_consume(queue='data_queue', on_message_callback=callback, auto_ack=True)
19
20   print("Waiting for messages")
21   channel.start_consuming()
```

Fig. 7. The code used to generate the data as a "subscriber". Source: Own study

data presentation environment. Relationships between Publisher and Subscriber and relationships between services are shown in Fig. 8.

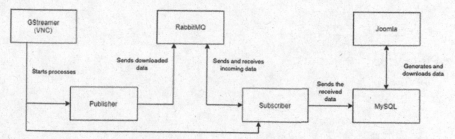

Fig. 8. Dependencies in the stack named "Joomla, MySQL, GStreamer, RabbitMQ and Php-MyAdmin". Source: Own study

The launch of these services will enable the creation of a configuration based on which the publisher will generate data. The consequence will be adding them to the queue and downloading the data using subscriber, then saving the data in the MySQL database and presenting them in the Joomla environment. The entire process will run in a parallel development environment. Due to the fact that machines in both environments will differ in computing power and resource availability, it is worth paying attention to the differences resulting from these dependencies.

The result of the experiment is to verify the correctness of data generation and retrieval by means of MQTT communication and the transfer of this data to the MySQL database presented in the experiment. Thanks to a fully working stack, we can observe the correct generation of data to the RabbitMQ server and the correct download of the generated data and save them in the database.

3.2 Model Verification - Research Experiment No. 2

In the second research experiment, processes that create services using the Stack are launched. These services, working together, will process the video into individual frames, which will then be converted into a bitmap and sent to the PostgreSQL database. The result of this process will be converting bitmaps into an image and displaying this data in a presentation environment such as CMS Joomla.

The second experiment starts with stopping the stack of the previous experiment. Stopping is done by going to the "Stack" tab and then selecting the appropriate stack to be stopped. In this case, it is "Joomla, MySQL, GStreamer, RabbitMQ and PhpMyAdmin". Then go to the button next to "Edit", expand the menu and select the "Deactivate" option (Fig. 9). This sequence of actions results from using the same ports and sharing two services (GStreamer and RabbitMQ). After performing the above steps, the second Stack was created, which is a combination of: Joomla, PostgreSQL, GStreamer, RabbitMQ and PgAdmin.

After starting the environment, it goes to the GStreamer website, which is located under port "9000". The Visual Studio Code environment is run on it, and then the

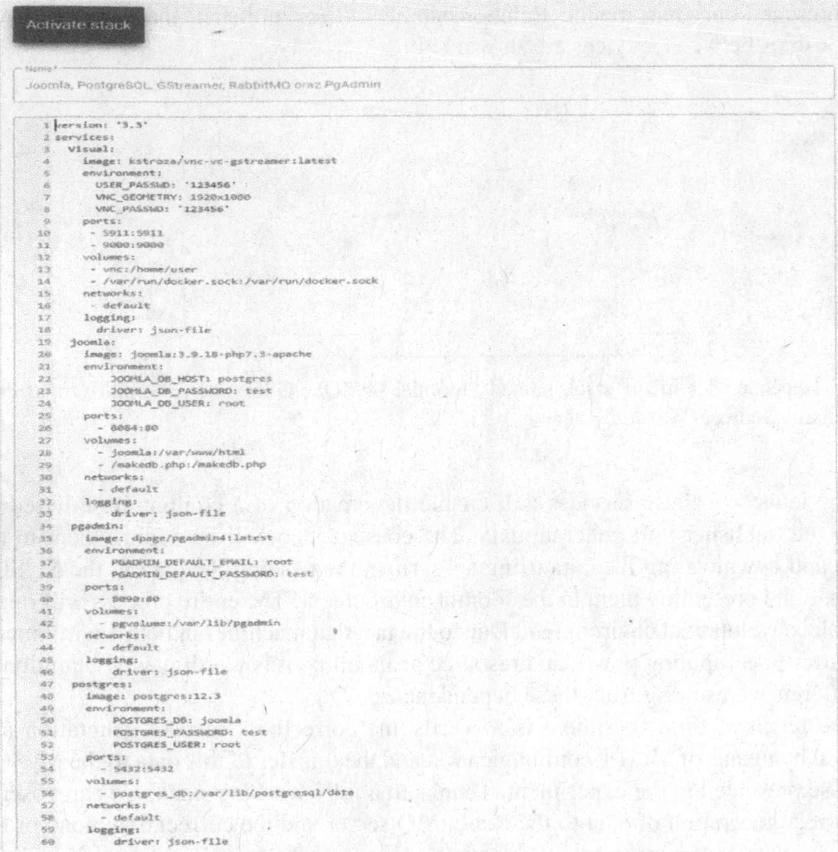

Fig. 9. A fragment of the Docker Compose code used in the implementation of the "Joomla, PostgreSQL, GStreamer, RabbitMQ and PgAdmin" environment. Source: Own study

Python script named "GStreamer.py" is implemented. The code is shown in Fig. 10. The launch is identical to the previous experiment via the "python3 GStreamer.py" command line. The code runs until the entire recording is processed and all images are sent to the PostgreSQL database. The course of this experiment is identical to the process of the first experiment and takes place on two different machines of a parallel design environment. Links between these services are presented in the figure below (Fig. 11). The consequence of sending the images to the database is their presentation in Joomla. The aim of the experiment is to check the correct handling of the database and reading these images with Joomla

The process of generating images in GStreamer is done through Pipeline, which makes it faster than the video itself. The video duration is 4 seconds and the video processing time is 2 seconds. The data sending process runs in the background, therefore you cannot notice the data transfer to the PostgreSQL database. The result of the experiment is the image correctly converted by GStreamer and the software prepared using Python to the appropriate format and sending the result to the PostgreSQL database.

```
1    import os, psycopg2, sys
2
3    def convertToBinaryData(filename):
4        # Convert digital data to binary format
5        with open(filename, 'rb') as file:
6            binaryData = file.read()
7        return binaryData
8
9    os.system("mkdir /home/user/Desktop/images")
10   os.system("gst-launch-1.0 filesrc location=/home/user/Desktop/Clock.mp4 ! decodebin ! videoconvert ! pngenc ! multifilesink location=/home/user/Desktop/images/%d.png")
11   conn = psycopg2.connect(host="postgres", database="joomla", user="root", password="test")
12   cursor = conn.cursor()
13   cursor.execute("CREATE TABLE IF NOT EXISTS images (photo BYTEA NOT NULL)")
14   conn.commit()
15
16   for x in range(len([1 for x in list(os.scandir("/home/user/Desktop/images")) if x.is_file()])):
17       data = convertToBinaryData("/home/user/Desktop/images/" + str(x) + ".png")
18       cursor.execute("INSERT INTO images(photo) VALUES (%s)", (data,) )
19       conn.commit()
20
21   conn.close()
22   os.system("rm -rf /home/user/Desktop/images")
```

Fig. 10. Code used to process and generate image data via GStreamer and Python. Source: Own study

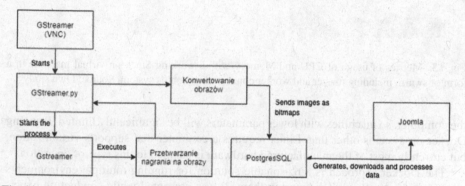

Fig. 11. Dependencies in the stack named "Joomla, PostgreSQL, GStreamer, RabbitMQ and PgAdmin". Source: Own study

4   Analysis of the Results and Conclusions

The results of the conducted experiments show that the created environments communicate very well with each other. It is also worth noting that creating such projects in pairs allows people with different experiences and skills to look from different points of view. Collaborating on code elements and discussing each problem results in higher quality and faster delivery of environments. This approach makes it possible to supplement good and bad practices, which in turn causes the transfer and automation of various types of tests, facilitating work on IaC environments.

Looking at the Swarmpit-generated metrics shown in Fig. 12 and Fig. 13, it can be seen that the CPU usage increases only during the start of the environment, while the Memory utilization increases and remains at the same level. As you can see, the virtual machine has lower CPU consumption due to the lack of background processes, unlike a physical machine where normal work is performed in the meantime. It can therefore be concluded that to run more services or Stacks requires exponentially more RAM.

The conclusions drawn from the experience gained while creating the environment and conducting experiments indicate the importance of software development and testing processes in a parallel environment, especially for people working on the Linux system. In the case of virtual machines, the environment depends on the computing power of

Fig. 12. Metric of CPU and Memory utilization when Stack is running on a physical machine with Ubuntu system. Source: Own study

Fig. 13. Metrics of usage of CPU and Memory within working Stack on virtual machine in a form of swarm including master and worker connected to Centos system. Source: Own study

the computer, so machines with lower parameters will be significantly limited. Running Docker on systems other than Linux requires a computer that supports virtualization, but currently most of the manufactured hardware is adapted to this type of operation.

The Docker approach is a reasonable solution for running multiple environments where we frequently switch between them. It was presented while conducting experiments. Additionally, the time of launching and creating such environments is much faster, as shown in Fig. 1, where the differences between a virtual machine and Docker are presented. In the Docker environment, we can build stacks from any image located on the Docker Hub or created by us. It is also worth noting that Docker is an increasingly desirable technology and more and more used by developers, which is why the resource of Docker Hub images is constantly growing.

Problems that can be encountered are often discussed on internet forums, which are worth supporting in the process of creating the environment. It should be noted that when creating the environments presented in this article, a parallel environment helps to find errors automatically.

The simplicity of creating Stacks allows you to build virtually any environment. When running the experiments, you will notice that the Docker image does not change size, so it does not take up much disk space. However, when returning to the state from the previous session, we use a variable in Stack called "volume". The disk space begins to be allocated and the progress is saved there, which can be seen in the "Volumes" tab of the Swarmpit, where the created memory slots can be seen. The consequence of this approach is the generation of large data sets, as is the case with virtual machines. However, this data is not as large as in virtual machines, due to the fact that libraries are shared and we declare resources. This approach means that we only save the missing libraries and all kinds of files created by us.

Based on the experience gained during the experiments, it can be safely stated that it is a very good tool that has a large impact on the development of IoT technology and the IaC approach. Thanks to the introduction of the CI/CD approach, we also have much greater control over the environment, which additionally allows us to automate most of the processes related to testing.

References

1. CI/CD: Continuous Integration & Delivery Explained - Semaphore. https://semaphoreci.com/cicd. Accessed 05 Sept 2020
2. Overview of Docker Compose I Docker Documentation. https://docs.docker.com/compose/. Accessed 05 Sept 2020
3. Docker Stacks and Why We Need Them — NimbleCI Blog. https://blog.nimbleci.com/2016/09/14/docker-stacks-and-why-we-need-them/. Accessed 05 Sept 2020
4. Docker vs Virtual Machine - Understanding the Differences - Geekflare. https://geekflare.com/docker-vs-virtual-machine/. Accessed 20 Aug 2020
5. What is Docker? I Opensource.com. https://opensource.com/resources/what-docker. Accessed 23 Aug 2020
6. What is a Pipeline? - Definition from Techopedia. https://www.techopedia.com/definition/5312/pipeline. Accessed 06 Sept 2020
7. MQTT - najłatwiejszy sposób przesyłania danych do chmury! - MOXA. https://moxa.elmark.com.pl/2019/09/19/mqtt-iothinx/. Accessed 05 Sept 2020
8. "What is MQTT and How Does it Work?" https://internetofthingsagenda.techtarget.com/definition/MQTT-MQ-Telemetry-Transport [dostęp z dnia 31.08.2020],
9. What Is a Database I Oracle. https://www.oracle.com/database/what-is-database.html. Accessed 03 Sept 2020
10. Docker Basics: How to Use Dockerfiles – The New Stack. https://thenewstack.io/docker-basics-how-to-use-dockerfiles/. Accessed 06 Sept 2020
11. What is GStreamer? https://gstreamer.freedesktop.org/documentation/application-development/introduction/gstreamer.html?gi-language=c. Accessed 31 Aug 2020
12. "MySQL vs PostgreSQL -- Choose the Right Database for Your Project I Okta Developer." https://developer.okta.com/blog/2019/07/19/mysql-vs-postgres [dostęp z dnia 06.05.2020]
13. docker swarm init I Docker Documentation. https://docs.docker.com/engine/reference/commandline/swarm_init/. Accessed 06 Sept 2020
14. Install Docker Engine on Ubuntu I Docker Documentation. https://docs.docker.com/engine/install/ubuntu/. [Accessed 06 Sept 2020]
15. Wysocki, W., Orłowski, C.: A multi-agent model for planning hybrid software processes. Procedia Comput. Sci. **159**, 1688–1697 (2019)
16. Pastuszak, J., Czarnecki, A., Orłowski, C.: Ontologically aided rule model for the implementation of ITIL processes. In: Advances in Knowledge-Based and Intelligent Information and Engineering, vol. 11(2012)
17. Orłowski, C., Kowalczuk, Z.: Knowledge management based on dynamic and self-adjusting fuzzy models
18. International Conference on Knowledge-Based and Intelligent Information and 112006
19. Orłowski, C., Ziółkowski, A., Orłowski, A., Kapłański, P., Sitek, T., Pokrzywnicki, W.: High-level model for the design of KPIs for smart cities systems. In: Nguyen, Ngoc Thanh, Kowalczyk, Ryszard, Orlowski, Cezary, Ziółkowski, Artur (eds.) Transactions on Computational Collective Intelligence XXV. LNCS, vol. 9990, pp. 1–14. Springer, Heidelberg (2016). https://doi.org/10.1007/978-3-662-53580-6_1
20. Pastuszak, J., Orłowski, C.: Model of rules for IT organization evolution. Trans. Comput. Collective Intell. IX **55–78**, 10 (2013)

21. Chabik, J., Orłowski, C., Sitek, T.: Intelligent knowledge-based model for IT support organization evolution. In: Szczerbicki, E., Nguyen, N.T. (eds.) Smart Information and Knowledge Management. Studies in Computational Intelligence, vol. 260, pp. 177–196. Springer, Cham (2010). https://doi.org/10.1007/978-3-642-04584-4_8

22. Stóżański, K.: Docker development environment project for IoT systems supported by the environment local and orchestrators. Unpublished materiałs, Gdańsk (2020)

23. Bufon, M.T., Leal, A.G.: Method for identification of waste in the process of software development in agile teams using lean and scrum. In: Uden, L., Ting, I.-H., Corchado, J.M. (eds.) KMO 2019. CCIS, vol. 1027, pp. 466–476. Springer, Cham (2019). https://doi.org/10.1007/978-3-030-21451-7_40

24. Kulkarni, V., Kolhe, A., Kulkarni, J.: Intelligent software engineering: the significance of artificial intelligence techniques in enhancing software development lifecycle processes. In: Abraham, A., Gandhi, N., Hanne, T., Hong, T.-P., Nogueira Rios, T., Ding, W. (eds.) ISDA 2021. LNNS, vol. 418, pp. 67–82. Springer, Cham (2022). https://doi.org/10.1007/978-3-030-96308-8_7

25. Antonova, A., Aksyonov, K., Ziomkovskaya, P.: Development of a method and a software for decision-making, system modeling and planning of business processes. In: Succi, G., Ciancarini, P., Kruglov, A. (eds.) ICFSE 2021. CCIS, vol. 1523, pp. 148–157. Springer, Cham (2021). https://doi.org/10.1007/978-3-030-93135-3_10

26. Ayala, C., Martínez-Fernández, S., Rodríguez, P.: 2nd QuASD workshop: managing quality in agile and rapid software development processes. In: Kuhrmann, M., et al. (eds.) PROFES 2018. LNCS, vol. 11271, pp. 373–377. Springer, Cham (2018). https://doi.org/10.1007/978-3-030-03673-7_28

27. Komiyama, T., Konno, S., Watanabe, T., Matsui, S., Kase, M., Igarashi, I.: Improvement of agile software development process based on automotive SPICE: a case study. In: Walker, A., O'Connor, R.V., Messnarz, R. (eds.) EuroSPI 2019. CCIS, vol. 1060, pp. 518–531. Springer, Cham (2019). https://doi.org/10.1007/978-3-030-28005-5_40

Author Index

Printed in the United States
by Baker & Taylor Publisher Services